FRAUD EXPOSED

FRAUD EXPOSED

What You Don't Know
Could Cost Your Company Millions

Joseph W. Koletar

*To: Mike Gips -
with best wishes -
Joe Koletar*

WILEY

John Wiley & Sons, Inc.

This book is dedicated to the memory of my parents,
John Edward Koletar, of Shamokin, Pennsylvania, and
Margaret Ruth McAbee Koletar, of Spartanburg, South Carolina.

CONTENTS

PREFACE

This book was begun in October 2001, as an attempt to gather and articulate thoughts that had been with me for some time. After 35 years in security, law enforcement, and forensic investigations, I began to wonder if some of the techniques that were apparently having success in the broad field of law enforcement might also be useful in addressing fraud in the workplace. Thus began this journey. During it, the initial focus grew beyond the confines of law enforcement, as my research took me into areas as disparate as neuroscience, linguistics, and game theory. I also encountered issues of defining fraud and trying to get a handle on how big it is and what causes or impedes it. Even such apparently elemental tasks proved formidable.

Then, Enron. While at this writing the full implications of Enron are still being revealed and discussed, the name alone has become a catch phrase in public discourse, much like Watergate. Its very utterance conveys substantial volumes of meaning and emotion and has become a sort of shorthand metaphor for things that may be wrong in corporate America.

While I have mentioned Enron several times in this work, and speculated on its meaning for the forensic profession, the thrust of this book remains unchanged—thoughts as to how we can become more effective in dealing with occupational fraud (that is, fraud committed by employees against their own organizations). Enron may prove, as time passes, to be a tidal wave—massive and destructive, but by definition rare. If tidal waves occurred every day they would not be tidal waves, but merely exceptionally high tides. While the tidal wave and its hugely destructive effects rightfully capture our attention, it is the rivers that concern me. The rivers—slow, steady, and unrelenting—carve out huge canyons and forever alter the landscape. Enron is, perhaps, a tidal wave. Occupational fraud is the river that is slowly carving its way through most of the organizational landscapes we call home.

Joseph W. Koletar

ACKNOWLEDGMENTS

It is impossible to attempt a work such as this without substantial support from others, near and far. To this group I am eternally grateful for their wisdom, generosity, assistance, and encouragement. To these same friends and colleagues I offer an apology for any weaknesses or errors in this book; should such occur, they are solely my responsibility. I also apologize to any whose contributions I may have overlooked—such oversight was not a reflection of the worth of your thoughts and observations, but merely a function of my carelessness.

First, to my friend and mentor, Joe Wells: The founder of the Association of Certified Fraud Examiners, Joe saw the possibility of answers before others even knew there were questions. To Marie Simonetti Rosen, the gifted and dedicated editor of the *Law Enforcement News*, who has forgotten more about policing in the United States than I will ever know. To Dr. Edwin J. Delattre, a dear friend and valued resource, whose voice, wisdom, and resolve have immeasurably advanced the state of higher education and law enforcement in the United States and abroad.

Although this work is solely mine and does not reflect the views or opinions of the partners or employees of Ernst & Young LLP, to Mike Emmert and my colleagues at that firm, for welcoming me into their midst and always encouraging the pursuit of excellence.

To all in law enforcement and the forensic profession, who labor mightily under trying conditions to ensure that the bad guys do not always win.

Others, whose generous contributions were gratefully accepted, include Don Barnes, George Campbell, Chief Steve Cherry, Carson Dunbar, Tracey Foley, Dr. Gil Geis, John Kane, Tom Pickard, Frank Purdy, Jim Roth, Brian Sanvidge, David Sawyer, Steve Seliskar, Gary Stoops, Representative John Sweeney, Alan Trosclair, Fred Verinder, Miriam Weinstein, and David Zornow.

To my beautiful and talented daughter, Lauren, who makes me prouder each day to be her Dad.

And, finally, to my lovely wife, Martha, without whose patience, support, prodding, counsel, humor, and occasional questions as to exactly when I was going to get this mess off the dining room table, this book could never have been completed.

INTRODUCTION

This book will be long on questions and short on answers. It will, however, offer a few suggestions. It is about occupational fraud (that is, fraud committed against organizations by persons who are members of those organizations). It is written in an effort to stir debate, foster dialog, and encourage research. It is meant to provoke comment, both positive and negative, but all helpful to the process of discovery. It is written in a spirit of friendly ignorance, admitting that even after 35 years in the related fields of intelligence, security, investigations, and forensics, I do not pretend to know it all or, probably, even much of it. It is also written in the sure knowledge that collectively we know more than we individually realize. In short, it is an attempt to begin a process.

I sincerely hope, when this work sees the light of day, to receive any number of irate communications saying, in so many words, "Koletar, you idiot, weren't you aware of Professor "X's" theory of "Y" fraud causation? Have you no idea that the "Z" corporation has reduced occupational fraud to less than 1 percent by using cranial obfuscation analysis?" The more of those communications I receive, the happier I will be, for part of my mission will have been achieved. I have tried, to the best of my ability, to learn what I could about occupational fraud and its dimensions and causation. I have spent 35 years in the business, conducted research, and talked to some of the leading practitioners in the field, but I am sure I could double that amount of effort and still fall short. It is simply too large an undertaking for one person in any reasonable amount of time.

The mathematician Henri Poincare once likened facts to stones. Facts, in and of themselves, prove little. Only when they are compiled into a theory do they have potential utility. As he put it: "Science is built up with facts, as a house is with stones. But a collection of facts is no more a science than a heap of stones is a house."[1] Welcome to my house; let us see if it withstands the winds of debate, analysis, and dissent.

There are, I am sure, innovative and forward-looking control and compliance programs that have been highly effective in reducing occupational fraud. I presume they exist, but I also presume most of us in the forensic profession are unaware of them. Otherwise, why are we awash in fraud? Why do we continue to do more of the same, then bemoan our collective lack of success?

Former New York City Police Commissioner Benjamin Ward once referred to the fact that most crime committed in our country against minority citizens is committed by minority citizens as "our dirty little secret."[2] We in the forensic profession have our own dirty little secret: We are remarkably ineffective in dealing with fraud. There may be an excellent reason for this failure. Perhaps it cannot be done. Fraud, like murder and sin, has been with us throughout recorded history. It is part of the human condition. Eons ago, it is highly probable that one prehistoric man traded a club to another prehistoric man for some berries, knowing the club had a crack in it, but failing to tell his partner. A fraud was committed—perhaps two, for the berries may have been spoiled.

We can argue, successfully, that we are not ethicists, educators, lawmakers, human resource executives, or persons of the cloth. We are not in the morals business; we are in the investigations and prevention business. As far as that goes, it is true; however, I suggest that as a profession we need to do more, lest we cede the field to the others named or be relegated to the role of the people who follow the elephants in the parade with brooms and shovels. We need to become researchers, thinkers, experimenters, writers, rabble-rousers, and seekers of truth wherever we find it. We need to think deeply about what we do and why it happens in the first place.

In short, we need to devote more time to the improbable goal of putting ourselves out of business. It will never happen, but it is a worthy goal for any profession, ours included. To be free of disease, hunger, crime, and strife is the ideal of every civilized society. We will not see it in our lifetime, but that is not the point. If we have such ideals as goals, it is more likely that we will get closer to them than if we do not.

Speaking to this point, and cautioning that such activities cannot occur in an organizational vacuum, Erroll J. Yates, former chairperson and managing director of Kodak Limited, U.K., offered the following observation in Internal Auditor magazine in 1977:

> The Institute of Internal Auditors has published aims for the development of internal auditing. Its plans for education and research clearly demonstrate a growth in status. . . . All professions need such a foundation of technical excellence if they are to grow. But technical excellence is in itself not sufficient to guarantee growth. Those whom the profession serves must also support it. And that support should come from the highest level.[3]

I am primarily directing this work to those who are auditors, investigators, and compliance professionals in organizations, and others interested in workplace fraud, for three reasons: (1) you are the majority of the professionals in the field; (2) organizations are where most of us live and spend our professional lives; and (3) the ills of society, and the acts of fraudsters preying on other individuals, are beyond my mental radar range. Would that we begin to deal with the issues that occur in our organizational homes before we extend our efforts to the society at large. We have more than enough to do at home, right now, to keep us busy for a very long time.

It is also my fervent hope that some outside the immediate field of forensics will also find this work of interest. You should. It is not only our assets that are at risk, but yours—be you employee, shareholder, taxpayer, retiree, executive officer, or member of the board. In calling our collective lack of success a dirty little secret, I seek to grab the attention of my fellow forensic professionals, but our secret is a sticky one, and it clings to all who touch it. If you have accepted, tolerated, ignored, rationalized, or chosen to remain ignorant about fraud in the workplace, then you, too, share in the secret and are part of the problem. You are also a valuable ally as we seek to move forward. Welcome aboard.

In beginning to think about fraud in the workplace, or occupational fraud, it is important to understand three things: what it is, what it is not; and why it is important.

Occupational fraud occurs millions of times a day in the United States. Much of it is trivial and petty, but it is cumulatively expensive nonetheless. Such acts include showing up late for work, making personal telephone calls against company policy, removing supplies for home use, taking long lunch breaks, calling in sick, and copying personal papers on the office machine. These acts are important in the aggregate, but the focus of this book will not address them in great detail. Such transgressions are important to "slippery slope" and "broken windows" theorists and, in that regard, are the essential bedrock of an organizational compliance program based on those concepts. We shall discuss in more detail how such constructs operate and why focusing on small acts may help prevent bigger ones. At the same time, we shall also explore organizational issues to be considered when crafting a compliance program around such ideas.

We will spend the majority of our time exploring issues pertaining to more egregious forms of occupational fraud—willfully crafted schemes by which dishonest members of the organization loot its assets. They may do this through kickbacks, large-scale diversion of goods and services, creation of ghost vendors and employees, or hundreds of other techniques. Certainly, some of the petty offenses may grow into major league proportions. The employee who removes a few pens each week for home use may graduate to taking out a trunkload of supplies each day and selling them on the black market. In that regard, we must pay due heed to the "slippery slope" and "broken windows" theorists.

At the same time, if the statistics available to the profession are accurate, organizations in America already have a full roster of major league players. Occupational fraud in the United States is estimated to be a $600 billion per year problem, and it is growing. According to the Association of Certified Fraud Examiners (ACFE) in its *2002 Report to the Nation*, occupational fraud is fairly well distributed throughout organizational America: publicly traded companies (30%), privately held companies (31.9%), government agencies (24.7%), and not-for-profits (13.4%).[4] When we get into an examination of the definitions used in the field, the $600 billion figure cited by the ACFE may begin to seem small.

For those not familiar with this field, a word of explanation may be useful. One will frequently encounter the term *white-collar crime*. Generally speaking, this refers to a category of crimes that may be defined by the nature of the crime itself—from forging a check to illegal dumping of toxic waste and hundreds of things in between. The crime can be defined by the nature of the offense (if you commit offense "A" it is by definition a white-collar crime) or by the characteristics of the offender (if a corporate executive commits most offenses they are white-collar crimes). The latter example begins to bring into play some of the nuances that bedevil the field. A corporate executive who murders his or her spouse has not committed a white-collar crime. The same executive who trades on inside information has done so. Many scholars and theorists have spent many hours debating these definitions since they first were brought into play in 1939 by Sutherland, a scholar credited with creating the term *white-collar crime*.

Another category of white-collar crime is usually called corporate crime. These are offenses committed by an organization or members of the organization to enrich itself. Such offenses might include actions as varied as price fixing, mislabeling of products or contents, illegal dumping of toxic waste, and failure to provide a safe work environment for employees. Again, much debate appears in the literature as to how these offenses occur, why they occur, and who is responsible—the people, the organization, or both.

Finally, we come to that category of white-collar crime this book deals with— occupational fraud. Throughout this book we refer to white-collar crime and corporate crime, but the distinctions are important. Occupational fraud is crimes committed by employees (and, I will argue, others) against their organization. Even here, simple definitions can be strained if one pushes hard enough. If a sales manager creates phony sales to qualify for an annual bonus, that is occupational fraud. If the same sales manager creates phony sales at the urging of superiors to make the company look good, that is corporate fraud. The sales manager will still get the same bonus, but the motivation is different.

Throughout this book one will encounter the term *organization*, and at times it may appear stilted. *Company* seems to roll off the page more smoothly. The choice of terminology is, however, intentional. Occupational fraud in the United States certainly occurs in the private sector in massive proportions. It also, however, is common in public sector and governmental agencies, not-for-profit organizations, and voluntary associations and groups. Thus not all persons engaging in occupational fraud are employees working for companies.

Regarding the importance of occupational fraud, we shall see that it dwarfs many legitimate industries several times over. The cost of occupational fraud does not simply go away. It results in higher prices to consumers, lower profits to companies and shareholders, higher cost to taxpayers, lower bonuses to managers and executives, poorer performance on Wall Street, negative impacts on pension and retirement plans, and the failure of more than a few businesses.

The forensic profession, as it deals with the detection, investigation, and prevention of occupational fraud, is built on a foundation of failure. It rests squarely on four substantial columns of support that have allowed it to develop, evolve, mature, and prosper. The first of these columns, and arguably the most important, is the moral failure of the individuals who commit frauds in an astonishing variety of manners and circumstances. The second is the failure of the organization's internal controls to prevent these individuals' actions or, usually, to detect them quickly. Indeed, it is not uncommon upon discovery for some perpetrators to make comments to the effect of "What took you so long?"[5] The third failure is that of the managers, executives, boards of directors, and shareholders to recognize that fraud is a significant part of the life of most organizations and to act accordingly. The fourth failure, resting on our doorstep, is the failure of the forensic profession to be more effective in developing ways to minimize fraud in the first place.

While many in the field, myself included, have built rewarding and satisfying careers because of these interlocking failures, I believe we have a responsibility to look beyond our traditional activities and interests. Otherwise, we are doomed, personally and as a profession, to more of the same. The same in this context may be development of professional credentials and sharing of professional knowledge; development of new and improved techniques to detect, prevent, or prove fraud; the apparently never-ending quest for adequate funding and resources; and the recruitment of new and promising people into our profession.

All of these activities are good and worthy, appropriate to any profession, and they should continue; however, we are spending our time, resources, talents, and tools addressing symptoms, not causes. In this regard, we are not unlike our law enforcement counterparts who believed strongly for many decades that more cops and more arrests meant better law enforcement. In terms of professional growth and quantifiable outcomes, it was a powerful argument. More cops do generate more arrests, and more arrests were visible evidence to the public (the shareholders, if you will) that professionals were working hard on their behalf.

I have also been asked by knowledgeable reviewers if I am perhaps not being a bit too ambitious. They asked how I realistically proposed to write a book that, if I was successful, would have utility and meaning across thousands of types of organizations, great and small, public and private. Again, I can only speak from my experience and that of my professional colleagues. I have conducted forensic inquiries in retail, manufacturing, not-for-profit, health care, educational institutions, financial services, entertainment, hospitality, advertising, waste management, energy, television, and many other industries. Each has its peculiarities, but the base-level issues of occupational fraud are remarkably alike. Regardless of the business, there are only so many ways you can run a kickback scheme, a ghost vendor scam, or an inflated invoice fraud. There are a lot of ways to commit murder—shooting, stabbing, choking, beating, pushing, smothering, immolating, or poisoning—but to an experienced homicide investigator they all look pretty much the same. So, too, with fraud in the workplace. It may take an hour or two to figure out the industry-specific twist in a given matter, but thereafter it reverts to a fairly predictable form. Thus the source of my ambition with regard to occupational fraud. I think we have huge, but generic, issues on our collective plates, and I think we can benefit from a general consideration of the reasons they occur and how we can improve our ability to prevent and detect them.

We shall start our search for better answers to the problem of occupational fraud by looking at the police, whose problems were in many ways similar to ours, and also at some of the radical steps they took to address them.

CHAPTER 1

CRIME AND THE LAW ENFORCEMENT RESPONSE

The history of modern policing as we know it can be traced to London in 1828 when Sir Robert Peel introduced a bill to provide for a trained and uniformed police force. The force, because of Peel's backing, quickly became known as bobbies or peelers. Encouraged by this development, New York City followed the same path in 1844, when the old Night Watch was legislated out of existence. In 1845 the first shield was introduced. The device has a rather peculiar history. Up until that time the police preferred to patrol in civilian clothes, seeing uniforms as a British custom not befitting freeborn Americans. The eight-pointed, star-shaped copper shield was worn on civilian clothes to denote the wearer as a police officer. These persons quickly became known as coppers or cops. In New York City, formal training and official uniforms would not appear until 1853.[1]

Although there is much detailed history related to the subsequent development of policing in New York City and other locations throughout the United States, from this simple beginning the structure of modern law enforcement was laid. As it grew and evolved, it faced challenges both great and varied: draft riots during the Civil War, bandits of various ilk in the unsettled West; the fear of sedition during World War I; Prohibition and the rise of organized crime; black marketeering and military preparedness during World War II; the civil unrest of the 1960s; and, of course, drugs.

As the 1960s began to meld into the 1970s, despite the best efforts of law enforcement, crime continued to be one of the leading concerns of the public. In 1968, crime was the number-one domestic issue cited in the Gallup poll, the first time that had ever occurred. Crime rates were soaring, with the FBI reporting the following increases per 100,000 persons in the U.S. population between 1969 and 1970:[2]

Murder	Up 56 percent
Aggravated Assault	Up 92 percent
Forcible Rape	Up 95 percent
Robbery	Up 186 percent
Burglary	Up 113 percent
Larceny ($50+)	Up 240 percent
Auto Theft	Up 150 percent

Rader and McGuigan commented on these times in the following manner in 1983:

Either crime has been increasing over the last decade or clocks are ticking slower. In 1971, Americans could expect a murder every thirty minutes, a rape every thirteen minutes and a violent crime every thirty-nine seconds. In 1981, murders were occurring every twenty-three minutes, a rape every six minutes, and a violent crime every twenty-four seconds. Moreover, the average American is experiencing crime firsthand more often. A 1981 study by the Department of Justice found that 25 million American households (30% of the total) were victims of crime. Accordingly, U.S. families are more prone to have a member attacked in a serious crime (rape, robbery, or aggravated assault) than to have a residential fire or have a member injured in an automobile accident, and more likely to have a member robbed than to have a member stricken by cancer or heart disease, the nation's leading health problems.[3]

Were this not bad enough, urban America—Baltimore, Chicago, Detroit, Miami, Newark, and Washington, D.C.—experienced major riots, and significant parts of some of these cities went up in flames. Police control was tested, with the National Guard and even regular Army units being called up to assist. Serious commentators were debating the proper role of the military in assisting the police in the discharge of their duties and the Constitutional issues this would raise.[4]

Thomas Repetto, the head of the New York City Crime Commission, has commented on the state of crime in that city during the era. In 1961, the NYPD reported 390 murders; by 1964, the rate was 637, an increase of two-thirds in just three years. By 1972, the rate was close to 1,700, quadrupling over a single decade. The number of robberies reported had risen from 23,000 in 1966, the first year statistics for such crimes had been kept accurately, to nearly 90,000 at the beginning of the 1970s.[5]

New York City was hardly alone in its crime problems. Meltzer observes that other cities had their issues as well:

Bad as the situation in New York was, it was worse in other cities. In 1987 New York ranked ninth in murder and manslaughter among the twenty-five largest cities. Detroit was first (with a rate two and a half times that of New York), and New Orleans was second in rates per 100,000 people."[6]

The United States was also not faring well when compared to other countries, as Meltzer also notes:

The United States has a higher homicide rate than any other industrialized country. In the 1980's about 20,000 murders a year were committed in the United States. Each year 10 Americans of every 100,000 were murdered. In West European countries the homicide rate was fewer than 2 per 100,000. Taking Australia, Canada and New Zealand together, the homicide rate was less than 3 per 100,000.[7]

At the same time, he advises, the overall level of violent crime in the U.S. was beginning to show signs of declining, by 21 percent in the period 1980–1984.[8]

Some argued that public concern about crime was merely a function of awareness and perception. To quote the old newspaper adage, "If it bleeds, it leads." As the 1980s approached, sometimes-sensational coverage, aided by smaller and more mobile remotes and eye-cams brought crime into our living rooms. Like the Vietnam War, daily doses of near-real-time carnage had a powerful impact on the public psyche. Reality television producers realized that for the cost of a camera crew, powerful entertainment could be put forward without the need to build sets and pay actors and scriptwriters. Even the search for fugitives, one of the most basic elements of law enforcement for centuries, could be transformed into a long-running television series.

Such respect for the power of the media has not abated. At the 2002 American Bar Association meeting of its White Collar Crime Section, two entire tracts were devoted to media matters: "High Visibility White Collar Crime Cases: Will the Media Shape Your Case?" and "Inherit the Wind—Dealing with the Media in the 21st Century." Considering that these topics were competing for scarce presentation time with items such as "International Investigations—The Expanding Extraterritorial Jurisdiction of the United States and the Bill of Rights" and "Grand Jury Reform," it appears the criminal bar is appropriately sensitive to the influence the media can wield. Indeed, the proceedings of this meeting contained no less than 14 newspaper articles that were believed to bolster the argument for the media's ability to shape public perceptions.[9]

Others saw broader societal forces at work, affecting not only street criminals but many institutions and professions as well. The Hastings Center, in an ethics report at the end of the 1970s, noted:

On the societal level, our newspapers and pundits have bemoaned symptoms of a moral vacuum...a sense of moral drift, of ethical uncertainty, and a withering away of some traditional roots and moorings. There is a concern about juvenile delinquency, about white-collar crime, about a culture of narcissism, about the absence of fixed and firm guidelines for both personal and institutional behavior... almost all the professions are beset with criticisms concerning the moral behavior of their members... A recent Carnegie study emphasized widespread unethical practices by college students. The list of public complaints is long, and the professions have seen a comparative drop in public confidence.[10]

Law enforcement budget enhancements were sought, even in times of fiscal austerity elsewhere in the public domain. One writer noted: "[T]he police administrator is faced with the problem of obtaining more productivity from existing levels of resources, knowing full well that those resources will probably diminish in the future in the face of an increasing demand for the output of those resources." The writer concludes that the answer lay, in part, through increased officer productivity measured through improved performance appraisal systems. Again, the answer offered is more arrests.[11]

Another writer saw promise in the developing field of *futuristics*, the "use and application of forecasting techniques as an aid in law enforcement decision-making."[12] He went on to note, however, "In spite of the advances that have been made in policing in the past two decades, American law enforcement continues to operate much as it did at the beginning of the century."[13] This translates, roughly, into "find the bad guys and lock them up."

Still others sought understanding in the causal roots of criminal behavior:

[A] decline in family influence in an increasingly youthful society; a permissive attitude toward much criminal behavior; the deterioration of many of our major cities and rapid unplanned growth of suburbs; the failure of our criminal justice system to deal promptly and fairly with persons accused of crimes; the failure to rehabilitate those convicted of crimes. Overlapping most of these factors are the opportunities for crime in today's society and the problem of drug addiction.[14]

Gangs, too, began to become a more significant factor in the nation's crime problems. From being present in 54 cities prior to 1961, they had grown to inhabit more than 170 cities by 1980. By 1992 they were present in 766 American cities, including 91 with a population less than 10,000 persons.[15] By 1992, 54 percent of cities with gangs had from one to five gangs present, and an astonishing 30 cities, 4 percent of the total, had over 50 gangs each.[16] Gang violence had a corrosive spillover effect, not only in terms of violence gang members did to one another or rivals, but also to the uninvolved. One study conducted with data from the Los Angeles Police Department indicated that when gang homicides were compared to nongang homicides, the following characteristics emerged. Gang homicides:[17]

- More often occurred in the street
- More often involved autos
- More often involved guns
- More often involved injuries to other persons
- More often involved victims with no prior relationship to their assailant(s)

In 1980 there were 351 gang homicides in Los Angeles County, a number that would decline slightly for the next several years, before beginning to rise substantially in the late 1980s and early 1990s.[18]

Some theories of gangs and gang behavior saw a set of factors as promoting gang membership and growth. As we shall see shortly, these factors are remarkably similar to issues raised by "root cause" theorists of crime in general:[19]

- Sufficient number of minority youth, that is ten to thirty
- Absence of appropriate jobs
- Absence of acceptable alternative activities
- Concentrated minority populations
- Comparatively high crime rate
- Absence of community and informal controls

Given the beginning growth spurt of gang activity in the time frame of the 1960s, it is perhaps less than coincidental that the most famous and successful gang movie of all time, *West Side Story*, debuted in this era. The artistic merits of that film aside, gangs were rapidly becoming yet another problem for law enforcement to deal with.

More traditional organized crime groups were active as well, prompting the 1967 President's Commission on Law Enforcement to comment: "If organized criminals paid income tax on every cent of their vast earnings, everybody's tax bill would go down, but no one knows how much."[20]

As the 1970s and 1980s passed, the face of organized crime in the United States became more varied. The old group, the mafia or La Cosa Nostra, was in full flower, especially in major cities, but they were being joined and pushed by newcomers on the scene—highly organized and often-vicious gangs from Mexico, China, Cuba, Colombia, and Jamaica.[21]

As a result of these pressures, more prisons were built, often bringing badly needed jobs to communities suffering economic blight. The Federal inmate population alone increased over 600 percent, from 21,266 in 1970 to 131,419 as of October 2001.[22] Overall, at the midyear point of 1998, there were estimated to be 1.8 million inmates in the United States, double the number of a decade earlier.[23] The private sector saw opportunities and responded, with private prisons coming into being.[24] The defense industry, impacted by the effective end of the Cold War, saw growing law enforcement needs as an alternative market for their products and technologies. Legislatures and jurists combined, somewhat uneasily at times, to produce mandatory sentences, sentencing guidelines, "three strikes, you're out" legislation, and other remedies. The number of persons in various forms of incarceration in various jurisdictions began to put a strain on some budgets.[25]

The public's fears also spilled over into other areas, again funding private-sector growth. The Security Industry Association, a trade group, reported that U.S. businesses spent $82.3 billion on security systems and products in 1996.[26] Personal safety products and services sprouted; guard and alarm companies prospered; professional associations thrived; and near-endless meetings, symposia, roundtables, and conferences were held.

Former New York Police Commissioner William Bratton captured the tenor of these times when discussing the earlier stages of his law enforcement career. He noted that in the 1970s the guiding principles of much of law enforcement were the three R's: rapid response, random patrols, and reactive investigation.[27] In many ways, these precepts make perfect sense. Rapid response to a call for service can be vitally important; the sick or injured are tended to sooner, a fleeing perpetrator may be caught close to the scene of a crime, and valuable witnesses and evidence may be secured before they are lost. Much was made of measuring average response times down to the fraction of a second on a city-wide basis. Random patrols were meant to discourage criminal behavior by making the criminals unsure when or where a cop would appear. Reactive investigation was designed to place detectives and investigators at the scene of serious incidents. In theory, it made sense; however, structural issues soon came into play.

Many police departments operate on a clearance system. A call for service, measured for speed of response, can be cleared in a number of ways. A criminal can be arrested in the case of a robbery, an ambulance can be called in the event of a heart attack, a tow truck can be called in the event of an accident, and an unruly group can be dispersed in the event of a noise or nuisance compliant. Clearance rates are also tracked as an indicator of the responsiveness and effectiveness of police services. The widespread adoption of the 911 system in most major cities, designed to speed the rate of response, only operated to exacerbate already existing problems with how the public and police interacted. Calls for service flooded the systems, the vast majority of them for nonemergency matters, and the incentive within police departments was to move them through the system as quickly as possible. Little thought was given to what the net impact of all this activity produced.[28]

Bratton recounts one extreme example that highlights the flaws in this system. During his career in Boston, there was one corner where a gang of local juveniles liked to hang out at all hours. An older man lived above the corner and called to complain about the kids and the disturbance they were creating. A car with two police officers would be dispatched, arrive quickly (response time), and disperse the kids (matter cleared). Within minutes, the kids would return and the scenario would repeat itself. In one year there were 1,300 calls for service at this one corner! Each one was cleared and the situation never changed.[29]

The important element to appreciate in thinking about response time is that it is the junk that clouds over the truly important issues. In my 25-year career in the FBI, I have been on both sides of the response time issue; many times I responded, and a few times I was responded to. In both situations, time is critical.

Bratton comments on the effects of this mentality when he took over as the Commissioner of the NYPD some years later:

> The police department has always thrown numbers at the community. "Look at all of our arrests, look at our activity." But the department only measured activity, it didn't measure results. Civilians who complained about the squeegee men were in the same situation as the guy at I Street and East Seventh in Southie who placed 1,300 calls to 911 and never got satisfaction. The cops were a powerful group who could walk into community meetings and say, "It's the criminal-justice system that doesn't take this seriously, it's the judges who let these squeegee guys go, it's the society who created them in the first place. Don't blame us." People would back off because the numbers don't lie, and so nothing ever got done.
>
> But it was a lie. The strategies the NYPD was using were not effective, and the department knew it. They'd go after squeegee people and for a month show substantial arrests and summonses, but there was no urgency. They'd go after them for an hour, once a week. It was the same as working with prostitutes; if you tell them "Friday is sweep day, I'm going to arrest you; the rest of the week you can make all the money you want," you are inviting failure. Success comes with constant attention.[30]

That this system was ineffective is beyond the point. Measures define success and measures drive systems, to include police departments. By the measures used at the time, this was successful police work. There were other problems as well—a major disconnect between what the police thought was important to the public and what the public actually wanted. The police took the common-sense view that since serious crime was by definition, serious, it was high on the public's list of expectations. Resources were budgeted and deployed accordingly. The public, meanwhile, actually had much more mundane issues they wanted the police to do something about.[31] The police thought as long as they focused on the big things, the public would tolerate and accept the smaller ones as less important in the great scheme of things. The public, meanwhile, fully expected the police to handle the big issues and do something about the small ones as well.

Recognizing the apparent disconnect between public expectations and law enforcement objectives and strategies was not an act of obstinacy or stupidity. Rather, as Peter Manning points out, it was in many ways a logical consequence of the basic societal foundations of the policing function. Manning has devoted a considerable amount of time to the study of the police, mainly in the United Kingdom but also the United States, and has speculated on the nature of the social contract they hold with society, the implications of it, and how their efforts to fulfill that contract and survive as an institution have shaped their mission, organization, and self-perception. He notes that early pressures to regulate the possibility of violent intervention to effect their responsibilities relied on a system of strict accountability, a military rank structure, rigid control over communications, and constant supervision. As a result of these factors, the police came to be what he calls a "symbolic bureaucracy."[32]

Manning also describes eight attributes he believes characterize the nature and limits of police power.[33] From our perspective, it is useful to think of these attributes in two lights. The first, which we examine in this chapter, is the set of elements that tended to work to produce the types of responses that characterized the law enforcement mission for the first seven decades of this century in the United States. The second, which we shall examine in the next chapter, is how these same elements figured into the rethinking necessary to effect improvement in the police function:

1. The police symbolize the state, both in the sense of representing its political unity and also in being the arbitrators of adherence with its dictates.

2. They characterize their activities as being based on political consensus and serving society as a moral whole.

3. Although they are charged with enforcement of the law, they frequently encounter situations where the law is a weak resource.

4. They must do their work with few procedural guidelines while observing various constraints designed to protect individual rights.

5. From prior experience with criminals they often believe they should, or must, decide guilt or innocence before an arrest.

6. The police are highly dependent on the gathering, receiving, processing, and use of information.

7. In theory the police are apolitical.

8. Although the police often claim active control over issues of crime and public order, they are in reality highly dependent on information from others to even begin to approach the discharge of their duties.

Because of these factors, Manning theorizes that the law enforcement function often displays highly representative characteristics. First, while the police typically characterize themselves as crime fighters, they more often are involved in helping or order-maintenance roles.[34] Second, they are, by the nature of their mission, often put into roles wherein the demands being made on them are contradictory or incapable of logical resolution. Manning notes:

> The demands made on the police lead them to pursue both contradictory and unattainable ends. Further, the nature of their problems does not permit them to devise anything approaching a "solution." They lack a practically relevant theoretical understanding of the causes of crime, and even possession of that knowledge might not yield satisfactory crime control. . . . Rather than educating the public about their limits, the police have manipulated public opinion and have sought an uncritical public acceptance. To accomplish these goals, they adopt a vocabulary describing their conduct and aims as "professions."[35]

The result of these pressures, objectives, and mandates, Manning finds, is a movement toward bureaucracy, with the prototypical police organization being one that is rational, efficient, scientific, and technologically sophisticated. Also, as one might expect, one that is oriented toward the maintenance and use of statistics.[36] By and large, these statistics are the result of what gets reported to the police and are easily characterized by them as crime, and not necessarily the primary issues present in the social environment in which the public understands and lives.

In trying to understand the logic of these divergent perceptions of police activity and public expectations, Bratton is instructive. He notes that when he took over the New York Transit Police in New York City in 1990, more than 3.5 million people used the subways every day. For many, it was their only way to get to work and move around the city. Robberies had jumped by 48 percent in the past two years, and with other problems, like aggressive panhandlers and sleeping drunks, the subways had become an issue in the eyes of many New Yorkers. Bratton recounts that even after this increase in robberies, with a peak of about 55 per day, the total number of crimes that occurred in the subways was only about 2 percent of all crime in New York City. Fifty-five robberies a day is a small percentage when viewed from the perspective of 3.5 million daily users, yet these and other crimes made subway use problematic, especially at night, and especially for women.[37]

When Bratton involved the Transit Authority's (TA) director of corporate communications, John Linder, in the effort to better understand the public's perception of crime on the subways, the results were telling. Bratton recounts them as follows:

> Linder's focus groups told him that despite the fact that the TA had virtually wiped out graffiti on the trains, about 20 percent of the respondents said it was still there. Things had gotten so bad, people didn't even believe what they

saw. In one set of focus groups, Linder asked women what percentage of the city's crime they thought was committed on the subways. They said 30 to 40 percent. Homicides? Forty to 50 percent. When he asked men, crime came back at 20 to 30 percent, homicides to 30 to 40. In fact, 3 percent of the city's felony crime and between 1 and 2 percent of its murders happened on the subways. "What would you think if I were to tell you that 3 percent of the city's crime happens on the subway?" he asked the women. "Would that change your level of fear toward the public-transportation system?" They answered, "Absolutely not."[38]

Thus was a crime problem defined by the populace, and not the police.

Although the public defined what crime was and was not, from their perspective, the police defined the response to crime. Bratton recounts the results he encountered when he had one of his key lieutenants, Jack Maple, conduct a study of how the NYPD was approaching the crime problem in New York:

When Maple analyzed the Bureaus, the news got worse. The Narcotics Bureau, he discovered, worked largely nine to five or five to one, Monday through Friday. The warrant squad was off weekends. Auto-crimes squad, off weekends. Robbery squads? Off weekends. The community-policing officers— those six thousand baby-faced twenty-two-year-olds who were going to solve all the neighborhoods' problems—off weekends. Essentially, except for the detectives, patrol officers, and some other operations going round the clock, the whole place took Saturdays and Sundays off. The criminal element was working nights, they were working weekends, they worked the late shifts and legal holidays. They were working harder and smarter than we were. No wonder crime was up; and prevention was down.

The NYPD had people bluffed. They had a reputation as the greatest crime-fighting machine in the history of policing, but the big blue wall was a lot of blue smoke and a few mirrors. They were good at responding to crime, they just weren't very good at preventing it. They weren't even trying to prevent it. They were cleaning up around it.[39]

Part of the reason for this orientation, Bratton learned, was the manner in which over time both the Department and its officers had come to perceive themselves, their work, and what elements of it were important. Upon taking command of the NYPD, Bratton formed a series of 12 reengineering teams, staffed by 300 NYPD personnel. They surveyed more than 8,000 NYPD officers and made more than 600 recommendations for change. Bratton observed that he was astounded by their findings. With regard to the Department itself, he learned:

At the highest levels of the organization, the basic aim of the NYPD was not to bring down crime but to avoid criticism from the media, politicians, and the public. As one police executive put it, "Nobody ever lost a command because crime went up. You lose a command because the loudest voices in the community don't like you, or because of a bad newspaper story, or because of corruption.

The greater the distance from headquarters, the lesser the trust from one rank to the next. Exclusion was the rule. Creativity was actively discouraged. One commander said of his troops, "I have three hundred potential (career) assassins in my unit."

Police officers believed the department had not backed them up, even when their actions were warranted.

The department was structured to protect its good name (and the careers of its senior executives) rather than to achieve crime-fighting goals.

The Internal Affairs Bureau was seen as intent on tripping up officers for minor infractions rather than rooting out real corruption.[40]

Because of such deeply seated organizational assumptions within the Department, Bratton notes, it was also not surprising that there were significant discrepancies between how the rank and file saw what was expected of them, as opposed to what they thought was important. Bratton summarizes these disconnects as follows:[41]

Considered by officers to be most important to the department:

1. Write summonses

2. Hold down overtime

3. Stay out of trouble

4. Clear backlog of radio runs

5. Report police corruption

6. Treat bosses with deference

7. Reduce crime, disorder, and fear

Considered by officers to be most important to themselves:

1. Reduce crime, disorder, and fear

2. Make gun arrests

3. Provide police services to people who request them

4. Gain public confidence in police integrity

5. Arrest drug dealers

6. Correct quality-of-life conditions

7. Stay out of trouble

While one can overemphasize the findings with regard to one large department, given the prevailing attitudes and assumptions of the era, it is likely that many, if not most, police departments viewed their tasks in a similar light. They were in the business of producing numbers in the face of a burgeoning level of crime, and the better they produced those numbers, the better off they were.

One should be cautious in thinking that the police were some sort of aberration on the organizational landscape because of this behavior. There is perhaps no force so great in organizational psychology as what is familiar. Graham Alison, in his remarkable book on the Cuban missile crisis, *Essence of Decision*, has commented insightfully on the tendency of most organizations to see the world in terms of what he refers to as their "organizational routine." During that critical moment in modern American history, the State Department saw the event as essentially a diplomatic problem, while the military saw it as fundamentally a military situation. Both were viewing it from the perspective of their organizational skills and mindset, while discounting other explanations of the situation.[42]

Thus, too, the police. With more than a century of organizational history behind them, they had concluded that the solution to crime was arrests, just as it always had been. If there was an abnormally large amount of crime, there would have to be an abnormally high number of arrests to solve it, and this would probably require an abnormally high number of cops.

In an environment in which *case processing*, a term we shall later examine in more detail and context when used by Kelling, was the norm, so was the response. The police saw themselves largely as a production line, ruled by the theories of "scientific management" and "Taylorism." The object was to get greater production out of the line, much like Henry Ford when he began to build his fortune in the manufacture of cars. Former NYPD Chief of Detectives Al Seedman describes what was at the time a radical concept within the NYPD in the early 1970s to improve detective efficiency. For scores of decades, detectives were assigned to each NYPD precinct, normally occupying the second floor, with the uniform cops on the first floor. They investigated the more serious crimes within that precinct. Whether their caseload was high or low, there was always a certain complement of detectives assigned to each precinct, because that was how it had always been done.

Seedman came up with and implemented the radical idea, under then-Commissioner Patrick Murphy, of having detectives grouped into detective districts. The old squads would be disbanded, and each district would have four groups of detectives assigned on a functional basis: homicide and assault, burglary and larceny, robbery, and narcotics. The more routine matters they had handled in the precincts would now be handled by the patrolmen. Further, caseloads could be studied between districts and detectives assigned as needed to produce more even workloads. An additional benefit was increased specialization.[43]

Such changes now, in retrospect, seem minor and even obvious, but at the time they were profound. It is more telling that these were essentially

Tayloresque modifications to what was in many ways an assembly line, albeit an assembly line of crime processing. There was some specialization, and also some prioritization, as detectives handled more serious matters and patrolmen less serious offenses, but these were really slight nudges to a massive system that remained essentially in place.

Irwin Garfinkel, in the foreword to Murray Edelman's book, *Political Language: Words That Succeed and Policies That Fail*, notes the position Edelman takes on such phenomena: ". . . he argues that public bureaucracies are more effective in using language to shape beliefs about what they do than they are in dealing with the chronic social problems that they are supposed to ameliorate."[44]

Michael Lipsky, in the introduction to the same work, refers to Edelman's work in helping disclose the role that social facts play in public discourse and political debate.[45] The NYPD, it would appear, had conceptualized the crime problem by setting forth the social facts of the situation as they understood them. Once these facts were in place, there followed logical answers. In the case of Seedman's decision, the answers were increased specialization and improved balancing of detective workloads.

This action was neither coy or duplicitous on the part of the NYPD, for they were as much a captive of the prevailing political constructs of their time as the criminals or the public. They saw their world through the prism of their training and experience and accordingly ordered a social definition that seemed to make sense. As Edelman points out, this is more a function of language and its symbolic evocations than of conscious malicious intent: "Only rarely can there be direct observations of events, and even then language forms shape the meaning of what the general public and government officials see. It is language that evokes most of the political 'realities' people experience."[46]

He then goes on to describe the effects of this proposition, once played out in the interactions among social issue(s), governmental response, and public understanding:

> . . . governments shape many public beliefs and demands before they respond to the people's will. Eagerness to believe that government will ward off evils and threats renders us susceptible to political language that both intensifies and eases anxiety at least as powerfully as the language of religion does.
>
> If political language both excites and mollifies fears, language is an integral facet of the political scene: not simply an instrument for describing events but itself a part of events, shaping their meaning. . . [47]

While the focus of Edelman's work is on poverty and the role of governmental programs in affecting it, his observations hold true as well when thinking about crime and the law enforcement response. He notes, for example, that there are two prevailing schools of poverty causation. The first, essentially, is a collection of beliefs that basically say, "They brought it on themselves, by being lazy, immoral, etc." The second says that the poor are at root helpless victims of vast political, economic, and social forces beyond their control. Edelman notes, as I contend with regard to crime and law enforcement, that it is more common than not for policymakers to hold both beliefs, if not individually, then certainly collectively. If this is in fact the case, there are obvious and logical policy responses to the problem at hand, be it poverty or crime. Given that there are conflicting theories of causation, there will likely be varying responses. Because policy response is grounded on social facts that are politically created and cannot be proved in an objective sense, to some degree one answer is as good as another. If this is the case, the objective becomes regulation of the problem, rather than solution.

This is much the situation the NYPD, and many other forces, were in at the time. They had a monster—crime—by the tail; they had no firm idea of what caused or motivated it; and they knew they could not control it. The objective became to just hang on.

From time to time, if events (or, perhaps more accurately, perceptions) warranted, a crisis could be declared. We are all familiar with these phenomena; at the national level we have seen come and go the energy crisis, the inflation crisis, the health care crisis, the Social Security crisis, and many more. Edelman notes several of the attributes of a crisis and comments on how they tend to operate in the political and governmental arena:

> The word "crisis" connotes a development that is unique and threatening. When applied to a set of political events, the term is a form of problematic categorization because the development it highlights can also be perceived as recurring rather than singular and as an instance of arbitrary labeling. What events mean for policy formulation depends on whether they are defined as exceptional or, alternatively, as one more set of incidents in a world that is chronically in crisis.... [48]

In Edelman's conceptualization of crises and their impact on the public policy scene, he notes that crisis declaration has interesting properties. It may uncover or mask facts; it may generate activity and political will; but, most important, it conveys a sense of temporal finality. A crisis, by definition, is an exceptional event, and exceptional events do not occur all the time. If they did, they would be routine, and not exceptional. A crisis, therefore, has a limited life, after which some degree of victory can be claimed, and the ongoing work of problem regulation resume.

So, thus, did the police operate, albeit unconsciously. We have seen come and go the drunk driving crisis, the crack crisis, the gang crisis, the juvenile-offender-committing-adult-crimes crisis, the going postal crisis, the guns-in-school crisis, and more too numerous to recount. Regulation, however, was the norm to which we tended to return, once the crisis was over.

The pressures brought about by swollen crime rates also had other, more troubling consequences than mere organizational inefficiency, significant as that may be. Some officers, believing they had been placed into an impossible situation, came to believe drastic measures were justified. Bratton comments on these unfortunate perceptions as follows:

> Some cops lie. We as a profession have finally matured to the point that we can admit that dirty little secret. Cops often lie for what they consider to be the greater good. They lie to get around the exclusionary rule. The Constitution as interpreted by the U.S. Supreme Court has very specific rules concerning how evidence is gathered. Evidence obtained outside legal boundaries is excluded. In an effort to put bad guys behind bars, throughout history cops have gone outside that boundary.[49]

Integrity is indeed a high price to pay to try to achieve greater organizational efficiency, no matter how worthy the cause, for it has a corrosive and lasting quality to it. Once the line of honesty has been crossed, if not the first then surely the second or third time, when is confidence ever restored? Even among fellow cops, not to mention superiors, prosecutors, defense attorneys, judges, victims, and even perpetrators, there will always be doubt, even in instances where none need occur. Such is the price of lies; they eat at the soul—the soul of the officer who mouths them, the souls of everyone who has reason to hear their testimony and wonder if it is accurate, the soul of the court system, which relies on truth as the fuel that drives it, and the soul of the community, which sooner or later concludes that in the fight on crime you cannot trust the cops either.

Professor Edwin Delattre, educator and the leading authority on law enforcement ethics in the United States, refers to this as "noble cause" corruption, which he describes as follows:

> What does taint us as moral agents is an arrogant appraisal of ourselves that concludes, "I am entirely justified in my means because my end was noble," or a cowardly response to demands, such as "I'm damned if I do and damned if I don't, so it makes no difference."
>
> Such flattering self-appraisals and failures of nerve are the two forms of noble cause corruption. Arrogance and cowardice imperil the ideals of a constitutional republic, because they are marks of individuals who despair of rising to the ordeal of command. In my experience, the republic has little to fear from officials who face up to ordeals and do not try to get off the hook by complacently justifying themselves or by whining that "the world isn't fair." What is fearful are the officials who believe that their ends always justify or excuse their means or who give up in despair but remain in office nonetheless.... Arrogance corrupts by obscuring the need for thought, and cowardice corrupts by denying the point of thought, thus forsaking judgment to the whims of impulse.[50]

To some extent, such problems were not new and existed in times of low crime rates as well as high, but as a mechanism to deal with surging levels of crime, lies were a disaster that took many years to overcome.

Despite all the numbers the police were trying to put forward, the public fear of crime persisted.[51] In the earlier years, the late 1960s, part of this problem could be traced to simple neglect. In 1970 the total spending for law enforcement—federal, state, and local—and including police, prosecutors, courts, and corrections, was barely $5 billion. This compared to $9 billion spent on tobacco products and $12.5 billion spent on alcoholic beverages.[52] In this regard, the state of the police was not dissimilar to that of the forensic profession. While by 1999 total U.S. law enforcement spending in all categories for all services had risen to $174 billion, numbers alone were hardly the answer.[53] In many regards, the law enforcement and security professions were in the state the forensic profession finds itself in today. They were trying everything they could think of, they were getting bigger, smarter, and faster, they were working hard, but they could not get the problem under control.[54]

CHAPTER 2

RETHINKING THE ASSUMPTIONS

In the late 1970s and early 1980s the tide, slowly, began to turn. It would take the better part of 20 years to have a significant impact, but the movement had begun. In the opinion of many theorists and students of criminology. these changes were caused by law enforcement seeking other alternatives to their traditional activities.[1] Four distinct, but related, theories began to emerge which, when implemented, are credited by many observers with making the first significant impact on crime rates and, perhaps as important, the public's perception of them. The elements of many of these theories, having to do with the importance of the community, had been discussed for some time.[2] The trick was in how to make them operational; to move them from the realm of lofty ideal to practical reality that could be grasped, understood, implemented, tested, and improved with increased experience.

The first of these concepts was problem-oriented policing. To understand it, we must review a bit of history. In 1960 a nonpracticing attorney, Herman Goldstein, then in his thirties, was serving as an executive assistant to O.W. Wilson, the Superintendent of Police in Chicago. Goldstein spent countless hours in the field, day and night, observing what police officers actually do in the course of performing their duties. From these efforts came a seminal article, "Police Discretion: The Ideal Versus the Real," published in 1963.[3] The article was a sea change in how people thought about the police and, even more important, how the police thought about themselves. Its central thesis was that policing was a highly discretionary undertaking. That is, the average police officer on the average beat had and exercised considerable discretion in how the law was, or was not, enforced.[4]

Over time, police discretion and the nonscientific nature of many law enforcement actions would come to be widely recognized. In one court decision, dealing with whether police could stop persons when the description of a criminal suspect consisted primarily of the suspect's race and gender, and absent any showing of discriminatory intent, the court held: "Officers rely on their ability to act on nonarticuable hunches, collected experience, intuition, and sense impressions— all of which are crucial in carrying out a criminal investigation. Officers would be forced to justify these intuitive considerations in order to meet an accusation that race was the sole factor motivating the encounter. The unworkability of such a regime is self evident."[5] In 2000, when this decision was rendered, it seems reasonable to acknowledge that much of police work is discretion and judgment, but in 1963 such an acknowledgement was shocking to most people.

In 1964, Goldstein joined the faculty of the University of Wisconsin Law School and continued his work on policing and the police function. In 1979, he wrote an article that some knowledgeable observers have said would "pave the way for policing in the 21st century."[6] As Marie Simonetti Rosen, the long-time editor of the *Law Enforcement News*, and one of the leading authorities on policing in the United States noted, "'Improving Policing: A Problem-Oriented Approach,' which appeared in the journal *Crime and Delinquency*, prompted a number of progressive police departments, including those in Baltimore County, Md., Newport News, Va., and Madison, Wis., to experiment with this bold new method of thinking about and conducting the business of law enforcement."[7] In 1990, Goldstein followed with a book, *Problem-Oriented Policing*.

Goldstein describes problem-oriented policing as a process that "places the major emphasis on the need to re-conceptualize what the police are doing more generally, to focus attention on the wide range of specific problems that police confront and to try to encourage a more analytical approach to those problems. Then, as a result of that analysis, to think through different strategies"[8]

As simple as this may sound, it was a new way for police to look at themselves and their jobs. It was not more of the same: hire cop, train cop, put cop on beat, cop locks up bad guy, repeat as necessary. It was an attempt to define the true crime problems in the community, study what was causing them, develop strategies to stop them, and then test those strategies in real time and adjust as necessary. Problem-oriented policing might well engage elements of the community or of the civil service infrastructure in unique, never-before-tried partnerships and, if they did not work, disengaged from those partnerships. It might mean changing shifts, patrol patterns, equipment, uniforms, procedures, or literally learning a new language. (In areas with heavy immigrant populations, communication, particularly in times of stress, can be difficult and could lead to unfortunate con-sequences. Simple words and phrases in another language, like "police," "stop," "put your hands up," "are you hurt?" and "do you need help?" can make a world of difference.) Essentially, the possibilities were endless, as long as they seemed to make sense and were directed at the problems. It was, perhaps, the ultimate in police discretion: not the routine discretion of old, to lock up or not to lock up, but the discretion to define the function's mission in a way that seemed to make more sense, both to those charged with carrying it out, the police, and those for whom it was intended, the citizens.

As problem-oriented policing developed, it did not do so in a vacuum. Other theories were talked about and other initiatives were being tried. Over time, some of them began to touch, then blend somewhat and, in a few instances, become almost synonymous with one another. One of these was community policing. Goldstein describes it as follows:

> I've always assumed that community policing, and the package of changes commonly conveyed by that term, is designed to place emphasis on one great need in policing, which is to engage the community, to emphasize the point that the job of social control essentially in our society depends upon networks other than the police, that the police can only facilitate those networks and support them.[9]

Goldstein recognizes that community policing is also a concept that brings some powerful political baggage with it, usually positive, noting:

> Community policing in particular has a very strong, positive, value attached to it in the political forum because it conveys a sense of a more intimate, caring relationship on the part of the police for the community. The term itself almost conveys a sense of added security, and that has enormous attraction to political leaders. They are likely to buy into it for that reason, which has the positive value of increasing support for the efforts. But to the extent that it is not a very well informed perspective, it can create problems down the line.[10]

Community policing is a concept implemented, or attempted, in many police departments, great and small, in a variety of formats, and with varying degrees of success. It is an effort to conceptualize the police as part of the community and not, as one senior NYPD commander once referred to it, "an army of occupation." Its facets can be few or many and can include, in part:

- Taking officers out of patrol cars and putting them on foot patrol to increase interpersonal interactions
- Opening one and two officer substations in neighborhoods or, even, apartment buildings
- Reaching out to community leaders and groups to help in defining crime problems and structuring solutions
- Spending more time on social service issues of import to individuals and the community
- Learning a foreign language

When such programs are effectively implemented, they can be successful. No one knows the true nature of crime problems in the community better than the residents. They also may well know who the bad guys are and be willing to point them out. Juveniles playing sports in a school, church, or police league are better off than hanging out on the corner looking for ways not to be bored. The abusive husband may be located and counseled before the battered wife becomes another crime to solve. The disaffected daughter may be placed into a special counseling program before she takes to the streets to sell the only thing she has of value. Positive role models and frequent communication as human being to human being may improve minority recruiting. The promising student of little means may not know how to go about applying for a scholarship and gain a chance to change his or her life. The elderly shut-in on Social Security may look forward to the daily chat and the weekly cup of soup, paid for out of the officer's own pocket. The weed-filled lot strewn with crack vials and cheap liquor bottles may become a playground again.

Such initiatives can also save money. Carson Dunbar, the former Superintendent of the New Jersey State Police Department (NJPD), has observed that that agency, seeking to increase minority recruiting, spent around $1 million on such efforts. He has noted that other departments, such as the NYPD, approached the $10 million mark in their campaigns. When the results of all these efforts were analyzed, the NJPD discovered that the most effective method of attracting minority candidates to their ranks was personal contact with minority officers. The same held true for women officers. The common-sense rationale behind this is that most persons tend to have extensive networks of friends who are like them in terms of age, race, and gender. Thus contact with these people allows more persons to become exposed to law enforcement career opportunities and to learn, first hand, what the job is all about.[11]

To a degree, Goldstein sees the police operating in a community-policing mode as being the pathologists of the community, probing for social disease, weakness, and dysfunction, then seeking the right treatment.[12] This role, while potentially invaluable, is not without its risks and cannot function in a vacuum. As Goldstein notes:

> If they're thoughtful and analytical, they see where the problems are arising and an enlightened city government will look to the police to help identify the most critical issues so that it serves as a really solid basis for directing resources. If that's done in a thoughtful way, I think it can be very helpful and very productive. If, on the other hand, it's not thought through, then the police just come to be seen as pests who are demanding a disproportionate amount of time from other agencies, and the other agencies come to resent the fact that there's an implication that they're supposed to drop everything they're doing and respond to an agenda set by the police. That's just not going to work unless there's leadership on the part of the municipal executive to

orchestrate this, and make clear to all agencies what is expected of the police, and how police operations and needs are to be integrated with those of the other agencies.[13]

Goldstein's observations are well founded and offer a cautionary note to the adoption of community policing, or any other model, as a panacea that will produce results without costs. This consideration will be pertinent to our examination of the transferability of law enforcement models to the fraud environment later in this book. Even Goldstein, after more than 40 years in the field, is realistic about how much can get done, while remaining an advocate of trying:

> The word "reform" in other areas sort of characterizes periods of change, but my experience is that reform is a permanent part of the language of policing. We're constantly in a state of reform because we're constantly trying to catch up. . . . The bottom line is that if you think about the growing task and the fact that police are being looked upon to handle such a heavy load today, as some of our other social networks deteriorate and more and more shifts to the police, the police job, despite all the efforts that we've made, despite all the catch-up, seems to be increasingly an almost impossible sort of job. When you add to that fact that the police are dependent so heavily on the criminal justice system, and that system is totally overwhelmed and often unavailable, and add the fact that all of our urban areas are under such enormous financial constraints, and the police are being expected to do more with less, the picture is not a very encouraging one. In fact, it can be a bit overwhelming.
>
> As you look at that, at the same time you see very highly motivated police people at the top and at the bottom of our organizations trying to cope with that, saying we've got to do something to enable us to deal with this problem. Out of that are coming a wide range of different departments doing different things in order to respond to that, and I find all of those innovations very exciting. I think it's important for us to focus on the specific innovations more so than it is to worry about the way in which they're labeled, because in my view the elements of the various programs, the various innovations and the need for them is going to remain, and they're going to be met regardless of what the current flavor of the month . . . happens to be.[14]

There are, obviously, areas of overlap between problem-oriented policing and community policing and even some in the field use the terms interchangeably. Goldstein recognizes this, and notes: "There's a big difference, but I think the difference is primarily in emphasis. We need more engagement in community; we also have a critical need for thinking differently about what the police are expected to do and investing heavily in the systematic analysis of the various pieces of police business."[15]

As police thinking and theoretical development continued, one of the next major concepts came from an unlikely source. The March 1982 edition of

Atlantic Monthly carried an article entitled, "The Police and Neighborhood Safety: Broken Windows," by James Q. Wilson and George Kelling. In the words of one present-day police chief, a lieutenant at the time the article came out, it "knocked his socks off."[16] Marie Simonetti Rosen, the editor of *Law Enforcement News* who conducted an interview of Kelling 17 years later, noted the article "would provide the theoretical and practical underpinning for much of the crime decreases that have been occurring nationwide for the past several years. Moreover, the term 'broken windows' has become a metaphor, a law enforcement catch phrase, for increased police attention to quality-of-life crime and rescuing neighborhoods and public spaces from decay."[17]

Authors Lardner and Repetto have attempted to put "broken windows" theory into a somewhat broader context, noting it "dovetailed with ideas articulated two decades earlier by urbanologist Jane Jacobs. In her book, *The Death and Life of Great American Cities*, Jacobs portrayed the police as subsidiary partners in the enterprise of crime control; the first line of defense, according to Jacobs, was a critical mass of confident and engaged citizens actively monitoring the scene."[18]

It is, however, a highly useful concept that must be applied carefully, for many policies can sprout from its roots. Rosen addresses this point in her interview with Kelling, observing he "finds it interesting to have a long 'relationship with a metaphor that I helped to create'." He goes on to observe that the strength of the metaphor is that it:

> "helps people to wrap their minds around a fairly complex issue." The disadvantage is once the metaphor "gets a life of its own, it begins to block thinking." In addition, as has happened with the "broken windows" concept, a metaphor can breed "bastard children" like zero-tolerance campaigns, crackdowns and sweeps, terms that Kelling declares are "anathema" to his philosophy of policing. His is a philosophy that is based on a community policing model in which police and residents know and work with each other to solve neighborhood problems, policing activities are decentralized, and officers are given the proper legal tools and guidance in the wise use of police discretion—discretion that does not use race as a factor."[19]

So concerned was Kelling with a drifting away from his original ideas, that in 1998 he and his researcher-wife, Catherine Coles, wrote a book, *Fixing Broken Windows*, on issues of application of the concept he and Wilson originally developed.[20] Rosen further notes:

> To be sure, "broken windows" has not been without its critics, and of late that criticism has focused on the argument that order-maintenance campaigns are a veil for police harassment of minority groups. With such criticism having swelled in the aftermath of the police shooting of Amadou Diallo in New York, Kelling views such critics as opportunistic and politically motivated, eager to

attack Mayor Rudolph Giuliani despite his administration's dramatic success in reducing the city's crime rate using the "broken windows" approach. As important, Kelling believes that some of the criticism currently being leveled at "broken windows" stems from those who still cling to the belief that crime stems from "root causes" that police can do little to effect. In the 1960s, according to Kelling, many police scholars and police executives bought into the idea that "crime is caused by poverty, racism and social injustice [and] if you wanted to deal with crime, you have to deal with root causes." Since police could do nothing about root causes, the argument went, they could do nothing about crime. This way of thinking, Kelling says, helped turn police into "case processors" who responded to crime but could not prevent it.[21]

Ramsey Clark, the former Attorney General of the United States, spoke on behalf of many "root cause" theorists in his 1970 book, *Crime in America*. Among the major factors he saw promoting social dysfunction and crime increases were population growth, concentration of minorities and the poor into slums, economic disparities, poor housing, lack of adequate social assistance, disease, despair, mental retardation, lack of proper education, discrimination, and unemployment.[22] Interestingly, advances in medicine and the ability to better understand the functioning of the human brain have also contributed to more recent developments in "root cause" theory. Malcolm Gladwell, in a 1997 *New Yorker* article called "Damaged," cited medical studies and research as providing indications that some violent criminals have suspicious histories of child abuse, brain injuries, and psychotic symptoms that may explain some of their subsequent acts.[23]

Clark and Gladwell have somewhat abundant company. One of the more vociferous root cause advocates appears to be criminology and sociology Professor Richard Moran, of Mount Holyoke College. He contends that a new factory in a neighborhood does more to reduce crime than anything the police do, and he is especially dismissive of the effectiveness of the tactics associated with community policing and other law enforcement innovations of the 1970s onward. He argues that such efforts were merely a rain dance, and when it began to rain, credit was wrongly given to the dancers, the police. He believes that while crime did decrease during this period it was due to an improved economy, the lessening of the crack wars, and increased periods of incarceration for young offenders. To support his position, he notes that one of the poorest cities in the country, East St. Louis, Illinois, had an even sharper drop in crime during this period than did New York City, but the police there introduced no new programs. Indeed, he contends, due to budget constraints, the police department in East St. Louis often lacked enough gasoline to keep all its cars running.[24]

Others have been less accepting of the root causes explanation, noting that for much of the last half of this century various members of the learned classes in both the United States and Europe have marched in a sort of mental lock-step to place the blame for crime in every conceivable place but the offenders hand.

While their prostelyzing has certainly colored the debate on the subject and likely affected the thinking of judges, legislators and others key to the criminal justice system, it has also not gone unnoticed by the very persons who cause the criminal justice system to exist in the first place—the offenders. Some believe we may have inadvertently schooled several generations of offenders with the idea that their acts are not really their fault.[25]

Russell Kirk offers a historical perspective on the utility of the "root causes" argument, noting:

> The meliorists of the Nineteenth Century took it for granted that by a century after their time—by the year 1982, say—violent criminality would be virtually extinguished through universal schooling, better housing, better diet, general prosperity, improved measures for public health, and the like. They assumed that capital punishment was a relic of a barbarous and superstitious age. Capital punishment, they thought, was merciless; and they were themselves evangels of mercy. Their intellectual descendants did succeed, by the 1950s, in abolishing the death penalty throughout most of the civilized world.
>
> But they did not succeed in abolishing hideous crimes of the sort formerly named "capital." In the most affluent of great countries, the United States, the rate of serious crimes rose most steadily and rapidly. At a time when the need for restraints upon criminality appeared to be greater than before, penalties were diminished. All this was done in the name of mercy.[26]

One is tempted to speculate if the meliorists would argue today that the benefits they associated with a prosperous society have simply not reached those who commit serious crimes, or if they would take the tack that they have done so, but there is still a relative imbalance that fuels antisocial behavior. If the latter, we are left to ponder how to achieve a completely level playing field in a free society.

Stanmeyer comments on this question in his 1983 article, "Making Criminal Justice Work":

> Short of improving the personal character of an overwhelming majority of its citizens—a gradual task even harder than improving their economic well-being—there is little that government can do through indirect means that will have an early impact on the crime problem. To "abolish poverty" will not in turn abolish crime; during the Depression years poverty was high but crime was low; whereas in the last decade wealth was widespread but crime was spreading even more widely.[27]

Robert Kelly, likewise, has written of his interviews with numerous inmates in the Central Punitive Segregation Unit in New York City's Riker's Island prison. He notes that many inmates offer a surprisingly varied range of excuses or rationalizations for their acts:[28]

- A violent robber would not have shot a customer if that person did not "choose" to enter the store at the wrong time.

- Since bullets were "flying everywhere" during a driveby shooting, it was just unfortunate that an innocent person happened to get shot.

- An auto thief only stole expensive cars, since the owners could obviously afford the loss, but avoided the vehicles of poor people.

- A sexual predator admitted making rude and vulgar remarks and displays to women, but prided himself on the fact that he never actually physically assaulted them.

From such stories, there may be validity to the "trickle down" theory of explanation for behavior that "really wasn't my fault."

Kelling, in the course of his interview, sets forth the basis from which his original concept sprung, research he conducted in Newark, New Jersey:

I learned about the idea of order maintenance by watching foot patrol officers in Newark, N.J. negotiate a standard behavior for street persons that they and the community could live with. That is, they would remind people, warn people, occasionally arrest people, but nothing much would happen to the arrests or follow-through because prosecutors weren't interested in minor offenses or in dealing with the troubled population that oftentimes is involved in disorderly behavior. So, I think the biggest change is that, starting in the late 1980's, police departments started to conduct order maintenance officially, and that lead in turn to changes in prosecutions because, if police were going to handle disorderly behavior officially and process the cases, prosecutors had to start taking it seriously as well. All of which, I think, suggests that police and prosecutors are listening more carefully to the demands of citizens for order.[29]

In approaching "broken windows" or quality-of-life issues, Kelling seems to rely on two separate, but interconnected, themes. The first, as we have seen with other approaches, is a sense of partnership. It is partnership with the community, but partnership also with other municipal services and agencies, in recognition of the fact that badges and handcuffs are not necessarily the answer to every civic problem. It is also a recognition that many lesser crimes can produce the environment conducive to the commission of many greater crimes.[30] The armed robbery of a store affects a relatively few people very much, but the aggressive panhandler or public drunk may affect hundreds or thousands of people to a lesser degree. Common sense and experience tell us that crime is more likely in the red light district than on the parish grounds.

"Broken windows" is not an attempt to turn the entire city into the parish grounds, although a few commentators have bemoaned the fact that Mayor

Rudolph Giuliani's cleanup of Times Square has caused it to lose its character and zest. Usually, they compare the new Times Square, long a haven of bars, prostitutes, and strip joints, to a sort of midtown Manhattan Disneyland, suitable for family entertainment, but bland. A counterpoint is offered, however, by the observation that the new Times Square now draws 30 million tourists a year.[31]

The objective, following Kelling, is an attempt to prevent deterioration to the point that higher crime rates will almost surely follow. As he puts it, it is an attempt that "should lead to high levels of police activities, but decreasing numbers of arrests. That is, once it becomes clear that certain behaviors are no longer tolerated, arrests should go down."[32]. It is important to understand how Kelling views arrest rates in a "broken windows" strategy environment. He supports a higher number of arrests for lesser offenses, if that ultimately means a lower number of arrests for serious offenses, to make the point that the police and the community have decided that certain types of behavior are unacceptable. Or, as he puts it, "So if it means we're going to be jailing more people for short times, but in the long haul we're not going to be imprisoning people for long periods of time, I'll live with that."[33]

Kelling also addresses issues of organizational continuity, which he believes are highly important to the effective implementation of any crime reduction strategy. This, he believes, can be a problem, particularly in cities and departments with a history of somewhat rapid turnover at the top. He notes, for example, that the average tenure of a New York Police Commissioner is usually about two and one-half years. Those programs that have survived turnover in New York and elsewhere are usually the result of a long-tenured executive or the grounding of the program so effectively into the culture of the department and the community that it is resistant to change at the top.[34]

The final development in the resurgence of the effectiveness of American policing involves not only a theory, but also our old friend, the computer. Police departments, particularly big city police departments, can have thousands, perhaps tens of thousands, of officers, plus administrative and support personnel. They are small communities with their own histories, cultures, and ways of doing things. While they can be highly resistant to change, they can also be remarkably difficult to maneuver. They have been likened, in this regard, to aircraft carriers.[35] Part of the Compstat process, at least in New York City, involved that Department "reinventing itself as speedy, maneuverable 'task force' of dozens of smaller 'ships'—precincts and other field units which, acting as a coordinated whole, have realized the seemingly impossible dream of reducing crime in the Big Apple to a degree nothing short of eye-popping."[36]

Originally a computer program to compare statistics (hence the name), Compstat grew into a management philosophy that places high levels of responsibility on police commanders, down to the precinct Captain level, to understand the crime problem in their areas and create effective strategies to deal with it. Under the New York model, all commanders are debriefed every two weeks at

Police Headquarters to test their understanding of their area's problems and to defend their track record in dealing with it. As Dodenhoff has noted:

> In fact, to assume that Compstat was merely some sort of executive inquisition would be to miss the point utterly. Compstat is enabling the NYPD to pinpoint and analyze crime patterns almost instantly, respond in the most appropriate manner, quickly shift personnel and resources as needed, assess the impact and viability of anti-crime strategies, identify bright, up-and-coming individuals from deep within the ranks, and transform the organization more fluidly and more effectively than one would ever expect of such a huge police agency.[37]

He attributes these positive developments to the four guiding principles that make Compstat work:

1. Timely and accurate intelligence
2. Use of effective tactics in response to what that intelligence tells you
3. Rapid deployment of personnel and resources
4. Relentless follow-up and assessment

Since its inception in 1994, Compstat has continued to evolve to the point that it is now a much more robust and comprehensive crime-fighting tool, as noted by William Rashbaum in *The New York Times*. He observes that the system, which went on-line in 1994, now measures 734 "indicators," from gathering spots for prostitutes to complaint rates against police officers. In effect, Compstat has become a living map of the city and, as such, a valuable diagnostic tool and targeting tool.[38]

It must be acknowledged that crime causation and prevention is a terribly complex business, and one must tread cautiously before crying "Eureka!" about any potential solution. Given that injunction, however, it seems clear that the four theories discussed previously have had at least some role, and perhaps a great role, in reducing crime and the public perception of crime as a threat. A *New York Times* article reviewing the law enforcement achievements at the end of the Giuliani administration in New York City noted that in 2001 violent crime registered its biggest drop in any of the previous five years, and even in those prior years it dropped an average of six percent a year. The article observed, however, that crime control may be affected by many factors, to include "general societal trends like a decreasing teenage population and declining use of crack cocaine, as well as crime-fighting tools Mr. Giuliani and his police commissioners introduced." The article went on to note that in many other parts of the country crime seemed to be rebounding.[39]

What do these concepts have in common?

1. *They are about community.* Community is the common thread, and both the objective (to better serve the community) and the means (to interact with the community to more accurately assess needs and partner in solutions). Community may take many forms in these constructs. It may be residential, as in a neighborhood where people live, or conceptual, as with Times Square, where relatively few people live but thousands have business or other interactions each day. It is, most of all, bonded and defined by self-interest. It is a place where people have an interest in its well-being since this affects, or can affect, them.

2. *They are all mental reconceptualizations.* There is precious little technology here. Even Compstat is not driven by any computer program not readily available to most corporations. Vincent Henry, in his history of the development and utilization of the program, noted it used off-the-shelf software and a couple of personal computers and was, in its first incarnation, nothing more than an automation of the old push-pin maps that used to hang in precinct houses.[40] These theories are grounded in a rethinking of assumptions, objectives, and relationships, which leads to a rethinking of strategies and tactics.

3. *They are to some degree about partnerships, be they partnerships with the community or partnerships with other municipal agencies.*

4. *They are about intelligence.* Not intelligence in the IQ sense, but intelligence about what is going on in the environment, whether that environment is the community or the police department.

5. *They are about change.* Not change for the sake of change, or replacing one massive bureaucratic structure with another, but change in the sense of experimentation, innovation, evaluation, and willingness to discard what does not work.

A survey of recent initiatives may be instructive in elucidating the forms and varieties of police activity that have evolved from the aforementioned concepts. The Herman Goldstein Award for Excellence in Problem-Oriented Policing is given by the Police Executive Research Forum (PERF) to police officers in the United States and abroad who engage in innovative and effective problem-solving efforts and measurably reduce problems of crime, disorder and public safety." PERF notes in its annual awards announcement that the awards are meant to recognize efforts that are consistent with Goldstein's theory that police should act to solve problems, rather than rely exclusively on the mechanisms of arrest. Or, put more generally, attempt to treat the causal conditions, rather than only the symptoms.[41]

In 2000, awards were made to six departments for the following initiatives:[42]

1. *Mid-City Division, San Diego Police Department: Graffiti Prevention and Suppression.*

2. *Kansas City, Missouri Police Department: Reported Gas Thefts at Service Stations.*

3. *Charlotte-Mecklenburg, North Carolina Police Department: Problems at the Homeless Men's Shelter.*

4. *Joliet, Illinois Police Department: Licensing Rental Property.*

5. *San Diego Police Department: Reclassifying A Home For People With Mental Illness.*

6. *Vancouver Police Department and Grandview-Woodland Community Policing Centre, British Columbia, Canada: Showdown at the Playground.*

In 2001 Goldstein awards were again granted to six departments for activities in the following areas of community concern:[43]

1. *California Highway Patrol: Corridor Safety Program: A Collaborative Approach to Traffic Safety.*

2. *Buffalo, New York Police Department: Workable Solutions to the Problem of Street Prostitution.*

3. *Chula Vista Police Department: Designing out Crime: The Chula Vista Residential Burglary Reduction Program.*

4. *Rogers County (Oklahoma) Sheriff's Office: Targeting the Market for Stolen Goods: Putting a Needle in the Haystack.*

5. *Salt Lake City Police Department: The False Alarm Solution: Verified Response.*

6. *South Euclid (Ohio) Police Department: The South Euclid School Bullying Project.*

These examples of police innovation are from 172 programs nominated for award consideration in a two-year period and are hopefully illustrative of the degree to which the police in the United States. and elsewhere have been successful in redefining their roles and mission. These programs are notable not only for their success, but also for the open manner in which police enlisted help from any source that seemed to make sense in the context of the situation at hand.

We shall examine shortly what value application of such conceptual approaches may bring to the forensic profession. There is, however, a cautionary note: Even with all the innovation and the apparent evidence of successes in many forms and locations, crime and the criminal justice system are still an expensive proposition. In 1999, the last year for which figures from the Bureau of Justice Statistics are available, the cost of fighting crime in the United States was $147 billion, or about four times the amount spent, $36 billion, in 1982. Nearly 2.2 million people work in the criminal justice system, including 1 million police officers, 717,000 prison and jail guards, and 455,000 people in the courts. These expenditures amount to about 7.7 percent of all state and local government spending. Federal increases were even more pronounced, with spending rising from $4.5 billion in 1982 to $27.4 billion in 1999.[44] As we shall see shortly, these numbers, impressive as they are, when combined are less than one-half of the estimated annual fraud loss.

Given the massive amount of criminal justice spending, some have argued that any potentially positive outcomes are likely the result of simple math; with huge numbers of people incarcerated, there is of course going to be less crime. While some favor this argument, others see it as less clear-cut. Marc Mauer, the assistant director of The Sentencing Project in Washington, D.C. and the author of *Race to Incarcerate* (New Press) counters this proposition in the following fashion:

Recent scholarship on crime reduction in the 1990's suggests that perhaps 25 percent of the reduction in violent crime can be attributed to prison-building. Significant? Yes, but this also obviously tells us that 75 percent of the reduction was not related to prison. Other factors that have likely contributed to this trend include an improved economy, strategic changes in policing, reduced demand in the drug trade, and demographic shifts.[45]

Bratton, too, rejects the "simple math" argument, that crime reduction is largely a function of the number of persons in jail, the number of cops available to put them there, or some demographic shifts. In recounting the successes of his tenure as New York City Police Commissioner, he advances the following arguments:

The drop in New York's crime rate reflected a national trend. We were the national trend. According to FBI figures, in the first six months of 1995, serious crime throughout the country went down by 1 percent, or about 67,000 crimes. In New York in that same period, there were 41,000 fewer crimes, a 16 percent drop. We were two-thirds of the national decline in reported crime.

New York's teenage population, which was responsible for a significant portion of the city's violent crime, was on its way down, and many of them were dead or in jail. "Jail? Who put them there?" Did all the sixteen-year-olds suddenly become fifty?" The number of sixteen-to-nineteen-year-olds in New York City was actually going up, not down.

Crime dropped simply because we had more cops. The NYPD reached its staffing height in September 1994 and lost about 1,400 each year thereafter through attrition until the next recruit class replenished the previous year's losses. Overtime was slashed. We were losing people and crime was still going down in double digits.

The crack epidemic that fueled the crime wave had ebbed. Heroin, a depressant, was now the drug of choice. This was the "all the criminals are nodding" defense. We spot-tested regularly in Central Booking and found that the percentage of people who had cocaine in their system when arrested remained the same or higher than it had been at crack's height. In Manhattan in February 1995, that number was 78 percent.

It was a particularly cold winter, which traditionally holds down crime. Come on. All the criminals stayed indoors? It was cold up and down the Eastern seaboard and those cities' crime figures didn't vary drastically. Were Boston's or Washington's criminal element more hardy than New York crooks?

Homicides were down because all the gangs had made peace with one another. The DEA had listened in on over 400,000 wiretap conversations, and we had never heard a word about this supposed treaty. And, if the gangs made an agreement not to kill each other over drugs, did they also agree not to rob anybody, or steal cars, or commit burglaries or shoot people?[46]

It is said that politics makes strange bedfellows—so too, may crime. At least one vocal death penalty opponent, John Bessler, an attorney and adjunct professor of law at the University of Minnesota Law School, has advanced the argument that rather than impose the death penalty as a crime-fighting tool, which he does not believe it is, we as a society should look toward earlier resolution of criminal issues. In this regard, he is not far removed from the position taken by Kelling and others that more less-serious arrests may lead to a reduction in more serious arrests. Bessler advances his position as follows:

Instead of putting needles into criminals who are brain-damaged, mentally retarded, or who do not share our value for human life, our crime-fighting efforts should focus on real solutions such as tougher gun-control laws, stiffer penalties for violent offenders, better child-protection laws, and combating truancy to keep kids in school and out of gangs.[47]

Thus, in the space of roughly 20 years, a significant number of police departments—organizations rooted in quasi-military traditions of unity, conformity, obedience, silence, and isolation—had transformed themselves and in the process had transformed crime rates in many cities. They were still cops, with guns and badges, and they still locked people up and got in shootouts from time to time, but the basic assumptions that had dominated their thinking for decade after decade had changed. By 1999, the last year for which the Bureau of Justice Statistics of the U.S. Department of Justice has published figures, more than 90 percent of police departments serving 25,000 or more residents had some type of community policing plan, and most departments serving populations of 50,000 or more had a formal, written plan. Nearly two-thirds of departments, 64 percent, had full-time community policing officers, and it was estimated that nationwide 91,000 law enforcement officers, 21 percent of all local officers, were regularly engaged in community policing activities.[48]

As these new theories in law enforcement began to enter their third decade, the results still appear positive, although experts continue to debate exactly what the figures mean and what caused their decline. The Law Enforcement News (LEN) reports that FBI Uniform Crime Report data for 2001 appears to show that the era of broad decline in crime may have bottomed out, but that some cities are still reducing the level of criminal activity, noting: "Exactly why crime has fallen seems to be somewhat of a mystery. Experts say that although policing strategies have played a role in many areas, the fall in local crime has been so precipitous that other factors had to have been at work. Just what those were, however, no one seems to know."[49] LEN goes on to note, for example, that major crime in Miami dropped in 2001 to the lowest level in 23 years, and in New York City the predicted murder rate in 2002 is expected to be at the 1958 level. One veteran police official is quoted as observing, " Homicide detectives are beginning to feel like Maytag repairmen, the number of homicides is so low."[50]

Absent further research and analysis, we can only speculate what portion of this decline was caused by the police redefining their roles and operations; however, it seems without question that such changes in priorities and strategies had at least some, and perhaps a dominant, share of the responsibility. Before we speculate on what value their experiences may hold for us, we must now consider the state the forensic profession finds itself in today.

CHAPTER 3

THE STATE OF OCCUPATIONAL FRAUD

To those of us in the forensic profession, the experience of law enforcement and its search for answers to apparently intractable problems must sound familiar. We, too, are awash in fraud, much of it within the organizations we call home. In his 1993 book, *Handbook on Corporate Fraud*, Jack Bologna cites the Hallcrest Report II, which estimates that economic crime in the United States cost consumers and businesses $144 billion in 1990 and represented about 2 percent of the nation's gross national product.[1] Recognition of the importance of this phenomenon is also not late in coming. Bologna cites a statement in 1970 by Henry S. Ruth, Jr., then the director of the U.S. National Institute of Law Enforcement and Criminal Justice: "[T]he entire field of white-collar crime represents a national priority for action and research—to define the problem, to examine its many faces, to measure its impact, and to look for ways in which its victims can be helped."[2]

The Association of Certified Fraud Examiners (ACFE) in its *1996 Report to the Nation* announced that responding members, Certified Fraud Examiners, estimated that their organizations/employers lost about 6 percent of revenues to fraud and abuse. In his 1997 book, *Occupational Fraud and Abuse*, ACFE founder and President Joe Wells notes of this figure, "If multiplied by the U.S. Gross Domestic Product—which exceeds $7 trillion annually for the latter 1990's—then the total cost to organizations in the U.S. exceeds $400 billion annually. It is a staggering sum, twice what we pay to defend our country. It is more than we spend on education and roads, not to mention six times what we pay for the criminal justice system."[3]

Based on the research conducted in assembling the *1996 Report* and updated by the *2001 National Fraud Survey*, the ACFE set forth the following statistics concerning occupational fraud:[4]

- The average organization loses more than $9 per day per employee to fraud and abuse.

- The average organization loses about 6 percent of its total annual revenue to fraud and abuse committed by its own employees.

- The median loss caused by males is about $185,000; by females about $48,000.

- The typical perpetrator is a college-educated, white male.

- Men commit nearly 75 percent of the offenses.

- Losses caused by managers are four times those caused by employees.

- Median losses caused by executives are 16 times those of their employees.

- The most costly abuses occur in organizations with less than 100 employees.

In 2002 the ACFE issued its most recent *Report to the Nation*. This document is based on the findings of 663 Certified Fraud Examiners (CFEs) who investigated fraud cases totaling more than $7 billion in losses. Again, as in 1996, the CFEs estimated their organizations will lose about 6 percent of revenues to fraud, now about $4,500 per employee. Applied to the U.S. gross domestic product, these loss ratios mean it is now possible that occupational fraud in the United States is a $600 billion annual problem. Of the losses investigated, more than half were in excess of $100,000 and nearly one in six caused a loss in excess of $1 million. Other findings of the report include data that indicates:[5]

- Over 80 percent of the occupational frauds involve asset misappropriation. Cash was the target in 90 percent of the incidents.

- Corruption schemes accounted for 13 percent of all occupational frauds and on average they caused more than $500,000 in losses.

- Fraudulent statements were the most costly form of fraud, with median losses of $4.25 million per scheme.

- The average fraud existed for 18 months before it was detected.

- The most common method of exposure was a tip from an employee, customer, vendor, or anonymous source. Accidental discovery was the second most common means by which frauds were detected.

- Organizations with fraud hotlines cut their fraud losses by approximately 50 percent per scheme. Internal audits, external audits, and preemployment background checks also significantly reduce fraud losses.

- The typical perpetrator is a first-time offender, at least insofar as having a criminal record. Only 7 percent of perpetrators had a prior conviction for a fraud offense.

- Small businesses have the greatest vulnerability. The average scheme in a small business resulted in a $127,500 loss, while for larger companies the average was $97,000.

Wells is not alone in these dire assessments. One author and researcher, writing of the savings and loan debacle, has estimated it alone may cost the U.S. taxpayer $1 trillion over the next several decades.[6] The Attorney General of the United States, in the U.S. Department of Justice (DOJ) *Fiscal Year 2000 Performance Report* and *Fiscal Year 2002 Performance Plan*, notes that the DOJ has requested to expend 9,807 full-time equivalent positions in 2002 on white-collar crime alone. This report also contains input from the Inspector General of the Department of Health and Human Services (HHS), which states that while audits conducted by that office indicate improper payments to health care providers are down to only 8 percent, this still accounts for $13.5 billion in losses each year.[7] We should note, however, that both the DOJ and the HHS figures pertain to all forms of fraud, not just occupational fraud. Certainly, some of the resources requested by the DOJ and some of the fraud reported by the HHS is occupational in nature, (i.e., it is committed by employees against their employer). Likewise, the Office of Management and Budget reported that in fiscal year 2001 the federal government paid out $20 billion in erroneous payments.[8] Presumably, this figure includes payments of the type reported by the Inspector General of the HHS, and certainly some portion of it is occupational fraud. Unfortunately, we do not know how much.

Milton Meltzer, in his book *Crime In America*, offers the following figures to begin to comprehend the size of white-collar crime in the United States:[9]

- Fraud by business costs the nation over $100 billion per year, reports the National Association of Attorneys General.

- In sum, the dollar cost of corporate crime in the United States is more than ten times greater than the combined total from larcenies, robberies, burglaries, and auto thefts committed by individuals."

We must note that Meltzer is describing the apparent size of white-collar crime, which he defines as, "crime committed by a person in a position of trust, for his or her personal gain."[10] While the figures he cites are certainly impressive, especially noting his book was written in 1990, we do not know what portion of these crime figures represents occupational fraud. Certainly, some does. This is an area we will address further with regard to definitions and how they affect our understanding of occupational fraud and its dimensions.

The National Public Survey on White Collar Crime may also offer some useful data. Published in 2000 by the National White Collar Crime Center (NWCCC), the survey was supported by a grant from the Bureau of Justice Assistance, Office of Justice Program, U.S. DOJ. In the first quarter of 1999, the survey collected data from 1,169 U.S. citizens, using a set of rigorous telephone interviewing techniques. The survey was also subjected to various forms of statistical analysis and controls to improve the utility of its data. In its introduction, the survey notes that in 1968 the President's Commission on Law Enforcement and the Administration of Justice "concluded that the public was indifferent to white collar crime and in many cases, actually sympathized with white collar offenders."[11]

The Survey goes on to note several facets of this crime problem that seem to bedevil the best efforts to deal with it: flat funding, a poor understanding of the size of the problem, a nagging suspicion that such crimes' cost dwarfs that of street crime, and the fact that in the decade of the 1990's, while arrests for more routine crimes fell, arrests for white collar offenses rose.[12]

While such figures are certainly interesting, we should note that they may or may not say much about occupational fraud. We shall deal with issues of definition later, but for our purposes a fraud or embezzlement resulting in an arrest reported to the FBI may be the act of an employee, in which case it would be occupational fraud. We cannot tell from the figures what percentage of reported arrests fall into that category. Certainly some does, we just do not know how many.

Likewise, in dealing with the NWCCC survey and its results, it is important to note the definition used. The survey defined white-collar crime as "'planned crimes that involve cheating or lying that usually occur in the course of employment.' Respondents were told that white collar offenses included crimes like fraud, embezzlement, and crimes against the public health and safety."[13]

In a conversation with John Kane, of the NWCCC, he confirmed that the survey was in fact a victimization survey, designed to discover how people felt about white-collar crime, if they or a household member had been victimized, and so on. Kane noted that part of the thrust of the survey was to try to determine if, among other offenses, a homeowner had been victimized by an unscrupulous contractor or an unscrupulous employee working for a legitimate contractor. Thus, he noted, there was an interest in persons associated with companies or organizations who used their positions to victimize other members of the public. The survey was not intended, per Kane, to try to determine if employees were victimizing their employers.[14]

Among the survey's findings were the following:[15]

- One in three households had been victimized by white collar crime.

- There was a disparity between how people said they would react to being a victim of white collar crime and how they did act. Nearly all the sample (95 percent) indicated they would report an offense, but less than half advised they had actually done so.

- Less than one in ten incidents were reported to a law enforcement agency.

- There was significant sentiment for increasing the punishment of white collar criminals.

The survey sponsors voiced their belief that there was a definite need to increase public awareness of victimization factors and also their level of reporting these incidents.

The work of the NWCCC is invaluable in gaining an understanding of yet another element of the U.S. white-collar crime problem, but has only limited applicability to improving our understanding of the dimensions of occupational fraud.

In 1999, the professional services firm of KPMG released its *1998 Fraud Survey*, which polled 5,000 leading U.S. publicly held companies, government agencies and organizations, and not-for-profits. Respondents were queried to determine the size and scope of a variety of organizational frauds, such as financial misstatements, check fraud, inventory theft, expense account schemes, inventory losses, and the like. The survey found that while all forms of fraud had increased, medical insurance claims frauds had the greatest average cost per incident, while the costliest of incidents was financial reporting frauds.[16]

Also in 1999, the Institute of Management and Administration (IOMA) and the Institute of Internal Auditors (IIA) issued the results of their joint *Business Fraud Survey*, which polled more than 300 internal auditors from organizations with average annual revenue of $2.8 billion and average annual audit budgets of $900,000. A variety of industries and governmental agencies were included. Half of the respondents said that internal fraud represented a greater threat to their organizations than external fraud or even management fraud, although 15 percent said that management fraud did represent the greatest fraud risk.[17]

In May 2000, Ernst & Young LLP released its report, *The Unmanaged Risk: An International Survey of the Effect of Fraud on Business*. This survey queried senior executives from 10,000 major organizations representing more than 30 industries in 15 countries. The survey concluded that 82 percent of all known frauds were committed by employees, and about one-third of these were committed by management. While managers did not commit the preponderance of frauds, one can conclude that as a percentage of the total employee population, their fraud rates were significantly higher than the general fraud population. Also, one would suspect, given their higher levels of influence, scope, and authority, their frauds were likely to be more serious.[18]

Even among security professionals, persons usually concerned with matters of executive protection, workplace violence, terrorism, and drugs in the workplace, occupational fraud may be found to exhibit a rather high profile. In 2002 Pinkerton completed its ninth annual *Top Security Threats and Management Issues Facing Corporate America* survey of Fortune 1000 corporations. Asked to rank 23 security threats, from workplace violence to product diversion/transshipment, fraud/white-collar crime was viewed as the sixth most important threat area, surpassed only by workplace violence, business interruption/disaster recovery, terrorism, computer crime, and employee selection and screening. Since 1997, fraud/white-collar crime had never ranked lower than seventh on the prior surveys and was once ranked as high as third. In terms of industry sectors, fraud/white-collar crime in 2002 ranked highest in retail (third) and lowest in utilities and manufacturing (eighth). Such perceptions on the part of security professionals are perhaps made more remarkable by the fact that only 3 percent of them report to the audit department of their corporation and only 33 percent have any formal coordination arrangement with that department.[19]

There is perhaps yet another way to try to comprehend the enormity of the occupational fraud problem in the United States as estimated by Wells. If we think of all the hamburger chains in the United States, all of the chicken chains, all of the taco chains, all of the pizza chains, all of the donut chains, indeed, all of the fast-food business, we are dealing with an industry that does $100 billion per year in business.[20] Fraud may be six times bigger.

Recently, during the course of a radio interview, Texas Ranger superstar short-stop Alex Rodriguez was asked how he felt about the state of baseball, which had been the subject of much talk about salary inflation, league contraction, and labor problems. Rodriguez replied to the effect that there was really nothing to worry about, since baseball was a $3 billion business.[21] I am sure Mr. Rodriguez is probably right about the gross revenues of baseball. There are 30 teams, and each plays from April to October, if they are lucky. Each has thousands of seats filled every night, parking, concessions, luxury boxes, logos on merchandise, television rights, and licensing deals. That is where the $3 billion gross number comes from. Yet, all of baseball in a given year may be less than three days of occupational fraud in the United States.

It has been publicly reported that credit cards are the most popular form of payment for purchases, totaling about $1.29 trillion last year, with about $400 billion of that amount being carried by consumers as debt. Compared to occupational fraud losses, then, all credit purchases are about twice as big and all credit card debt is about two-thirds as big.[22] Each year!

We hear much about the mind-boggling profits that are made in the drug trade and how these immense numbers provide the basis (and money) for the corruption of politicians, cops, judges, customs officials, and others around the world. Lest we wonder, please consider the magnitude of the drug dollars floating throughout the world. A United Nations' study estimates international drug profits to be $400 billion per year.[23] Impressive? Yes. But it is about where we were five years ago with occupational fraud in the United States and only two-thirds of where we believe we are now.

Finally, believe it or not, occupational fraud in a given year may be about two-thirds the value of the federal government, with a few important disclaimers. The *2002 Federal Financial Management Report*, reports this number thusly: "The balance sheet of the Federal Government shows a historical value of over $900 billion in physical and financial assets. This estimate is not comprehensive because it does not include natural resources, stewardship land (national parks, forests, and grazing lands), national defense assets, or heritage assets (e.g., the Hope Diamond)."[24]

Hopefully, such numbers provide us a rudimentary basis for beginning to comprehend just how big occupational fraud is today. The bad news is that we may not even have all of it counted, even at the $600 billion level.

The *2001 National Retail Security Survey* conducted by the University of Florida reported that U.S. retailers lost more than $32.3 billion in inventory shrinkage.[25] Some of that loss was caused by human error, damage, and theft by outsiders. But if only 10 percent was caused by theft by employees, that amounts to $3.2 billion dollars—larger than all of major league baseball. Informed observers from the NWCCC estimate the real percentage of such losses caused by the fraudulent actions of insiders to be about 40 to 45 percent—about five times the size of all of major league baseball![26]

Even figures this striking may be substantially incomplete. Computers are part of the high-tech world in which we live, and they are certainly involved in at least some portion, and perhaps a high portion, of the frauds with which we are concerned. But are these losses also covered, are they in addition to what we believe we know, or is there some element of double counting? Again, we do not know. There is no organization believed to keep accurate loss figures on high-tech and computer crime, and even the FBI, long in the crime statistics business, has difficulty capturing such data. Compounding this issue are organizational disincentives for revealing such data, to include negative publicity, decreased stockholder acceptance, and customer confidence. Given this state of affairs, organizations such as the Computer Security Institute, in conjunction with the FBI International Computer Crime Squad, conducted the 1999 *Computer Crime and Security Survey*. This vehicle revealed the following results:[27]

- 62% of organizations had a computer security breach within the last year
- 30% reported system penetration by outsiders
- 57% pointed to their Internet connection as the point of entry from outside intrusion
- 32% reported denial of service attacks
- 19% experienced sabotage of data or networks
- 14% were victims of financial fraud
- 90% had incidents of virus contamination
- 55% had incidents of unauthorized access by insiders
- 97% reported abuse of Internet privileges by their employees
- 69% lost laptops to theft
- 26% said they had experienced theft of proprietary information
- 32% of the responding organizations had reported serious incidents to law enforcement in the last year

- Losses due to computer security breaches totaled over $100,000,000 for the third consecutive year
- Of the 51% of organizations who acknowledged financial loss, only 31% were able to put a figure on their loss

While some of these statistics are of little relevance to our concerns (e.g., virus contamination, laptop theft), much of this data is directly on point to the problem of occupational fraud. Some organizations were clearly victims of computer-related financial fraud, more than half reported unauthorized access by insiders, one quarter suffered loss of proprietary information, and less than one third of those victimized had the ability to put a dollar value on their loss. These are disturbing numbers and, when coupled with incentives to underreport, appear to be indicative of problems we see in the larger arena of occupational fraud. To some degree we are being asked to solve a problem when we do not know its dimensions or, for that matter, its definitions. Some estimate that shoplifting in the United States costs retailers $13 billion per year, and that at least some, perhaps most, of this loss is caused by employees.[28] Are such figures captured as part of what we define as occupational fraud? We simply do not know.

Even the most cited of all crime indexes in the United States, the FBI's Uniform Crime Reporting Program (UCRP), or its newest incarnation, the National Incident-Based Reporting System (NIBRS), are of little use in any detailed analysis of occupational fraud. The primary reason is the method by which the data are captured. White-collar crime, and especially occupational fraud, is not a priority category for the UCRP. Second, to the degree that this data is captured at all, analysis is difficult because of the categories involved. A typical crime committed in an occupational fraud scenario may be charged in UCRP terms as larceny, larceny by trick, uttering a forged instrument (usually, writing a bad check), or some other offense category. The problem is you cannot tell from the data if the charge relates to an employee submitting phony vouchers for payment (an occupational fraud) or someone passing a hot check at a liquor store. To the police, the courts, and to the UCRP, all these offenses are the same. To us, the distinctions make a world of difference.

The *White Collar Crime Study*, released by the FBI National Press Office on March 6, 2002, indicates that white-collar crime, when extracted from the NIBRS, constitutes 4 percent of all crime reported and, further, that 4 percent of all arrestees in the system were there for bad check offenses. The report goes on to note that of all computer crimes, or technocrimes, 42 percent were deemed to be white-collar crimes, with the majority of these being larceny-theft. This figure is then broken out by specific offense type: fraud offenses are 9 percent, larceny-thefts are 31 percent, and 2 percent are embezzlements. The report notes that the NIBRS attempts to capture five categories of white-collar crime: fraud, bribery, counterfeiting/forgery, embezzlement, and "other offenses that in combination could constitute white-collar crime." The report also states that businesses are as likely as individuals to be victims of white-collar crime, and that white-collar crimes, on a per-incident basis, are more costly than property crimes.[29]

From my long experience in the FBI, I also believe federal offense data are of limited use. The White Collar Crime Section of the FBI's Criminal Investigative Division does keep track of white-collar crimes within the FBI's purview (not all are), mainly for program assessment purposes and use in preparing budget testimony. The vast majority of these are Bank Fraud and Embezzlement (BF&E) matters, but here again the utility of the data for our purposes falls off rapidly. A BF&E offense may be committed by an employee seeking to defraud the bank (an occupational fraud for our purposes) or an outsider running some sort of swindle. Even this data is tracked only because the financial institution is federally insured, which gives the FBI the basis for its jurisdiction in the first place.

Most occupational frauds (those involving other than federally insured institutions) are usually captured under one of several federal statutes, some of which may not even be within the FBI's White Collar Crime Program. Typical of these would be Interstate Transportation of Stolen Property, Fraud By Wire, Mail Fraud, and Conspiracy. In recent years, certain categories of computer crimes have been added to such statistics, as have violations of the Economic Espionage Act of 1996.

Again, we have the BF&E problem: From the statistics alone, it is difficult to determine if any of these acts involved an employee and were, thereby, an occupational fraud. Further, each judicial district in the United States, ninety-some in total, has prosecutive guidelines, which they use to prioritize prosecutions. Generally, these are set higher in urban areas than in rural locales. Thus, while a given statute may say that a theft of $5,000 or more will trigger federal prosecution, the reality is that the working number sufficient to arouse federal interest may be $50,000, $100,000, or higher. Depending on the district, matters below this threshold amount are not accepted into the federal system and, accordingly, are not considered federal crimes even though they are clear-cut violations of law.

This problem may, for all we know, be only the tip of a rather large iceberg. As Wells further notes with regard to the 6 percent figure:

> Considering everything we know, it may be the best number we can use for the present. It at least gives organizations a rough measure of their potential exposure. Whether or not that exposure is ever discovered is a different matter. We have seen examples of occupational frauds in this book that have gone undetected for years. Except for a fluke of circumstance, many of them could still be thriving today. That, of course, is the most troubling aspect of many occupational frauds: the longer they go on, the more expensive they are. People who start committing fraud will generally continue unless there is a compelling reason to quit.[30]

Were Wells' observations not dire enough, there is at least some research that indicates there may be powerful organizational imperatives toward fraudulent behavior. Research conducted in 1996 by Professor Arthur Brief of the Freeman School of Business at Tulane University found evidence that suggested a significant percentage of managers may forget their personal ethics when placed in a demanding business environment. In the study of about 400 executives, Brief found that 47 percent were willing to commit fraud by understating writeoffs that would cut into their company's profits. Commenting on these findings, Brief noted: "People in subordinate roles will comply with their superiors even when that includes wrongdoing that goes against their individual moral code. I thought they would stick with their values, but most organizations are structured to produce obedience."[31]

Brief's findings may perhaps find support in studies reported in a book by Michael R. Young, *Accounting Irregularities and Financial Fraud*. He cites several studies that may be a cause for concern, particularly given that they came in a pre-Enron environment. Young notes:

> A series of surveys conducted by PricewaterhouseCoopers shows that claims based on alleged accounting irregularities have increased from 25% of securities claims filed in 1997 to 49% just two years later. A similar study concluded that between 1992 and 1998, the number of securities lawsuits based on the need to restate audited financial statements increased by 750%. A separate survey of chief financial officers, conducted on a strictly anonymous basis, found that fully two-thirds had recently been subjected to pressure within their companies to misrepresent financial results. According to the survey, 55% had successfully resisted. At the same time, 12% had not.[32]

Holman Jenkins, writing in *The Wall Street Journal*, also notes that a variety of corporate executives faced civil and criminal sanctions well before Enron. Citing a number of these cases, he goes on to note one of the reasons for the increase:

> An astonishing number of business execs face jail or indictment for book-keeping fraud. Federal prosecutors, ... once left such behavior to the civil courts. Change was coming even before SEC Chairman Arthur Levitt began rallying opinion in the late Clinton years with speeches against "accounting hocus-pocus." ...[33]

L. J. Brooks also expressed concerns about the general corporate environment and the demands and pressures faced by U.S. corporations. He noted they will continue to be called on to address their ethical dimensions because of a number of factors:[34]

1. A growing crisis of confidence about corporate activity
2. Increasing quality-of-life issues

3. Growing expectations that corporations and individuals will be dealt with harshly for ethical and legal violations

4. The growing power of some special interest and watchdog groups

5. The general level of publicity generated by the previous factors

6. An enhanced recognition on the part of business executives and the greater business community of the legitimacy of longer-term versus immediate goals

Some of Brooks' concerns seem to have been borne out. Others, such as a long-term versus immediate orientation are not so clear, but the interesting thing is that Brooks made these observations in 1989, almost 15 years ago.

Kenneth Labich likewise speculated in 1992 on factors he believed would motivate businesses to deal more vigorously with issues of ethical compliance, among them:[35]

1. Increased media expertise in rooting out corporate misdeeds

2. Financial consequences of corporate ethical failures

3. Harsh federal sentencing guidelines for certain misdeeds

These figures, troubling as they are, may or may not represent occupational fraud. Normally, we think of such fraud as being the province of one or more employees abusing their organizational positions for personal profit. While we shall discuss such issues more fully in reference to issues of definition in the occupational fraud field, I would suggest incidents such as this are occupational fraud. The only difference appears to be that someone senior to the chief finan- cial officers is pressuring them to commit the fraud on their behalf. We can, should we so chose, term some incidents of this type *business reversal fraud*. That is a term Cressey, whose pioneering work we shall examine in Chapter 4, used to describe frauds undertaken for the primary purpose of saving a failing business, but they are frauds nonetheless.

While this book is about the state of occupational fraud in the United States, some statistics from Canada are perhaps pertinent. Their utility derives from several intriguing issues they raise—issues that may go to the heart of explain- ing some of the peculiar characteristics of the fraud phenomenon with which we are dealing. In 2000, Ernst & Young LLP—Canada commissioned a polling organization to conduct a random, confidential, statistically sound survey of Canadians. The poll randomly contacted 822 Canadians and produced results that are considered accurate to within +/– 3.4 percentage points, 19 times out of 20.

Those contacted were asked if they knew one of their co-workers was taking goods or money that did not belong to them, if they would report it if they were the only person with such knowledge. Eighty-four percent of the respondents said they were very likely or somewhat likely to do so (55% very likely, 29% somewhat likely). Respondents were then asked how big a problem they thought the following types of fraud were. Those responding cited the following areas as significant problems in the 7–10 range on a 1–10 scale:

Inflating expense accounts	68%
Taking items from the office	66%
Altering books to make profits or costs look better	57%
Pocketing money from cash sales	56%
Taking kickbacks from suppliers	51%
Creating phony supplier invoices	44%

Respondents were then asked if they were personally aware of any of these types of fraud in the past year involving either themselves or people they knew. Twenty-five percent responded positively and 74 percent responded in the negative. The most common offenses were taking items from the office (47%) and inflating expense accounts (21%). All other response categories were 13 percent or less.

The respondents were then asked, with regard to the previous instances, if they personally reported them. Thirty-four percent said they did and 66 percent said they did not. This is truly an interesting statistic and one worthy of further study. When asked in the abstract as to whether they would report fraud, 84 percent said they would. Later, when faced with a specific, actual event, only 34 percent said they reported the occurrence, a drop of 50 percent. Since the latter question queried them as to acts they may have personally committed, it is logical to assume they would not report themselves. But, it appears unlikely this accounts for all of the 50 percent difference in those who would report in the abstract but not in reality. This may be simply because it is usually easier to espouse good intentions, rather than act on them. Or, there may be flaws in the reporting mechanism(s) that dissuade persons from coming forward. Awareness of reporting channels did not appear to be an issue, since 89 percent of respondents said they knew who should be made aware of such events.

Finally, 21 percent of respondents said instances of workplace fraud had decreased in the past few years, 10 percent said it had increased, and 59 percent opined that it had stayed the same. Asked about the ease with which occupational fraud could be committed, 39 percent said they thought it was easier to accomplish, 41 percent said it had become more difficult, and 16 percent said it had not changed.[36]

Such studies are useful, but always leave one with questions: What if "taking things from the office" had been eliminated? Certainly, this constitutes occupational fraud, and if it means a trunkload of expensive inventory every other day,

I think we are all interested. But, what if it is the occasional pen or mechanical pencil? Still occupational fraud, but then so is looking out the window and day-dreaming about fishing, if we want to get technical about it. The issue of reporting is extremely important and is one, I believe, that warrants much further study. What the study seems to imply, nagging questions aside, is that there may be a significant amount of occupational fraud, of at least some sort, in Canada.

Given these characteristics of fraud, we in the forensic profession may, as the saying goes, "Be in a heap of trouble." We know we have a huge problem on our hands: it probably measures in at least the hundreds of billions of dollars annually. Every indication we have is that it is not shrinking much and may be growing.[37] We know from experience that most of it remains hidden and that it tends to continue unless stopped. That is one of the more interesting aspects of occupational fraud—it almost always keeps going. The person robbing a bank does not stand there, unless they are truly stupid, for six hours and keep robbing it. They would surely get caught. They might go down the street and rob another bank or come back a week later and rob this one again, but they do not continue to rob the same one in a temporal sense.

Fraudsters, on the other hand, and especially occupational fraudsters, usually do precisely the opposite. Once they have committed a fraud and not gotten caught, they gain a greater sense of confidence. They may repeat it endlessly at a like amount or increase the amount of their next take to test the system. Uncaught and absent some truly significant personal event to change their behavior, they may continue for years or decades. Thus the bank robber is like a shark that swims up, takes a quick, violent bite, and swims away. The occupational fraudster is more like the parasite that seeks to remain attached to the lucrative host for as long as possible, feeding constantly.

It may also be that some of these parasites travel in packs. A survey conducted of members by the ACFE in March 2002 asked the following question: In your latest internal fraud case, how many people were involved?

The results were surprising, since many in the general population and many in the forensic field consider fraud to typically be the work of the lone perpetrator:[38]

Number of Perpetrators	Percentage of Cases
1	41 percent
2	21 percent
3–5	21 percent
5–10	6 percent
Over 10	9 percent

We can only speculate at this point what these figures tell us. Are increasing numbers of people involved in the same instance of fraud because it is so complex that it requires a lot of assistance? Are these units or departments that have become infected and gone bad? Is this copycatting, where one employee sees another get away with something and decides, "Well, why not me too?" Or, is this some form of malevolent fellowship, where one dishonest employee shares his or her secrets with office mates, so others can dip from the well also? Unfortunately, absent further research, we can only guess.

While this may be interesting psychology or half-baked biology, it represents yet a further challenge to the forensic practitioner. Usually, time and experience have taught us to be wary of the strange—the strange person, the strange neighborhood, the strange noise, the strange food. With occupational fraud, the equation is reversed. New employees may possibly attempt fraud the first day on the job, but usually they do not. They need time to learn the policies, people, and procedures. As the saying goes, to "case the joint."

Our potential adversary is not the new face, but the one we are used to seeing— the longer-term employee we may be used to chatting with most days or waving at in the company cafeteria. Such is the inherent nature of occupational fraud, and it is a characteristic that tends to make our already difficult jobs even more troublesome. We do not have our innate sensitivity to strangeness to protect us. The very nature of the fraud(s) being committed may compel the fraudster to stick around, since continued access to books, records, and accounts is required to keep the fraud hidden from sight.

Not only are we often familiar with those who commit fraud in the workplace, but it is their very familiarity with us and our organizations that make them so effective in their schemes and so significant a threat to their organizational homes. Diane Sears Campbell, in discussing the threat of cybercrimes to organizations, quotes Donn Parker, the author of *Fighting Computer Crime: A New Framework for Protecting Information*. Parker notes that one of the things that computer criminals utilize to commit their crimes is that computers are by definition predictable. Parker notes:

> Among the 200 computer criminals I have interviewed over the past 35 years, I find that unpredictability of the environment and circumstances of their crime is the most important aspect to being successful in their crime.... The perpetrator has to be able to predict the circumstances and environment of his crime successfully or he will be caught and his crime will fail. So control over that environment or those circumstances is critical.... This is one reason that computers, as objects of attack, or as tools to engage in fraud, are so attractive, because computers are predictable. They will do exactly the same thing under exactly the same circumstances, predictably, whereas people are assured to do something different every time. People are unpredictable.[39]

Interestingly, while hackers and computer criminal stories seem to appear in the media with increasing regularity, the *1999 Business Fraud Survey* conducted by

IOMA and the IIA is reported to have found that 72 percent of respondents indicated their organizations did not even have fraud detection software in place![40]

These observations are supported by data and analysis provided by the ACFE. In reflecting on its *1996 Report to the Nation* occupational fraud survey, the ACFE reported that small organizations, those with fewer than 100 employees, are particularly susceptible to occupational fraud. In such organizations the median fraud loss was $120,000. The median loss per incident to occupational fraud goes down as organizations get bigger, up to 10,000 employees. Above the 10,000-employee level, fraud begins to go up again in terms of median size per incident.

This is particularly troublesome since smaller organizations are usually less likely to be able to absorb such a loss. Several of those cited in the study went out of business because of their occupational fraud losses. The ACFE proposes two theories to explain why smaller organizations have such heavy losses. The first is that they have fewer divisions of responsibility. Separation of duties is normally one of the more basic controls used to mitigate financial risk. We shall discuss controls in more detail later in this book, but we have recently seen from examples like Allfirst Bank and Frank Gruttadauria of Lehman Brothers that even large organizations can apparently have control lapses that lead to serious problems. The second rationale proffered is that in small organizations there is a greater level of intimacy and, therefore, trust. The ACFE notes this presents a challenge for executives in smaller organizations:

> [F]raud cannot occur without trust, but neither can commerce. If one makes controls and security measures too strict, one's business will suffer because it will be inefficient, . . . if one makes controls and security measures too loose, one's business will be a sitting duck for occupational fraud.[41]

Interestingly, the question of balance in approaching such issues was suggested in a poll conducted of ACFE members in April 2002. When asked what measures would be most effective in deterring fraudulent financial reporting, respondents offered the following as their top three recommendations[42]:

1. Encouraging whistleblowers (28%)
2. Surprise audits (25%)
3. Assigning at least one CFE to every public audit (24%)

The parity provided in these responses is perhaps revealing. Although the question and answers were not intentionally structured to provide relative choices, the fact that almost the same percentage of experienced practitioners suggested each of the techniques may argue both for the perceived effectiveness of each but also for the potential synergy to be obtained from utilizing all three in a coordinated manner.

No matter how deep our experience or well honed our professional skills, how-ever, we may expect occupational fraud to continue to evolve and grow. Each new technological advance triggers new opportunities for those so inclined to misuse it, whether inside the organization or without. Last year, for example, federal authorities conducted a series of inquires into various forms of Internet fraud that resulted in criminal charges being brought against 90 persons and businesses. Losses to victims were estimated to be $117 million.[43] Richard L. Johnson, the director of the National White Collar Crime Complaint Center, has been quoted as believing that Internet fraud complaints, now running about 1,000 per week, will soon reach 1,000 per day.[44]

Internet connections have, for the fourth year in a row, been cited as the most frequent point of attack in cybercrime incidents in the *2001 Computer Crime and Security Survey* conducted by the Computer Security Institute and the FBI. The rate of such incidents reported by respondents to the survey increased from 59 percent of those contacted in 2000 to 70 percent in 2001. Of the 538 computer security professionals surveyed in the project, 64 percent reported that these attacks resulted in financial losses to their organizations. One of the most com-mon potential sources of Internet-connected fraud, according to Howard Cox, acting deputy general counsel with the Office of Inspector General of the U. S. Postal Service, is: "Internal employees who use the Internet to anonymously gain access to data that is not related to their jobs and then misuse it for personal gain, compromising the organization's security. These people usually are about to be fired or are unhappy in their jobs."

Cox notes the Internet is favored by employees inclined to take actions against their organization's interests for three reasons: (1) more financial transactions are consummated on the Internet; (2) the Internet affords a relatively anony-mous venue to commit these acts; and (3) new laws acted to make obsolete some internal controls auditors have relied on in more traditional environments.[45]

The *2002 Computer Crime And Security Survey* of large corporation and gov-ernmental agencies is also revealing in grasping the dimensions of these prob-lems. It notes, in part, that while 90 percent of respondents reported computer security breaches, only 34 percent reported these to a law enforcement agency. While only 44 percent were able to put a dollar value on their losses due to com-promise of intellectual property, those that did estimated losses in excess of $170 million. Organizations reporting financial frauds estimated those losses as being in excess of $155 million. Finally, 78 percent of respondents advised their employees had violated Internet access and use policies.[46]

Unfortunately, the survey as released does not indicate what percentage of such incidents were committed or abetted by insiders, thus making them occu-pational fraud.

GartnerG2, a research service from Gartner, Inc., reported the following find-ings: "More than $700 million in online sales were lost to fraud in 2001, repre-senting 1.14% of total annual online sales of $61.8 billion. Online fraud losses for 2001 were 19 times as high, dollar for dollar, as fraud losses resulting from offline sales."[47] The persons who engage in such acts often show a great deal of ingenuity and resourcefulness, sometimes combining two or more technologies or techniques to make their tasks easier and ours harder.

Douglas Watson, writing in the March/April 2002 edition of *The White Paper*, likewise reports on a study conducted by the Nevada State Attorney General, who found that while the average bank robber gets about $2,500 and the average bank embezzler gets about $25,000, the average computer crime reaps about $500,000. The report further notes that the average computer-related fraud is $1.9 million. Such activities may be seen by the unscrupulous not only as highly profitable, but also relatively safe, since the report also indicates that only 1 percent of computer crime is detected, only 7 percent is reported to law enforcement, and only 3 percent of the cases that are investigated and prosecuted result in jail time.[48]

The Internet Fraud Complaint Center, a joint undertaking by the FBI and the NWCCC, reports that auction fraud is now the number one computer-related crime. Last year the NWCCC logged 7,193 complaints representing losses amounting to $5.4 million, and it estimated that fewer than 10 percent of persons defrauded even bother to file complaints. The usual reasons, we are informed, are because the victims are embarrassed or do not know where to turn. That one also sees such reactions on the part of many organizations, great and small, when they encounter occupational fraud does not give us great confidence that we shall know the true dimensions of organizational fraud anytime soon. Cameron, citing an April 2000 report by Meridian Research, notes that estimated credit card losses to U.S. business were $9 billion in 2001, and could reach $40 to $60 billion by 2005.[49]

Such scams, reprehensible as they are, do not directly affect us, since they do not meet the definition of occupational fraud. Yet the experience of the NWCCC is still instructive, for what we see developing in the commercial marketplace usually finds its way into our organizations. One technique now starting to appear involves combining a fraudulent sale on the Internet with identity theft (the assumption of another person's legitimate identity to commit or facilitate a crime). The more enterprising fraudsters now offer nonexistent goods for sale and ask the unsuspecting buyer to wire their money to a bank account. This often gives the buyer a level of assurance, since they falsely believe if the goods are not delivered they can use the bank account information to track down the other party.

Such, alas, is not the case, for the bank account is also fraudulent, having been set up with an identity stolen from yet another victim. The fraud perpetrator merely lets money accumulate, drains the account, and then repeats the process all over again.[50]

Such identity thefts are, unfortunately, perceived in some circles as a minor or nuisance crime. An article by Adam Clymer in *The New York Times* may help dispel this notion. Clymer notes: "Federal authorities announced a nationwide sweep of identity theft arrests today, charging the people with using false credentials to cover up a murder, sell homes belonging to the elderly, and exercise 176,000 stock options belonging to an unknowing company executive."[51]

Attorney General John Ashcroft has called identity theft "one of the fastest growing crimes in the United States," with an estimated 500,000 to 700,000 victims each year. He noted that U.S. attorneys around the country had brought 25 new identify theft cases in the last 24 hours before his remarks. While this level of increased enforcement is encouraging, a study of DOJ data conducted by the Transactional Records Access Clearinghouse of Syracuse University indicated that about one-third of those convicted of identity theft did not receive prison time and of those that did the average sentence was less than one year.

Clymer also noted that in one case a hospital worker stole the identities of 393 patients for the purpose of obtaining bogus credit cards, while more than one Web site actively advertises stolen social security numbers for sale to those interested in gaining false credit.[52]

Authors Ellingson and Williams have cited the California Public Interest Research Group to the effect that their research indicates that it takes two years and $18,000 for the average identity theft victim to clean up their stolen identity and remove fraudulent information from credit files.[53] Such time and expense is considerable both for the individual and to the country as a whole, when one thinks of the range of yearly victims cited by Attorney General Ashcroft. The cost to individuals alone may be $9 to $12.6 billion per year! Certainly, some part of this loss is caused by the improper activities of employees accessing customer data, much like the hospital worker. We simply do not know how much.

Lest we forget, the government is also an employer and, thereby, subject to some level of occupational fraud. Combining the local, state, and federal levels, there are millions of government employees in the United States. Trying to obtain comprehensive statistics on these workplace fraud losses is difficult because of the diffuse nature of the thousands of entities that can be termed governmental agencies. They range from the local school authority to massive federal agencies. One article, however, may provide some flavor of the scope of potential governmental problems.

In May 2002 the Associated Press reported that Inspector Generals from three federal agencies have advised Congress that they cannot even estimate the extent of credit card abuse by federal government employees. The article noted that at the Pentagon alone more than 46,000 employees had defaulted on in excess of $62 million in travel expenses charged to government credit cards. At the Education Department, the General Accounting Office could not find 179 pieces of computer equipment, worth more than $200,000, that had been charged to government credit cards. The total size of potential problems in this arena alone is unknown, but some idea of its scope is suggested by research conducted by the Associated Press. That organization learned in 2001 that the federal government had more than 3 million credit cards in its possession, one for three out of every four federal employees.

Gregory H. Friedman, the Inspector General at the Energy Department, advised a Congressional Committee that his agency alone had conducted 22 audits and criminal investigations of credit card abuse since 1998 and recovered more than $325,000 in unauthorized purchases. Among these violations, he noted, were kickbacks to suppliers for false invoices, goods bought for personal use and delivered to the employee's home, and ghost purchases in which all required paperwork was completed but no goods or services were ever received by the government. Inspector General Janet Rehnquist of the HHS advised Congress that last summer her office began to analyze all credit card purchases for unusual amounts or characteristics. As a result of this effort, they have already begun 24 investigations involving 43 employees of that agency.[54]

Given the size, scope, infinite variety, and hidden nature of occupational fraud, what do we do to defeat it? One of the obvious first steps is to try to determine why it happens.

CHAPTER 4

THEORIES OF OCCUPATIONAL FRAUD

I n his book, *Occupational Fraud and Abuse*, Joseph Wells sets forth several theories of fraud causation based on his many years of research in the field and his interactions with a number of academics and theorists interested in the subject.

One of the earliest researchers in the arena was Edwin H. Sutherland, a criminologist at Indiana University. Focused initially on the activities of the elite business executive, Sutherland rejected the conventional wisdom that the motivation to commit fraud was the result of some mental defect or socioeconomic deprivation. Sutherland coined the term *white collar crime*, although he used it in the sense of corporate acts and acts by individuals acting in a corporate capacity. Later, Sutherland developed his theory of *differential association*, which held that criminal activity is a learned behavior, much like the ability to learn a language or play a musical instrument. Criminal learning, he theorized, involved two separate but supporting areas of endeavor: achieving the technical competence to commit the fraud and "the attitudes, drives, rationalizations, and motives of the criminal mind."[1]

Donald R. Cressey was a student of Sutherland's who undertook his own research into the causation of fraud, especially that committed by embezzlers. Much of Cressey's work was based on his interviews with several hundred incarcerated embezzlers. As a result of this work, Cressey came to develop what Wells has characterized as the *fraud triangle*; that is, the three sets of conditions conducive to fraud taking place: (1) a perceived nonsharable financial need or pressure; (2) an opportunity to commit the act(s); and (3) a rationalization mechanism to permit the fraud to occur.[2]

Cressey opined that the nonsharable nature of the financial need was solely the perception of the individual involved and did not necessarily require any objective basis in fact. Thus the gambler who regularly loses more than he can afford might have either a sharable or nonsharable problem, depending on how he perceives it. Cressey then divided nonsharable problems into six subcategories:[3]

1. *Violation of ascribed obligations.* Simply put, this is the accumulation of debts, legitimate or otherwise, that the individual believes are incompatible with their social role(s) as husband, father, employee, friend, and so on, and, therefore, cannot be shared without embarrassment or loss of social standing.

2. *Personal failure.* While some issues in this category might be macroeconomic in nature (e.g., a recession), others are microeconomic and more intensely personal (e.g., poor investment decisions).

3. *Business reversals.* While similar to the personal failure category, Cressey here saw patterns of people willing to violate trusts to try to save a dying business.

4. *Physical isolation.* Some persons, faced with financial pressures, simply have, or perceive that they have, no one to turn to for help.

5. *Status gaining.* Some persons aspire to a certain station in life and want to associate with certain types of people. If their finances will not support these aspirations, they may view this as a nonsharable problem.

6. *Employer–employee relations.* Revenge is perhaps the dominant motive in these instances, where an employee believes he or she has been slighted and has no open or legitimate recourse to remedy the harm.

Dr. W. Steve Albrecht, trained as a Certified Public Accountant (CPA), is a researcher into occupational fraud and abuse and a person Wells credits with giving him some of the concepts necessary to start the Association of Certified Fraud Examiners.[4] Working with other researchers, and funded by a grant from the Institute of Internal Auditors Research Foundation, Albrecht studied 212 frauds committed in the early 1980s, employing extensive questionnaires directed to internal auditors familiar with the incidents. One portion of the research concentrated on the motivations for the frauds in question, and yielded some likely characteristics: gambling and personal debts; a desire for personal gain coupled with dissatisfaction with compensation; chumminess with customers; a motivation to "beat the system;" and a fast and loose attitude toward rules.[5]

Wells notes the similarity of many of these motivators to what Cressey referred to as nonsharable financial problems, and concluded that Albrecht had found three primary elements to be present in the fraud causation: (1) a situational pressure (normally financial), (2) an opportunity to commit the fraud, and (3) a rationalization for committing the act.[6] He notes that Albrecht and his colleagues found that "occupational fraud perpetrators are hard to profile and that fraud is difficult to predict." He further notes, as of the date of his book, 1997, that "Albrecht's research does not address—and no current research has been done to determine—if nonoffenders have many of the same characteristics."[7]

The final study Wells cites is that of Richard C. Hollinger of Purdue University and John P. Clark of the University of Missouri, which was a federally funded study of 10,000 American workers. They, unlike Cressey and Albrecht, "concluded that employees steal primarily as a result of workplace conditions, and that the true costs of the problem are vastly understated"[8] Hollinger-Clark did conclude, however, that five separate but interrelated sets of factors were significant in understanding occupational fraud. The first of these was external economic pressures, much like the unsharable financial problem that Cressey had hypothesized. The second hypothesis was that contemporary employees, especially younger ones (the study was published in 1983) were not as honest and hardworking as those of prior generations. The third premise was that any employee can be tempted to steal.[9] The fourth hypothesis was that most employee theft was to some degree a result of job dissatisfaction. The fifth hypothesis was that theft occurs because of the broadly shared formal and informal structure, norms if you will, of the organization.[10]

Wells notes that Hollinger and Clark made several attempts to draw inferences from the data they had collected. They compared income levels with incidences of fraud and found no meaningful co-relations, other than one between a person's concern about financial condition and the likelihood of resultant theft. This emphasis was repeated when respondents were asked to rank eight personal issues, such as health, educational issues, financial posture, and so on. They found that those who ranked finances as the first or second most important issue had higher incidences of theft as employees. They did note that there appeared to be few relationships as strong as that of youth and propensity to theft, hypothesizing that younger employees had less tenure and, therefore, less commitment to the victim organization.

To some degree, the Hollinger-Clark hypothesis may be borne out by more recent data. For example, the *White Collar Crime Study* issued by the FBI National Press Office on March 6, 2002, observes that: "The majority of white-collar crime offenders have had contact with their victims and are typically white males aged late-twenties to early-thirties."[11]

Other factors Hollinger and Clark found to be significant were organizational positioning, observing that employees with the greatest access to organizational assets were more likely to engage in theft than those who did not. They also noted that while all age groups of employees could be found to engage in improper or illegal behavior, the tendency was greatest among the younger age groups.[12]

From this point, Hollinger and Clark moved on to the obvious issue of organizational controls, asking if there was any co-relation between controls and organizational deviance. In this effort, they examined five areas of common controls: company policy, selection of personnel, inventory control, security, and punishment. Generally speaking, they found these mechanisms to have some degree of effectiveness. They found that company policy can be effective in deterring theft, as could educating employees. The other control mechanisms were believed to likewise have some deterrent effect, but their overall conclusion was mixed, at best. They opined that while organizational controls could be inferred to have some deterrent effect, it was neither strong nor consistent. The most realistic statement of their effect, they concluded, would be to recognize them as useful elements in a deterrence structure, but best understood as operating in conjunction with other factors less amenable to measurement or direct organizational influence. One of these factors was employee perception. Simply put, much like the child eyeing the cookie jar, employees who believed there was a high likelihood of detection and punishment were less likely to engage in improper behavior. [13]

Finally, Hollinger and Clark commented on the issue of formal and informal social controls within the organizational setting, observing that while both were important, informal controls, particularly the opinions of one's acquaintance and peers, were the most effective.[14]

Writing some years later on issues of ethical codes in organizations, James Bowman noted that in the absence of systematic guidance and sustained effort, it is likely that the average organizational member is being educated by happenstance events, idiosyncratic actions of individual persons and managers, or through the rumor mill.[15]

In his summary of Hollinger and Clark's work, Wells concludes that organizational management would be well served to pay particular attention to four aspects of workplace life: (1) develop a clear understanding of theft behavior; (2) continually disseminate positive information regarding company policies; (3) enforce sanctions; and (4) publicize sanctions taken.[16]

Having followed Wells and his mentors through this history of occupational fraud theory, what does it tell us? It seems, on first blush, that Cressey was onto something. Time and again, we come back to the iron triangle of fraud: perceived need, opportunity, and rationalization. Hollinger and Clark, and others, have done valuable work in expanding our understanding of the nuances of these elements and of the efficacy of measures directed toward fraud deterrence, but at root level we are pretty much where Cressey left us many years ago. Given that each of us has needs, much less perceived needs, and that these change, evolve, and develop as a result of scores of extraneous factors, how does the organization deal with what is going on in employee's heads and hearts? Further, perceived injustices within the workplace are legion, and if each is a potential motivation to fraud, must the organization create the world's first perfect society to remain safe? We are told that controls are effective, at least to some degree, as are sanctions, but must the defeat of the iron triangle of fraud causation be countered with an iron hand of organizational control? Are we prepared for the cost, both economic and psychic, of such a stance, even were one willing to pay it?

Jack Bologna, a 40-year practitioner and writer in this field, offers his own set of characteristics for fraud behavior, which tend more toward the operational than psychological. He finds a general sense of malaise within susceptible organizations, with scant attention paid to rewards, controls, discipline, positive reinforcement, and operations. Coupled with inadequate resources devoted to these dimensions, the organization becomes ever more susceptible.[17]

Bologna, while in some ways different than Wells, still seems to come back to Cressey's iron triangle of need, opportunity, and rationalization. The words and emphasis may differ, but the base mechanisms seem to remain in place. Bologna does, however, offer some thoughts on the nature of fraud-prone organizations, which may be viewed as an interesting complement to the earlier work on fraud-prone individuals. Obviously, when the two meet, one would suspect the likelihood of improper acts to increase. Bologna cites the following characteristics as being significant: a distant and self-interested top management whose focus is on short-term economic goals; poor controls; inadequate loyalty and commitment on the part of employees; high turnover, especially among those entrusted with financial oversight; cash flow problems, coupled with a weak relative position in the marketplace; inadequate pre-employment background checks; lack of any values other than financial success; poor track record of positive ethical training; and poor history of responding to customer and vendor complaints.[18]

We need to be mindful that Bologna is interested in fraudulent acts both by and against the corporation, and several of his warning signs are geared accordingly, but this does not sound like a great place to work. One would suspect that if an organization met all, or even most of, these criteria, an employee thinking about fraud would be tempted.

Cressey, among other theorists, has observed that revenge may be one of the motivating factors in employees committing frauds against their employers. If that is indeed true, one of the more classic euphemisms of the 1980s and 1990s may be providing more than enough rationale. *Downsizing*, driven by a variety of financial factors, became an all-too-frequent event for many U.S. workers. Lowell E. Hofmann, president of the National Organization of Downsized Employees, estimates that between January 1991 and April 1994, approximately 2.5 million Americans lost their jobs through such actions. *The New York Times* is reported to have conducted a survey in which it found that 72 percent of Americans had either been downsized themselves or had a friend or relative who had been. Mahiuddin Laskar, of the MBA program at the University of North Florida, cited a study by the American Management Association that found between one-third and one-half of medium and large U.S. firms had downsized every year since 1988.[19]

Several commentators and forensic investigators have speculated that in such an environment it is only reasonable that some employees will seek revenge, and a portion of them will resort to committing fraud against their employers. Were this not bad enough, even for those not directly affected by a given downsizing, the message may be clear. There is no longer an expectation of loyalty on the part of the organization; why should I be loyal in return?[20]

KPMG, in their *1998 Fraud Survey*, is reported to have concluded that the following factors seem to be causes or indicators of employee fraud:[21]

- Personal financial pressure
- Substance abuse
- Gambling
- Real or imagined grievances
- Ongoing transactions with related parties
- Increased stress
- Internal pressure to meet deadlines or budgets
- Short vacations
- Unusual hours

While the characteristics enunciated in the KPMG survey appear to be fairly similar to those of several other researchers, Gottfredson and Hirschi put forth a theory in 1990 that took a different tack. In the course of developing and presenting their work, *A General Theory of Crime*, they did not do specific research on workplace fraud in particular or, for that matter, white-collar crime in general.[22] Rather, after exploring the history of theories of human criminality, they examined competing theories of crime causation, such as those espoused by the schools of biologic, economic, psychologic, and sociologic positivism. Within each tradition and its constituent theories, they found what they perceived to be flaws of logic, weaknesses of research design, or both. Because of this, they argue, there is no robust, verifiable, general theory of crime. They are especially disdainful of those who contend that certain subspecies of crime, such as street gangs, have a special causation and dynamic that merits their being singled out to be the subject of a specialized theory. Given this position, they likewise reject the need for, or the accuracy of, any special theory devoted solely or primarily to white-collar crime or workplace fraud.

Gottfredson and Hirschi argue that criminals exhibit the following characteristics:

First, they opine that relative differences in levels of self-control tend to remain stable throughout life, even though they are established in early childhood. As a corollary to this, they believe that the mediating structures of adult lilfe, to include the criminal justice system, have relatively little effect in constraining those with low levels of self-control.[23]

Their theory rests solely on a basis of weak self-control, leading to a tendency to seek immediate gratification in varying forms—some criminal, some not. With regard to those acts in the criminal category, Gottfredson and Hirschi dismiss issues such as probability of arrest or length of sentence as irrelevant, arguing that from the perspective of the offender the decision to offend is not weighed or rational.

Second, they argue that since weak self-control is, in their theory, an inherent personality characteristic it is likely to manifest itself in any number of manners, from drug use through reckless driving. Because of this, they reject those theories that argue that one set of behaviors, say drug use, is likely to promote another, say committing burglaries to support that drug use.[24]

In this regard, Gottfredson and Hirschi appear to be close to the informal observations made by Leuci that 5 percent of the people in any organization are dirty. In Leuci's view, no matter what the organization does to police them, they are still going to try to beat the system. Without buying into all of the implications and conclusions of the general theory, it is easily possible to think of people we know and people we probably work with who always seem to have a deal or a scheme going, be it petty or significant. Some appear, by nature, to be interested in always pushing the envelope, and they may be quite successful in avoiding the consequences for lengthy periods. Whether this is an adequate theory of workplace fraud is, to my mind, another matter, at least at this point.

Gottfredson and Hirschi then go on to discuss the satisfaction and displacement aspects of their construct of criminal causation:

Third, they reject "root cause" determinates of criminal behavior by arguing that most criminal acts serve no purpose other than satisfaction of an immediate need. Accordingly, policies that seek to address theoretical "causes" such as poverty or drug dependency, are likely to meet limited success. Also, they posit that offenders are not pathologically "driven" to crime. Accordingly, preventive measures, such as automobile theft deterrent programs may, in fact, reduce auto theft. They note their theory does not predict that such a program would then increase the occurrence of another type of crime to offset the reduced levels of auto theft.[25]

Here, without meaning to oversimplify the general theory, it is important to bear in mind two things. First, Gottfredson and Hirshci are trying to literally put forth a general theory of crime, one that will be useful in explaining acts as disparate as murder and shoplifting. Accordingly, they must cover a lot of ground and circumstances. Second, in their theory the driving motivator is low self-control, whose consequences they see as a desire for immediate gratification with little or no regard for long-term consequences. Their position is, in rough terms, an inclination rather than a pathology. Thus they seem to accept that some acts by organizations or agencies may defer some acts of criminality, but there is no quota system in effect. The criminal is not, in their view, driven to commit a certain number of deviant acts each day, and if one need is satisfied will seek another outlet in the form of a different activity or a different location. At the same time, as we shall see next, they believe this inclination persists for a considerable period, tempered only, it appears, by age:

Finally, they note that they, too, accept the conventional wisdom that indicates crime rates decrease with age, but caution others to be wary of interpreting such changes to be the result of some criminal justice program or initiative.[26]

Here, Gottfredson and Hirschi are in concert with many other theorists and researchers in agreeing that the rate of criminal activity seems to almost always decrease with age, with the late teenage years into the early twenties being particularly active. We may recall also that Hollinger and Clark concluded that age was a significant factor in their study of workplace fraud published in 1983. The general theory seems to say that while the decrease is notable in terms of the individual's past transcript of offenses, those with low levels of self-control will likely always have incident rates higher than their better-controlled peers, regardless of age.

Since the concept of self-control, or the lack of it, drives their theory, it is useful to consider what Gottfredson and Hirschi see as being the consequences of the acts deriving from this deficit. In other words, when due to a lack of sufficient self-control, a person commits a criminal act, what happens? They posit the following conditions:[27]

1. *There is immediate gratification.* In their theory, persons with low levels of self-control respond greatly to stimuli in their immediate environment. They have a here and now orientation toward life and tend to seize on whatever (or whomever) they perceive as providing immediate gratification. Those with higher levels of self-control are not immune to the temptations the environment may offer; they simply usually chose to defer gratification.

2. *Acts emanating from low levels of self-control tend to be simple and/or easy.* There is no degree of planning or reconnaissance. Immediacy, in their theory, drives the person to seek money without work, sex without courtship, or revenge without consequence. The immediate nature of the action, in their view, almost precludes by definition that which is either complex or time-consuming.

3. *Again almost by definition, those with low levels of self-control are action people.* They are attracted to risk, excitement, and thrill. This is consistent with their here and now orientation and unlike the cautious, thoughtful, and verbal orientation Gottfredson and Hirschi believe characterizes those with high levels of self-control.

4. *The theory holds that criminal acts such as these provide little long-term benefit.* They are hardly the equivalent of a profession, career, trade, or job. Such impulsive acts actually detract from stability in vocation, marriage, friendships, or employment. In their view, the concept of a career criminal is

accurate in a semantic sense, but dead wrong in a causal sense. The popular usage of career criminal is one who chooses a life of crime as an alternative to gainful employment. There is an implication of a rough equivalency, at least in terms of continuing means of economic sustenance. Gottfredson and Hirschi would probably agree that a career criminal is one who has committed (or at least been arrested for) a large number of crimes. They would, however, argue that in purely economic terms the career criminal could make more money bagging groceries on a consistent basis. In their theory, the low-self-control crime is impulsive and almost always petty, at least in terms of economic benefit.

5. *Consistent with their view that these criminal acts are simple or easy, Gottfredson and Hirschi argue that these acts also require little skill or planning.* Again, this is consistent with their view that those with low self-control are unlikely to acquire substantial academic or vocation skills, since these pursuits run counter to their inherent nature. Accordingly, even in criminal acts they are unlikely to choose to commit those that require cognitive or manual skills they have not taken the time, literally, to develop.

6. *The general theory holds that while crimes often involve pain, loss, or discomfort to the victim(s), this fact is of little consequence to the perpetrator(s) driven by the confluence of opportunity for immediate gratification and low self-control.* These perpetrators, in Gottfredson and Hirschi's view, are far too self-centered and indifferent to attend to the needs of others or, probably, to even recognize that they exist. But, they caution, this does not mean that those motivated by low levels of self-control are necessarily sadists or pathological in their dealings with others. They postulate that some percentage of these offenders may exhibit traits of generosity and social adeptness, primarily because they have learned or intuited that these traits may be easy mechanisms for them to gain what they want with minimal effort.

One who is even somewhat familiar with the workings of the criminal justice system and with the denizens of its nether chambers would be inclined, I believe, to say "Yes!" to the elements that Gottfredson and Hirschi have described as typical attributes of crimes committed by those with low self-control. We need not think too long nor too deeply to recall any number of perpetrators who meet these characteristics to a tee. Depending on the era and venue, these persons are usually referred to as mopes, punks, losers, dregs, or any number of even more colorful terms. They are well known to law enforcement at all levels and in all locales; they are much of its clientele. They are usually the petty, self-centered idiots who do stupid things on the spur of the moment, often get caught, never learn from their mistakes, and blame everybody and everything but themselves. We would do well to recall Kelly's interviews with inmates and their self-serving explanations as to why they are really not bad people, or why some central element of their offense was really someone else's fault (see Chapter 2, note 28). The issue, however, is that Gottfredson and Hirschi are not seeking to describe a given subset of criminals or deviants, they are positing a general theory to describe them all.

While it would be interesting to examine, and speculate on, the rationale Gottfredson and Hirschi use while applying their general theory to street gangs, serial killers, and La Cosa Nostra, we must look within their theory to see what they have to say about occupational fraud. They devote one chapter of their book to a more generic version of the topic, white-collar crime, which shall suffice for our purposes. The particular value of the general theory in our consideration of workplace fraud is that it is considered by scholars and researchers in the larger field of criminology to be one of the more significant general formulations to be put forth in recent years.

They first note that it has been common in the literature to place white-collar crime into a special category. Part of the basis for this approach has to do with definitions formulated decades earlier, such as those by Sutherland and his theoretical descendents. White-collar crime has, in their view, been segregated from the general body of offenses because of early and continuing definitions that had it be a crime committed by corporate executives of high organizational and social standing and involving an inherent breach of social and fiduciary trust.[28] While Sutherland, like to some degree Bologna, was interested in crimes committed ostensibly on behalf of the organization, later formulations of the term *white-collar crime* came to the usage that it also meant crimes committed by persons in such positions for their personal benefit. Currently, as we have seen from examination of FBI Uniform Crime Report and National Incident-Based Reporting data, white collar crimes now include offenses as pedestrian as ATM and credit card fraud—offenses certainly not committed by persons of high social standing in most occurrences.

In thinking about white-collar crime from the perspective of their general theory, Gottfredson and Hirschi contend that persons of high social standing are not immune from committing a gamut of crimes of varying hues. While, they note, doctors can also commit murder, they—and others in positions of organizational, vocational, or professional power—can certainly use the access and opportunities such positions afford them to commit an impressive range of nonviolent crimes. These, however, they believe, fall well within the confines of their general theory.[29]

They begin by noting that the formulation of white-collar crime usually stands the crime-employment equation on its head. Many classical theories of crime contended, at least in part, that crime was caused by lack of employment or, at least, adequate employment. White-collar crime theories, they note, tend to reverse this equation and argue that it is precisely the fact of high-level, or relatively high-level, employment that creates both the opportunity and the means to commit these types of offenses. Given this apparent paradox, they then contend that both sets of theories have logical weaknesses:

In short, a finding that the employed are more likely to steal because of their employment no more justifies a unique theory of theft (white-collar crime) than a finding that the unemployed are more likely to steal justifies a theory focusing exclusively on the lower class (deprivation or strain theory).[30]

Since, in their view, employment is off the board as a causal factor, some other factor(s) must explain the causation of white-collar crime. They are likewise dismissive of concepts that attempt to treat corporate crime (crime committed by those with high organizational standing, but ostensibly on behalf of the organization) as a unique animal, contending that such theories lack the theoretical coherence and methodological support to provide them with viability.[31]

Gottfredson and Hirschi then examine whether white-collar crimes are essentially different from other forms of crime. On the surface, they might appear to be. Certainly, one must be employed in a bank, probably in a relatively high position, to commit mortgage loan fraud. Likewise, one must have access to the Medicaid system to commit Medicaid fraud. They ask, however, what is the essential difference—from the perspective of a theory of crime causation— between a pharmacist stealing drugs from a hospital pharmacy and a carpenter stealing lumber from a job site? What, they posit, is the difference between a bank manager embezzling and a gas station attendant doing the same thing?

In pursuing this line of inquiry, they recognize the conventional position that white-collar criminals are more damaging to society because they have betrayed a position of higher social standing and trust, and therefore, the causal motivation may be different. They see two problems with this line of analysis: (1) Are the causes of the offenses really the same? and (2) Is the seriousness of the offense compatible? Gottfredson and Hirschi take the position that many theories of crime causation in general and of white-collar offenses in particular create some linkage between these two issues, positing that if the offense of the white-collar criminal is more serious on societal terms, then the motivation must be different or more powerful. They contend there is no reason the seriousness of the offense must have an equally serious motivation, and they believe there is ample empirical evidence on this point. Further, they contend, there are good theoretical reasons why seriousness of offense and power of motivation should not be linked. While they recognize that a study of the varying types of white-collar crime may hold some utility in at least methods of investigating it, they argue that there is no theoretical or methodological benefit to be derived from thinking about different varieties of white-collar crime as distinct from one another. They argue that there is no point to thinking about white-collar crime as different from crime in general.[32]

They begin this line of argument by tying white-collar crimes back to the general population of criminal offenses:

White-collar crimes satisfy the defining conditions of crime.... They provide relatively quick and relatively certain benefit with minimal effort. They require no motivation or pressure that is not present in any other form of human behavior.

Since crimes involve goods, services, or victims, they have other constituent properties as well: they all require opportunity, and they are thought to result in punishment of the offender if he or she is detected. Yet such properties cannot account for the general tendency of particular individuals to engage in crime, and they are therefore not central to a theory of criminality.[33]

Having established this conceptual predicate, Gottfredson and Hirschi then apply their general theory of crime to white-collar crime. They begin by acknowledging that some aspects of the white-collar offender, at least in its most classic formulation, tend to be different from the norm most associated with general, or street, crime. Among these different characteristics are that the white-collar offender is more likely to be tied to a location in place and time (the workplace), is more likely to have some level of educational attainment, is required by the dynamics of the workplace to defer to some degree to the wishes and interests of others, and usually has to conform to some level of conventional appearance. Accordingly, they note, the demands of the white-collar environment tend to attract people with a markedly different set of personal attributes than the normal offender. The selection processes and criteria for upper-level positions make these distinctions from the normal offender even more pronounced.

Accordingly, they conclude, their theory would predict a relatively low incidence of white-collar crime, and they quarrel with other researchers whose findings indicate relatively high levels of white-collar crime. The basis for their disagreement, they note, is that they believe these researchers co-mingle personal and organizational crimes and usually adopt a longer period of analysis for crimes within the organization. Because of this, Gottfredson and Hirschi contend, the number of white-collar crimes is magnified when compared to the acts of the non–white-collar offender in a given year. When such factors are controlled for, they argue, the rates of offending for white-collar individuals should be lower than those of others, the differences being attributable to the non–typical-offender personal and occupational aspects noted in the white-collar population.

Unfortunately, they note, there are not sufficient empirical data available to adequately test this theory. They do report, however, that some studies indicate that as many as 90 percent of retail employees indicate they have never taken anything of value from their employer. While they take comfort in this study as confirming their position, they bemoan the research requirements of trying to obtain an adequate comparative fix on the incidence rates for white-collar offenders. On the one hand, they note, only persons in white-collar positions can, by definition, commit white-collar crimes. From a research perspective, they see two logical implications deriving from this fact: (1) either non–white-collar persons must be put into white-collar positions to see if their offense rates are higher or lower than their true white-collar counterparts, or (2) other settings and crimes must be construed, for the purposes of analysis, to be equivalent to white-collar crimes. They observe that the latter alternative is the one most often adopted by the criminal law and by the compilers of crime statistics.[34]

After commenting about the strengths and weaknesses of various forms of theory and analysis pertinent to white-collar crime causation, Gottfredson and Hirschi then discuss their research quandary and the quandary shared by all with an interest in this phenomenon:

> Experimental tests of our hypotheses could be achieved by distributing credit cards to junior high school students or by using banks for prison work-release programs. Without such tests, it is difficult to document the relatively low level of criminality among white-collar workers. Absent such tests, scholars will continue to argue that the criminal justice system favors white-collar workers; that businesses protect them to maintain their own reputations; and that white-collar crimes are relatively easily concealed. A case could be made that these arguments are themselves relics of a bygone age.[35]

To support this position, they note several studies that indicate that the probability of incarceration is as high for white-collar offenders as it is for violent criminals, and that both white-collar and non–white-collar offenders are subject to the same sentencing guidelines.

Issues of research design aside, we should consider what the general theory says about the causation of white-collar crime. Gottfredson and Hirschi contend that the common theories of white-collar crime differ from theories of general criminality that tie causation to biological, social, or psychological differences between offenders and nonoffenders. They note that Sutherland, with his theory of differential association, and other learning theorists such as Cressey, believed that some white-collar crime, most of which we today would call corporate crime, was learned by adopting the mores of the organization. Gottfredson and Hirschi observe their belief that such theories have survived and prospered because of their generality and that they explain activities that appear to be beyond those causal theories that rely on individual personal differences to understand criminal behavior on the part of some but not others.

The problem Gottfredson and Hirschi see with this position is their contention that white-collar crime is relatively rare. If the organization sells a paradigm of misconduct in pursuit of organizational goals as a matter of course, why do not more people commit offenses? A second problem they cite is that if such behavior is an organizational norm, the evidence they see for support from the organization or peers for such acts is limited, as they view the research. Indeed, they note, perpetrators of such acts usually seek to conceal them from both the organization and co-workers. A third issue they raise is temporal. If the organizational learning perspective is accurate, they contend that the more time one is part of the organization, the more opportunity one has had to learn misbehavior. Thus, they argue, one should see increasing rates of misconduct with age and organizational experience, rather than the common pattern of crime rates being highest among the young. The fourth difficulty they believe such theories encounter is that they are not general theories (i.e., they offer little utility in understanding ordinary incidents of crime and delinquency). They attempt to bolster their position by noting that while much research and theorizing has attempted to depict white-collar crime as long-term, sophisticated, complex, and high stakes, other research indicates that it is often more pedestrian. They believe, in this regard, it shares much more in common with run-of-the-mill street crime than some would have us believe.

In stating their theory of white-collar crime, Gottfredson and Hirschi argue the following points:[36]

- White-collar crime, like all crime in their view, will vary across social settings, and will be relatively low, depending on the selection criteria for admittance into the organizational setting. They state they are not bothered by issues of organizational or peer support for white-collar crime activities, since they contend that all crime is contrary to societal and organizational norms and interests and, therefore, has to take place in an environment of isolation.

- Their theory holds that those committing crimes will tend to have similar tendencies, regardless of the type of crime being committed. Accordingly, they contend that the difference between crime in the streets and crime in the suites is a distinction of offense type and not offender type.

- Their theory is one of crime in general and, if valid, should hold up under empirical testing regardless of the type of crime being committed.

Gottfredson and Hirschi have put forth a sweeping, and in some respects, controversial theory, at least insofar as it deals with white-collar crime in general and occupational fraud in particular. We shall consider some of the implications of and support for their theory in following discussions. First, however, it may be worthwhile to consider some of the response generated in the academic and theoretical communities to their formulation.

In 1989, Darrell Steffensmeier contributed a piece to the journal *Criminology* entitled: "On the Causes of 'White-Collar' Crime: An Assessment of Hirschi and Gottfredson's Claims." We should note that this response, in 1989, was a year in advance of their book, but in reaction to an article they had published in the same journal in 1987, entitled "Causes of White-Collar Crime." The article contained many of the elements of their theory later incorporated into their book. In his response, Steffensmeier countered their theory on three primary points:[37]

1. They misread the Uniform Crime Reports data from the FBI by inferring that the crimes of fraud, forgery, and embezzlement are reasonable indicators

of white-collar crime. Steffensmeier takes the position that this is not, in fact, the case, because these offenses are not good general indicators of white-collar crime, much less occupational fraud.

2. The demographic distributions presented or inferred by Gottfredson and Hirschi (i.e., sex, age, and race) for these three offense types are not the same as crime in general, whether one accepts the position that fraud, embezzlement, and forgery are legitimate representative white-collar crime offense types or not.

3. Gottfredson and Hirschi are incorrect in their assessment of the fact that these white-collar crime offenses are relatively rare. Steffensmeier sees them as being at least as common as other types of offenses reflected in commonly available data.

In pursuing this final point, Steffensmeier notes that many of the offenses recorded in the FBI's Uniform Crime Report data are for acts such as bad checks, credit card fraud, theft of services, falsification of identification, defrauding an innkeeper, small-time confidence games, and the like. Accordingly, he does not find them representative of white-collar crime in any meaningful sense. He believes Gottfredson and Hirschi erred in choosing such white-collar crimes that were actually close in many important aspects to typical street crimes.[38]

Steffensmeier also takes issue with the age characteristics Gottfredson and Hirschi apply to their formulation of criminal causality and the impact age has on it, at least insofar as white-collar offenses are concerned. We may recall that the general theory postulates that white-collar offenders mimic offenders in general offense categories, by peaking in their late teens and early twenties, then dropping off sharply thereafter. Steffensmeier presents an analysis of 1985 Uniform Crime Reports data in which he finds that the age curve for fraud offenders is both flatter and older than that for those committing general crimes such as larceny, burglary, and robbery. For example, he presents data that he contends shows that the peak age for fraud offenses is 24, the median age is 30, and it is not until age 41 that the offense rate is less than 50 percent of what it was at the peak offense period. By contrast, he argues, the peak age for burglary offenses is 16, the median point is 17.5 years of age, and these offenses drop below 50 percent of their peak occurrence frequency at age 20. Thus, he argues, white-collar crimes present a different profile than the general crimes Gottfredson and Hirschi believe are highly similar, if not identical.[39]

Without going into great detail regarding his arguments, Steffensmeier also contends that Gottfredson and Hirschi's position that white-collar crimes are relatively rare is also wrong. He notes that there are subtle but significant definitional distinctions, and he also raises questions about whether occurrence rates of white-collar crime are contrasted to the general population, only some of whom have the opportunity to even commit a white-collar crime, or the population of white-collar workers, each of whom he argues have such opportunities each day. The issue, he contends, is that this latter population is much smaller, thus driving up the frequency of offenses when considering the absolute number of offenses versus a smaller base population of only white-collar workers.[40]

The next notable commentary on Gottfredson and Hirschi's position appeared in 1996, when Reed and Yeager published "Organizational Offending and Neo-classical Criminology: Challenging the Reach of a General Theory of Crime." They began their critique by recounting a bit of theoretical history, noting that since Sutherland's work in 1939 criminologists have used the platform of white collar crime as a launching point for attacks on theories of criminal causation based on economic deprivation or personal defects. Conversely, many of these same theorists have constructed arguments that white collar crime exhibits characteristics unlike almost all other forms of crime.[41]

Reed and Yeager then go on to advance their critique by contending that Gottfredson and Hirschi selected those elements of white-collar crime that most closely resembled the general population of offenses committed by the young, typical, active offender. They then contrast a series of corporate white-collar offenses to show what they believe are the inadequacies of the general theory, noting that such corporate crimes are usually absent from much Uniform Crime Reports data. In this regard, we should note that while several theorists have also focused on corporate offenses, this is a stance markedly different from what we have been discussing as typical of occupational, or workplace, fraud.[42]

In supporting their position with regard to corporate crimes and the adverse implications its commission has for the general theory, they cite 18 studies on the frequency of such offenses, ranging from anti-trust violations to financial fraud to pollution violations. They note that these studies indicate these offenses, as opposed to the predictions of the general theory, are fairly frequently committed, even by large, powerful, corporations; highly complex in many instances; and distributed among both large and small organizations.[43]

They conclude their critique of the general theory, at least insofar as it fails in their view to address corporate crime, by noting that while corporate offenses such as embezzlement are roundly condemned and operate to benefit only the offender, the general theory is inadequate to explain those forms of corporate crime where the corporate entity itself benefits.[44]

Having spent some time examining the general theory and its critics, what are we to make of it? From a purely experiential perspective, it would appear to explain a fair amount of crime, particularly the type of street crime committed by the young. Unlike Reed and Cleary, whose focus was on corporate crimes committed on behalf of the organization, I believe we must also find weakness in the general theory as it applies to workplace fraud.

Certainly, some portion of occupational fraud is committed by persons motivated primarily by low self-control and the need for immediate gratification, and clearly some of these persons are young. The best evidence now available, however, suggests a different offender profile from that suggested by the general theory. The *2002 Report to the Nation* of the ACFE, reports the following offender and scheme characteristics:

- *Occupational fraud schemes reported in this survey had a median duration from inception to detection of 18 months.* Nearly two out of three schemes ran for a year before being detected.[45] It is important to note here that the fact of detection ended the scheme. Accordingly, it is reasonable to assume the scheme, and the offender(s), would have continued for some reasonable period past a year had they not been caught. Such findings run directly counter to not only the general theory's postulation that criminal acts are immediate, but also that they are simple. One could argue that even a simple scheme could continue for some time without achieving a degree of complexity. While that is true, a counterargument could be made that some degree of complexity is required to perpetrate even a simple scheme over a substantial period.

- *13.5 percent of schemes ran for five years or more before detection.*[46] This finding raises questions not only as to the general theory's predictions on immediacy and complexity, but also on the contention that crime is essentially unrewarding, being composed of a series of small scores. One could argue that an offender would continue a scheme for in excess of five years and be content to steal only $20 a week, but it strains credibility and common sense. Such long-term schemes might not achieve seven-figure headline status, but on the other hand they must have been worthwhile from a financial perspective if they were continued—at some risk—for that long a period.

- *The most common types of fraudulent disbursement schemes were billing schemes (45.5%) and payroll schemes (17.7%).*[47] This finding also suggests a level of complexity that runs counter to the position taken by the general theory. One suspects that were they presented with this finding, Gottfredson and Hirschi would reply to the effect that the instrumentality or mechanism of the criminal act does not impact their theory. I would envision their response being that white-collar crimes are, by nature, more complex than a simple act like putting a carton of cigarettes under your jacket and walking out of a store, but they are still simple in a relative sense. Certainly, creating a phony invoice from a nonexistent vendor or adding a ghost employee to the payroll requires not only knowledge of internal control systems, but some degree of financial and literary acumen as well. They would, I suspect, reply that within the range of possible white-collar offenses, these are still simple offenses and are, thereby, consistent with their general theory.

I see two problems with this line of argument, were it to be advanced. The first is that it implies, indeed requires, a typology and a hierarchy of white-collar offenses, so we can determine when the threshold of simplicity has been passed. Certainly, some white-collar offenses deserve to be considered complex. The question is, where is that line?

Second, the very nature of these two most common fraudulent disbursement schemes suggests a motive very much at odds with the general theory. It is doubtful an offender would go to the trouble of creating a nonexistent vendor or a ghost employee to only receive one vendor payment or one paycheck. The simple and immediate criterion of the general theory implies, if not requires, a smash-and-grab mentality, where the proximate target of opportunity is seized in the moment. A condition of the general theory is that these offenses are inherently unprofitable, thus defeating the notion of a life of crime as a viable and rewarding modus vivendi. While the white-collar offender indulging in a billing or payroll scheme usually might not gain enough to displace a legitimate source of income, there seems to be a permanence to these offenses that is inconsistent with the requirements of the general theory. This concept is borne out not only by the mechanism of the crime (creation of nonexistent entities and people), but also by the Report's findings as to the average length of these and other offenses. Billing schemes represented in the Report ran an average of 23 months and payroll schemes an average of 19 months. Were Gottfredson and Hirschi to respond that, like the issue of complexity, selected white-collar offenses must be viewed in the context of all white-collar offenses when considering issues of duration, the general theory does not gain much support. The longest-running white-collar scheme mentioned in the Report was fraudulent statements, and these averaged 25 months in duration, only slightly longer than billing schemes.[48]

The issue of age in offenses covered in the Report also appears to be inconsistent with the requirements of the general theory. Only 6 percent of offenders were reported to be 26 or younger, with 47.3 percent being 41 or older. Thus, in this cohort of cases, not only does the criminal activity peak not occur in early age, but it actually rises to a frequency peak in the 41–50 age bracket (30.1 percent of all offenders reported), then tails off to 14.7 percent of offenders in the 51–60 age bracket and 2.5 percent in the over-60 bracket. Such a distribution appears to at least partially support the position taken by Steffensmeier, who argued that the offense curve for the white-collar offenses he analyzed was flatter and longer than for general crimes. The Report's findings seem to support him on the issue of white-collar offenders' age distribution being different but contradicts the findings he saw in Uniform Crime Report data about at least some categories of white-collar offenses tailing off after the late teenage to early twenties period. In either event, the general theory appears to be challenged on the age distribution question.

An interesting corollary to the issue of absolute age is organizational age. Gottfredson and Hirschi raise this issue with regard to their analysis of the learning theory of corporate white-collar crime causation, arguing that if such behavior is, in fact, learned, one would expect long-term employees to exhibit more of it since they have learned more. This position is consistent with, in an obverse sense, the findings reported by Hollinger and Clark, who hypothesized that younger employees were more likely to commit workplace fraud since they had a lower sense of loyalty to the organization. When one considers that as many as 13 million Americans per month change their employment status, there are certainly significant percentages of new employees in most organizations.[49] Whether these persons present a special category of occupational fraud risk is an intriguing question worthy of further study and analysis.

Another challenge may be raised for the general theory when one considers the magnitude of frauds reported in the Report. Of the 620 cases in which respondents were able to provide loss data, over half cost their victims at least $100,000, and nearly one in six cost victims losses of $1 million or more.[50] Such findings appear to contradict the predictions of the general theory on two and perhaps three counts: (1) losses of this magnitude do not appear to be the minor and nonrewarding crimes the general theory tends to predict; (2) the likely complexity of these acts is again counter to the tenets of the general theory; and (3) the duration of these acts, while already established by other data in the Report, is certainly implied by the sums involved. Certainly, there may be one-time fraud events that net the perpetrator $100,000 or even $1 million, but experience and common sense indicate that a significant portion of these losses represent cumulative totals that have built up over time.

Two pieces of the general theory would seem to be supported by the Report, at least in appearing to be consistent with some of the logic of its position. The Report asked respondents to rate the measures they believed would be most effective in combating workplace fraud. They reported the following measures, in decreasing order of importance: strong internal controls, background checks on new employees, regular fraud audits, and established fraud policies.[51] Gottfredson and Hirschi theorized that some level of immediate-satisfaction criminality might be tempered by adequate rewards satisfying deprivation issues of the offender, noting that their general theory rejects deprivation as an adequate general theory of crime. To the degree that rewards temper deprivation and thus reduce the incidence of crime, we might also infer that reduced opportunity—in the form of strong internal controls—would likewise have a moderating effect. I am not sure Gottfredson and Hirschi would readily embrace this observation, but it seems logical that if positive elements in the environment (rewards) could have a moderating effect, negative elements (impediments in the form of controls) could have the same effect.

So, too, with the issue of background checks: In making their argument for the application of the general theory to white-collar crime, Gottfredson and Hirschi acknowledge that the educational, work, and selection criteria for entry into the white-collar work arena operate to eliminate entry of some persons with low levels of self-control. Again, the respondents seem to agree with this position, ranking preemployment screening as the second-most effective measure in reducing occupational fraud.

The educational profile exhibited by offenders cited in the Report seems to confirm part of Gottfredson and Hirschi's theory, noting the caveat that they carve out white-collar crime as a sort of special case, even within the confines of the general theory. The Report indicates that 32.7 percent of offenders cited had a bachelor's degree, while 10.4 percent had a postgraduate degree. The majority of offenses, 56.9 percent, were committed by those with a high school degree or less; however, the magnitude of these offenses, measured in dollar value, seems to exhibit peculiar characteristics. Those committed by persons with a high school degree or less had a median cost of $70,000, while those committed by persons with bachelor's degrees had a median loss of $243,000, or an order of magnitude of 3.5. Offenses committed by persons with postgraduate degrees had a median loss of $162,000, more than twice the high school or less category but one-third smaller than the bachelor's-level offenses.[52]

One may speculate, as do Gottfredson and Hirshci, that educational and screening mechanisms cause white-collar offenders to commit a different pattern of crimes than their street-level counterparts, and the loss figures in the Report would seem to bear this out. One can surmise that those with college degrees have access to higher-level and more powerful positions, thus they are in a position to do greater harm when they offend. The median loss profile of those with postgraduate degrees, almost splitting the difference between high school and less and bachelor's-degree offenders presents a quandary, absent further research. Could their offense record be because in most organizations, degree level and organizational position do not necessarily equate? Could it be that those with postgraduate degrees often occupy technical and administrative positions, thus limiting their access to organizational funds when they offend? Or, could one attempt to argue that those with postgraduate degrees exhibit an even higher level of self-control, as evidenced by their deferring gratifications in pursuit of such degrees? Were this the case, one would have to make a secondary argument that these characteristics, when they do offend, cause them to commit more measured or timid offenses.

While one could speculate endlessly about the dynamics of these offenses and the theoretical underpinnings behind them, it is probably best to say that absent more detailed data and further research, we just do not know. These parameters do, however, strongly suggest that if white-collar crimes are to be successfully included within the confines of the general theory, it may have to bend to accommodate them.

On the issue of collusion, the findings of the Report also appear to raise issues for the general theory. On the one hand, 67.6 percent of the offenders acted alone, with a median loss of $67,000. This would appear to support the general theory's requirement for a relatively simple, spontaneous act, although the dollar amount begins to look suspiciously high for a simple, spontaneous act. On the other hand, the 32.4 percent of offenders who acted with one or more accomplices had a median loss of $450,000, almost seven times the level of single offenders.[53] What does this tell us from the perspective of the general theory? While sole perpetrators were certainly the clear majority, the size of their haul notwithstanding, those who chose to partner in the offenses walked away with considerably more money. Gottfredson and Hirschi might argue that these persons are insignificant, in numerical terms, and the general theory is therefore capable of addressing white-collar crime comprehensively along with all other crime.

Were one to grant this point to the general theory, it then appears to back into other problems. The aforementioned statistic, 32.4 percent, is still one-third of all offenses cited in the Report, and these cases exhibit characteristics very different from those predicted by the general theory: they are at least somewhat complex, as they require help to consummate; they are therefore not inherently "spontaneous"; and, at a median loss of almost $5000,000, they are lucrative.

The findings set forth in the Report are also supported by a later poll conducted in March 2002 by the ACFE. In this online survey, responding CFEs were asked how many persons were involved in the latest internal fraud inquiry they conducted. The results (see Chapter 3, note 38) indicate that 41 percent were committed by one person and 21 percent by two individuals. Such findings might be argued to be consistent with the tenets of the general theory, which holds that most crime is committed by individuals or, alternatively, by small collections of individuals acting in a largely spontaneous fashion. The remaining 36 percent of frauds (the reported results appear not to have been rounded, thus not totaling 100 percent) appear to be inconsistent with the general theory. These frauds were committed by 3 to more than 10 persons; 9 percent of these frauds involved more than 10 persons.

In fairness to the general theory, one can surmise that at least some of these larger numbers are the reflection of "me too" forms of fraud—one person in a work unit beginning to submit inflated overtime reports and others following suit over time; however, it is equally unlikely that all of these larger fraud incidents are mere copycat violations. While more than 10 people is an awfully large or complex internal fraud, it is probable that a fair number of the reported frauds were complex and involved perhaps three to five persons. Were we to take a hypothetical fraud event involving large numbers of people that would most closely support the predictions of the general theory, there are still theoretical issues to be overcome. Say, for example, we use our earlier example: One person in a work unit submits inflated overtime reports, does not get caught, and next week nine fellow workers follow the example. One might say these were spontaneous events, consistent with the general theory, but even in this benign scenario, how can the issues of the length of the schemes and the financial benefit derived be made consistent with the tenets of the general theory?

Likewise, the Report's findings on the issue of criminal history appear to strain the general theory. As reported 68.8 percent of all offenders had no prior criminal charges or convictions. Only 6.9 percent had a prior criminal record, 2.9 percent had been charged in the past but not convicted, and 21.3 percent had an unknown criminal history.[54] Even allowing the unknowns and unconvicteds to fall into the convicted categories still leaves a significant hurdle for the general theory to overcome. Granted, Gottfredson and Hirschi carve out some portion of white-collar offenders in their exposition of the general theory, but at the same time their overwhelming and consistent depiction of those likely to offend as spontaneous and vicarious in all aspects of their lives seems inconsistent with this white-collar offender profile. They have contended that some white-collar crime is underreported by organizations concerned with embarrassment, and that is certainly true in my professional experience; however, even this argument causes problems for the general theory, since it means that while they predict white-collar offenses will be relatively rare, there are, by their own admission, certainly more of them than make it to the official record.

The general theory must also deal with that mass—more than two-thirds—of white-collar offenders with no criminal record. We saw earlier that the offenders cited in the Report did not display the normal youthful skew in terms of age at the time of the offense. Indeed, the peak offender age reported was well into middle age, 41–50 (30.1 percent of offenders). These are people clearly past their predicted offense years, from the late teens into the mid-twenties. How, then, can it be within the confines of the general theory that more than two-thirds of them have no criminal record? To use Gottfredson and Hirschi's argument of organizational coverup, did they make it through those supposedly turbulent times with an organization or family to protect them from acquiring a criminal record? Did they offend and not get caught, even once? Were they caught but diverted into some program that left no permanent record? Were their records expunged after a period of good behavior? All of these mechanisms are possible, but it strains belief that they were prevalent or consistent enough to account for more than two-thirds of all offenders. We must remember, the general theory of those with low levels of self-control purports to describe those oriented to risk, thrill, excitement, immediate gratification, and little concern for the consequences. Were that many people that lucky, or must the general theory be challenged?

What, then, may we say in retrospect about the general theory? My experience tells me that it may well explain a sizable portion of crime and perhaps much of street crime. I recognize that Gottfredson and Hirschi have carved out a segment that holds, within the general theory, that white-collar crime may exhibit different characteristics; however, from the data presented in the Report, it seems that the white-collar offender must be treated as more and more special as additional factors predicted by the general theory are considered. One could argue that the cases and offenders cited in the Report are a small portion of all white-collar crimes—however one wishes to define that term—and therefore are not a suffi-cient challenge to the general theory. That may be acceptable from a strict quanti-tative methodological perspective, but until the general theory proves it is capable of including such offenses without the creation of more and ever broader special categories around the white-collar offender, I will remain unconvinced.

Plus, my gut tells me the general theory is wrong. I have investigated too many middle-aged, middle-class, solid-citizen offenders to completely accept what the general theory says about their behavior. Certainly, there were a number of high-flying risk-takers also present, but until the general theory can account for Mr. Jones in the next cubicle with his kids' pictures on the wall, I find it incomplete.

CHAPTER 5

LIES, DAMNED LIES, STATISTICS (AND OCCUPATIONAL FRAUD)

The noted statesman, Benjamin Disraeli, once said: "There are three kinds of lies: lies, damned lies, and statistics."[1] During the course of my life and professional career, I have come to believe this position has merit. I suspect we have all seen numbers, in the right hands, do some truly impressive things.

In thinking about occupational fraud, the numbers are incredibly important. We have discussed some of the numbers—estimates, really—that are being used to describe occupational fraud and they are truly impressive. How accurate they are is totally another matter. There are several reasons for this. First among them is the simple fact that no one—not the FBI, the U.S. Congress, or any professional organization of which I am aware—keeps any comprehensive tally of occupational fraud losses. This is an issue we will discuss later in this work. The second, and potentially more troublesome, issue is that of definition. What do we mean by occupational fraud? Such questions are not uncommon in the social sciences, as John Rohr noted when trying to grapple with the topic of ethics:

It will come as a surprise to no one to learn that the field of ethics is chaotic. The term is undefined; the inquiry unbounded. . . . eleven years ago one of my tasks was to prepare an annotated bibliography on "Ethics In Public Administration." An ever-expanding definition of both ethics and public administration had to be justified to make any pretense of having done the job. . . . Today the problem is just the opposite. I find myself looking for reasons to cut the topic back to manageable proportions. . . . Clearly there is considerable overlap between ethics and administrative theory; but there is also an overlap between ethics and just about everything else in the field—personnel, budgeting, administrative law, and so on.[2]

Joseph Wells, in his seminal work *Occupational Fraud and Abuse*, defines *occupational fraud* as follows: "The use of one's occupation for personal enrichment through the deliberate misuse or misapplication of the employing organization's resources or assets."[3] This is a start. It is only when one goes in search of useful numbers with which to try to discuss occupational fraud that the woods get thicker. Much of this chapter is a discussion of a series of questions. There are questions because neither I, nor anyone I have been able to locate, seems to have answers. That such is the case means we have an awful lot of work to do to begin to tidy up this field. It can be done—it must be done—but it will not be easy.

At this writing, the Enron story is blaring from every radio and television, and filling up newspaper pages like some wild vine run amuck. Let us say that Enron plays out to have been caused by fraudulent behavior on the part of one or more corporate executives. Is it, then, occupational fraud? Are all the other corporate collapses that seem to shatter every now and then also occupational fraud? If so, fine, but how do we calculate the damage? Is it the money taken, directly or indirectly from the coffers of the corporation? Is it the loss in shareholder value or market capitalization? Is it the pensions and 401K benefits lost? Is it some combination of these factors? If it is pensions, for example, do we adjust for the future value of pension benefits now lost?

Such issues are more than a philosophical debate or parlor game. Until we begin to resolve them, through discourse, consultation, and research, we cannot truthfully say we have even defined our own field. The path may be strewn with pitfalls.

All measurement systems are subject to interpretation, if not outright manipulation, and this is a risk we run when we begin to think systematically about occupational fraud. Wells and his associates at the ACFE have done yeoman service in getting us as far as they have in our understanding of the scope of the occupational fraud problem in this country. But, even they, I am sure, would admit that their estimates, as good faith as they are, are only estimates. If we are to truly begin to capture numbers that will hold up to sustained analysis and analytical interpretation, we will have to develop a much more comprehensive and rigorous methodology to do so.

As I noted earlier, a collection and analysis entity is the necessary first step, but the second step may be a good bit bigger than the first. We need to decide what we are going to measure. In thinking about this problem, Enrons aside, I offer the following examples, some real and some hypothetical, of what we will need to address:

Co-generation. In my childhood we used to call these things dumps, but today they are big business. A co-generation facility is basically a power plant that runs on trash. Refuse is burned to produce electricity. This one had a problem. When trucks come into such a facility, they stop on an electric scale that weighs the truck, deducts the weight of the truck and the container, calculates the amount of garbage and the charge to the waste hauling company, and prints out a trip ticket. The truck then dumps its load, the garbage is burned, and the hauling company is invoiced. At this facility the scale operator had a scam. He would take cash from owner-operator-drivers to override the electronic scale and produce a handwritten trip ticket. He would pocket the cash, the driver had a trip ticket that allowed him to dump, but no invoice was ever generated. He could do this only because the scale was sometimes broken and handwritten tickets were needed. Obviously, no one ever stopped to ask why the scale was broken so many times when this chap happened to be working. This was clearly an occupational fraud; basically, a theft-of-service scheme.

We were hired by the company to try to calculate the amount of revenue it had lost through this scheme so they could file a fidelity bond claim with their insurance company. After three long, and smelly, weeks we came up with a rough number because it is difficult to determine how much garbage was or was not burned on a given day, and this scheme had been going on for two years. We knew how much the scale operator had pocketed, $200,000, mainly because he kept records for his own use and we got our hands on them, but coming up with a number to estimate the company's losses was much more difficult. These are the sorts of issues we will have to contend with if we are to calculate the true amount of occupational fraud in the United States. Theft-of-service schemes can be tough.

Manufacturing. This could be thought of as a mini-Enron. This company was publicly traded and its CEO wanted to look good for Wall Street. When business began to slow, he took work-in-progress and counted it as inventory, an accounting no-no. At the end of quarters, he would ship product to distributors on consignment and call it sales, another no-no. When times really got tough, he would ship product to distributors that had not even been ordered, book a sale, and deal with the returns later.

When this daisy chain finally cratered, what were the losses? To the company, to the employees, to the shareholders, to the vendors who would probably never get paid? Were the legal fees some of these vendors surely ran up trying to recover some portion of their money also losses?

Again, issues to be dealt with. This sort of list could go on forever, and there is no point in putting forth endless scenarios, but several additional questions may be in order. How do we categorize the employee who leaves the warehouse door open so his buddies can help themselves 'round about midnight? He has enabled others to remove company assets. Are we properly picking up such instances as occupational fraud?

The days of my father—35 years and a gold watch—are long gone. How do we handle frauds committed by contractors, vendors, joint venture partners, consultants, and temporary employees? Are they covered as having committed occupational fraud? They meet Wells' definition of using their occupation to deprive their employer of assets, but they are not permanent employees of the organization, which is the common-sense way we normally think of occupational fraud. Then again, if I am hired as a 30-day temp or consultant, is the entity paying me my employer?

Such issues are far from academic and may have profound tax and other consequences for the employing organization. An article in *Internal Auditor*, the magazine of the Institute of Internal Auditors, addressed such issues, noting:

> No single legal definition exists for classifying all workers. Most of the statutory definitions are circular, in that they include language such as "any individual employed by an employer." Because the application and the interpretation of tests by the courts have varied, the employer cannot rely on a definitive guideline for classifying a worker. Nevertheless, three tests have been widely used in determining proper classifications: the Common Law Test, based on a 1992 Supreme Court decision; the Economic Realities Test, based on the Fair Labor Standards Act; and the Right to Control Test from the National Labor Relations Board. A fourth classification test, the Internal Revenue Service's 20 Common Law Factors Test, builds on the Supreme Court decision by including eight additional factors."[4]

Not only, the authors contend, does the possibility of misclassification expose the organization to liability, but it may also operate as an irritant when employees believe they have been misclassified to their detriment. In such cases we may suspect, given what we have examined with regard to theories of fraud, that the temptation to commit fraudulent activities may be higher.

Government employees are surely employees of their respective department or agency, but do we accurately capture the amount of wrongdoing committed when they go bad?

How do we handle volunteers? If I steal from a house of worship, or school board, or local lodge, is that entity my employer if I am not paid for my services? The Red Cross, I am told, is the largest nongovernmental entity on the face of the earth, with more than 1 million persons affiliated with it. Is the Red Cross the employer of any of these persons? Such things do, unfortunately, happen. In my own little town in New Jersey the Chief of Police recounted an unpleasant investigation his department conducted after a suspicious series of incidents at a local church. The collections seemed to be down, even though the church membership was strong and growing. The police put a concealed video camera in the area used to count the collections and recorded a trusted church member stuffing money into his pockets as he had been doing, evidently, for many years.

Recent weeks have brought accounts of several prominent and successful historians who have admitted to instances of plagiarism in some of their most popular works. If I am under contract to a publishing house and I produce a work flawed by such practices, have I committed fraud against my employer?

Intellectual property is one of the fastest-growing sectors of our economy. This has caused a substantial rethinking of many traditional concepts in law, accounting, and finance, to name but a few fields. A number of articles have been written arguing, pro and con, that current accounting systems are incapable of adequately capturing the financial impact of such assets on balance sheets.[5] We as a society have come to the point that we are willing to pay large amounts of money for what is in people's heads, rather than the output of their hands. As one wit once put it, "My inventory goes home every night at 5 p.m." If I dream up a valuable idea on company time and then sell it in the market-place for my personal benefit, have I committed occupational fraud? This is not an absurd theoretical question; there have actually been lawsuits on this very issue.[6]

Some sense of the scope and significance of intellectual property, and its corresponding importance to American business operations, can be gleaned from the fact that IBM alone makes an estimated $1.7 billion each year on its patents. Two experts in the field, Kevin Rivette and David Klein, estimate in their book, *Rembrandts in the Attic*, that U.S. companies lose $1 trillion each year by not capitalizing on their patents.[7]

While the cases involving high-profile authors may grab the public's attention for a week or two, issues involving the compromise of intellectual property continue every day in a dizzying variety of fields:

- House designs[8]
- Real estate market data[9]
- Women's fashions[10]
- Automobile design technology[11]
- Music[12]
- Waste management data[13]
- Microchip trade secrets[14]
- Plant seeds[15]
- Adhesive labels[16]
- Photographic film[17]
- Motor oil additives[18]
- Glass[19]
- Videocassettes[20]
- Software[21]
- Soup[22]
- Plastics[23]
- Soft drinks[24]
- Oil field data[25]

The list, unfortunately, could easily be extended. To the degree insiders were involved in compromises of this intellectual property, an occupational fraud was committed.

The FBI, as we know, does keep statistics on crimes reported to it as part of its Uniform Crime Reporting Program and National Incident-Based Reporting System. Unfortunately, they do not capture much of the data that would be of interest to us, and even some of the data they do capture may be difficult to segregate in a fashion that makes sense for our purposes.

Consider, for example, a Member of Congress who is taking bribes in return for favors. The FBI would consider this to be a political corruption matter, a federal crime, and perhaps also a violation of the Fraud by Wire, Mail Fraud, Fraud against the Government, and Conspiracy statutes. If the matter were tried in a state court it could be a kickback, bribery, or even extortion violation. For our purposes, it is an occupational fraud—maybe. The member was using the authority of his employer to take things of value, not unlike a traffic policeofficer who is willing to forget about a ticket for a price. Now, the thing of value did not come from the employer's pocket, but the employer did suffer a loss, if nothing more than public trust and confidence in the institution. Are such matters occupational crimes?

Matters of definition are extremely important, but to the general public they may seem trivial. They are not. Jack Bologna, for example, defines the fraud he is interested in as follows: "Corporate fraud is a fraud committed on behalf of or against a corporation by its directors, officers, employees or agents."[26] Please note the difference between Bologna's definition and that used by Wells. Bologna is also including improper acts committed "on behalf" of the organization, a much broader definition than Wells. Such distinctions are significant in considering a field potentially as broad as occupational fraud.

The definition used by the FBI in its National Incident-Based Reporting System, unfortunately, only clouds the picture further, making side-by-side analyses of fraud data from varying sources even more difficult and frustrating. The definition offered by the FBI of white-collar crime is: "a crime committed by a person of respectability and high social status in the course of his occupation."[27] I have attempted to suggest the complexities of defining *occupational fraud*, much less dealing with the boundaries of "respectability" or "high social status."

This observation is not to quarrel with the FBI for not choosing a definition more in keeping with either Wells or Bologna. That is not the point. The confounding reality is that each group or association uses a definition that makes sense from their point of view. The definition used by the FBI may well make sense as it attempts to segregate white-collar offenses from the huge sea of other data it also tracks, like assaults, robberies, drunken driving, murder, drug offenses, and sexual crimes. Some idea of the complexity of the FBI's task is suggested by the subcategories in even its white-collar crime category (many of them reflecting common state charges, from which the FBI draws much of its reported data):

False Pretenses/Swindle/Confidence Game; Credit Card/ATM Fraud; Impersonation; Welfare Fraud; Wire Fraud; Bribery; Counterfeiting/Forgery; Embezzlement; and Arson/Fraud.

Milton Meltzer has defined *white-collar crime* as being "crime committed by a person in a position of trust, for his or her personal gain."[28] In this regard he is somewhat close to the FBI's definition, but we should note in the studies he cites he seems to be primarily interested in crimes committed by organizations, and not against organizations, especially crimes committed against them by insiders.

Lal Balkaran, writing of the importance of internal audit functions in controlling corruption within organizations, notes that it: "generally entails misusing one's position for private gain or an unauthorized end. It can involve financial and nonmonetary benefit. Bribery, extortion, influence peddling, nepotism and fraud are all acts associated with corruption."[29] He goes on to note that corruption can have a significant and corrosive effect on the organization, increasing business risk, eroding investor confidence, and stifling growth.[30] In offering this definition, Balkaran is somewhat close to Bologna, since he implies that both acts by the individual against the organization or acts by the individual against someone else on behalf of the organization meet the definition.

The National Fraud Center, Inc., published a study in December 2000 on "The Growing Global Threat of Economic and Cyber Crime," which utilized the following definition of *economic crime*:

> as an illegal act generally committed by deception or misrepresentation (fraud) by someone (or a group) who has special professional or technical skills for the purposes of personal or organizational financial gain (or attempt to gain) an unfair advantage over another individual or entity.[31]

We should note again that this study utilizes a definition that makes sense from the perspective of its objectives. These are crimes committed by persons usually having an organizational position or technical/professional standing, but they can be committed to benefit the person or the organization. These acts may, per this definition, be committed against the employing organization, another organization, or an individual within or outside the organization. For our purposes, there is certainly some occupational fraud within the confines of this definition, but there is also much other fraud.

Were the subtle but significant differences between definitions not enough for us to ponder, we must also contend with changes in the environment and peoples' motivations. Consider espionage, if you will. As practiced especially over the last 30 years in the United States, it is occupational fraud. There was a time in our not-too-distant past that a lot of espionage was committed for ideological reasons—Kim Philby and other British spies working for the Soviets in the 1930s through the 1960s, and the Rosenbergs in the United States in the 1940s and 1950s. But, consider the major U.S. spy cases of more recent vintage—John

Walker of the U.S. Navy, Ronald Pelton of the National Security Agency, Aldrich Ames of the Central Intelligence Agency and, I am sorry to say, Robert Hansenn of the FBI. While there were certainly some psychological elements to their activities—Walker fancied himself a dashing James Bond figure, Ames had drinking and career problems, Hansenn smoldered with deep resentment over perceived career development slights—money played a prominent role in each instance.

Think of the definitions offered by Wells and Bologna: each of these cases fits perfectly. These people used their occupation to take something of value (in this case secrets or, more generically, intellectual property) and sold it to a competitor (usually the Soviet Union). Must we retool our thinking and analysis to also include espionage? I believe the answer is "yes," and note this brings additional considerations to the fore. After each of these cases we were dutifully informed by the media, usually quoting senior government officials, that untold billions of dollars in damage had been done to U.S. operations, techniques, capabilities, and interests. How do we capture such losses? How do we value a specialized spy satellite whose effectiveness has been compromised? Some of this treachery has been reported to have led to the execution of as many as 10 or 12 highly placed, long-term spies working for the United States. How do we value such losses?

In addition to espionage, the compromise of governmental secrets, we now also face a significant and growing threat to commercial secrets. These can assume three forms, according to the Office of the National Counterintelligence Executive (NCIX): The first is Economic Espionage, which NCIX and the Attorney General define as "the unlawful or clandestine targeting or acquisition of sensitive financial, trade, or economic policy information; proprietary economic information; or critical technologies." The second is Industrial Espionage, which the Department of Justice defines as "activity conducted by a foreign . . . government or by a foreign company with the direct assistance of a foreign government against a private U.S. company for the sole purpose of acquiring commercial secrets." The third is Proprietary Information, which the NCIX defines as:

> information not in the public domain and that which the owner has taken some measures to protect. Generally, such information concerns U.S. business and economic resources, activities, research and development, policies, and critical technologies. Although it may be unclassified, the loss of this information could impede the ability of the United States to compete in the world marketplace and could have an adverse effect on the U.S. economy, eventually weakening national security. Commonly referred to as "trade secrets," this information typically is protected under both state and federal laws.[32]

According to the *2001 Computer Crime and Security Survey* conducted by the Computer Security Institute and the FBI, the most serious losses suffered by organizations attacked through forms of Internet fraud are those dealing with intellectual property compromises. Thirty-four respondents to their annual survey reported losses of $151,230,100 in trade secrets, as opposed to 21 percent who reported losses of $92,935,500 in fraudulent financial transactions.[33]

Such compromises are hardly new. The 1995 *Annual Report to Congress on Foreign Economic Collection and Industrial Espionage* revealed that many of the techniques used to improperly obtain such information were simply slight versions of classic intelligence collection methods, to include agent recruitment, soliciting volunteers, surveillance and surreptitious entry, specialized technical operations (wire-tapping and interception of other communications), economic disinformation, tasking of foreign students, tasking foreign employees, debriefing of foreign visitors to the United States, recruitment of émigrés and ethnic targeting, elicitation during international conferences and trade fairs, commercial databases and journals, private-sector organizations and front companies, joint ventures, corporate mergers and acquisitions, head-hunting, technology agreements, sponsorship of research activities, and use of information brokers and consultants.[34] To the degree an employee of the organization knowingly participates in any of these activities for money or compensation, occupational fraud has been committed.

A sense of the scope of such activities is likewise long established. In September 1996, John Harley, Deputy Assistant Director of the FBI's National Security Division, outlined some of these techniques in a speech to a National Seminar sponsored by the American Society for Industrial Security (ASIS). They include biotechnology; telecommunications; computer software and hardware; advanced materials and coatings; energy research; defense and armaments technology; manufacturing processes; semiconductors; proprietary business information, such as bids, contract, customer, and strategy information; and governmental and corporate financial and trade data. FBI investigations, at that point, had identified 23 countries actively engaged in the collection or attempted collection of such data from U.S. organizations and interests.[35]

In 1997, the ASIS conducted a survey regarding loss of intellectual property and reported, in part, the following findings:[36]

- Dollar losses from compromise of intellectual property may exceed $250 billion annually.

- 56% of companies responding reported one or more attempted or suspected information misappropriations.

- 62% of companies have no procedures for reporting information loss, and 40 percent do not have a program in place to protect proprietary information.

- Five times as many companies feel the issue of intellectual property loss is increasing.

- Persons with a trusted relationship pose the highest risk to a company's intellectual property.

- Employees stealing secrets and divulging secrets at a future employment are the two greatest risks to intellectual property.

- On average, companies spend less than 3 percent of their security budgets protecting intellectual property.

As indicated by the definitions, the threats to such information may come from a foreign government, a foreign company operating with the assistance of its government, or an individual, U.S. or foreign. Because of such threats, Congress passed the Economic Espionage Act of 1996 (Title 18 U.S.C. Section 1831). For our purposes, we need not discriminate as to whether the source of a threat to proprietary information is a foreign government or an American citizen. If the compromise of the information is knowingly aided by an employee of the organization in exchange for some monetary consideration, it is a form of occupational fraud, identical to that committed by Walker, Pelton, Ames, Hansenn, and others. Such threats and compromises were estimated to cost U.S. businesses between $100 to $250 billion in lost sales in 2000.[37] Some portion of this amount is surely occupational fraud.

That these issues are interesting and challenging is not the entire point. Just as changes in the motivations for spying have apparently driven espionage into the occupational fraud arena, so too will other changes in technologies, motivations, and methods. Ours is a problem not only of definition, but also of evolution, and we must be prepared to deal with it.

Finally, let us examine the great underbelly of occupational crime—that which never makes it to the official record. We have discussed the problems in trying to use public statistics, such as arrests and convictions, when attempting to assess the size of the occupational fraud problem. Let us now examine the process that leads up to these public records and begin to understand why so much of the wheat falls out of the basket at each step.

First, some employees commit occupational frauds. If they are never discovered, we never know about it. Some wheat is lost. Second, some frauds are discovered, but the company may decide to dismiss the employee and write it off. More is lost. Third, the company may or may not decide to refer some matters for investigation. More is lost. Some matters are accepted and actively investigated, and others are not. More is lost. Fourth, the investigators present the matter to the prosecutor, who may or may not choose to accept the case. A technical violation of law may exist, but the amount involved is not sufficient to meet the standards set by the guidelines most prosecutor's offices use. More is lost. Then, there may or may not be a conviction. More is lost. Finally, the conviction is duly recorded in a public records system, where we may find it if we can determine which Mail Fraud violation is an occupational crime and which is not.

I have been quite liberal in quoting Wells and the ACFE in this chapter, and I do not in any way mean to infer by the issues and questions above that their work is flawed. It is not, in any way. Were it not for them, the field of occupational fraud would still be an uncharted jungle. Their work in beginning to define and professionalize the field has been monumental. I do suggest, however, that for the field to continue to mature and develop, we still have a long way to go.

CHAPTER 6

THOUGHTS ON OCCUPATIONAL FRAUD

Joseph Wells has commented on the paucity of research in this field.[1] The National Fraud Center report concurs in this assessment and provides some of the supporting rationale why this is so, citing the lack of agreed-upon definitions, poor and incomplete data collection, and a tendency for those few conducting research in the field to concentrate on crimes committed by persons of high organizational status.[2]

Given that Sutherland first raised the call for additional research on white-collar crime in 1939, it appears that in more than 60 years we have made but limited progress.[3]

Why is it that a national problem that arguably costs organizations, their owners, employees, and shareholders perhaps $600 billion a year, and maybe much more, has received so little attention? One of the phenomena I have observed in my eight years of private practice in the forensic field, dealing with organizations great and small, is their remarkable tolerance for employee theft. Please note I said employee *theft* and not employee *misconduct*. In today's atmosphere of intolerance for instances of intolerance, sexual, racial, ethnic, or religious harassment will usually be dealt with promptly and severely.[4]

Yet, the 200 or so organizations I have dealt with in times of crisis usually exhibit attitudes toward employee theft ranging from indifference to fear. Perhaps 80 percent, and this is admittedly an inexact number, are shocked, ashamed, confused, and indecisive in their response to employee dishonesty. Often, their primary objective is to document the misconduct so they can successfully defend a wrongful termination suit once they take action against the offender(s). Some are interested in restitution and want a full accounting of the scope of the misdeeds. A few will make fidelity bond claims, and even fewer will make a referral to law enforcement. Perhaps half will want to know how the event(s) took place and what controls can prevent them from happening again. If the defalcation is large enough, and there is a suspicion that assets may still be reachable, some will consider civil litigation. A very few, perhaps 20 percent to be generous, will pursue every option available to them—dismissing the employee, referring to law enforcement, initiating civil action, fixing controls, and filing a fidelity bond claim.

This attitude may provide the answer to the question posed previously. These issues, although common and collectively huge, are the "way it is." They are part of the human condition and do not lend themselves to correction or change. Like "shrink" in retail (the disappearance of goods in retail outlets, arguably due to shoplifting or employee theft), employee fraud is the cost of doing business. Many years ago theorist Donald Schon referred to this phenomenon in another context as the "failure of success": the inability of some, perhaps most, successful institutions to deal realistically with their issues.[5]

I find this perspective odd. Let's assume the number enunciated in the ACFE's *Report to the Nation* is correct. Occupational fraud accounts for 6 percent of an organization's revenues. Then, for the sake of argument, let us reduce this number by half; it is now 3 percent. That means if we, as a profession, could create an effective set of solutions to these issues, we could improve the bottom line of the average organization by 3 percent. Were I to go to Wall Street tomorrow with this proposition clothed in any other format, say tax planning, inventory management, sales efficiency, or hedging of investments, I would be on the cover of every business publication within the week. Think, if you will, what a 3 percent bottom-line improvement would mean to General Electric, General Motors, DuPont, or any other corporate giant.

Insurance is really not a perfect solution to workplace fraud. The *2002 Report to the Nation* from the ACFE advises that only 61.1 percent of organizations defrauded in its survey even had insurance. Of those that did over half, 52.6 percent, recovered no more than half of the amount they lost.[6] Likewise, the 2000 international survey of 700 organizations in 15 countries, *Fraud: The Unmanaged Risk*, by Ernst & Young, indicates that the international experience is, if anything, even worse. Only 29 percent of losses were ever recovered from the perpetrators, and an even lower amount was recovered from insurance companies.[7] Given this poor level of coverage and recovery, one suspects this is not the sort of financial performance lauded on Wall Street.

Still, we as a profession have trouble selling our message or, in the current corporate vernacular, proving we add value. Why is this? One reason may be the inherent nature of organizations. They have been described as resistant to change—both by tendency and to some degree by design—and as being subject to a variety of pressures and influences that affect their objectives and strategies.[8] They are also characterized as having a near-obsession with a short-term, quantitative, bottom-line mentality.[9] Finally, they eschew matters incapable of precise measurement or ones that extend into the distant future.[10]

Courtney Thompson has suggested that some of the reasons organizations are not more aggressive and more effective in addressing fraud in the workplace has to do with at least three factors. The first is that the most effective frauds are those that can be explained away as errors. This provides highly effective cover for the person(s) committing the fraud and an excellent rationale for management to not pursue it further and have to potentially deal with hurt feelings and sticky questions. The second reason is that some cases are difficult, if not impossible, to prove. This may be true even if an experienced fraud investigator is involved. Issues of cost can come into play, as well.

Yet at the same time, organizations by their very nature are susceptible to fraud. Diane Vaughan, writing of corporate crimes, opines that they are facilitated by the following organizational characteristics: formal structures and mechanisms; intricate and specialized reporting and processing systems; a high reliance on trust; and general, rather than specific, systems of monitoring.[11] She notes that especially when one or more of these elements is combined, the possibility of corporate fraud may be enhanced because complex events within complex systems may be difficult to detect and track. From our perspective, I believe we may say the same thing about occupational fraud. The modern organization presents an almost ideal environment for those so inclined to carry out unlawful acts, for their deeds will often also be difficult to detect and track. Further, as Vaughan notes, a prevailing need for trust provides fertile ground for those inclined to abuse it for personal gain.

Also, note Shover and Wright, some organizations breed a culture that makes them ripe for abuses—either by them against others in the case of corporate crime or, in my view, by others against them in the case of occupational fraud. They believe corporate misconduct is more likely in an environment where "rationalizations, excuses, and justifications for illicit behavior. . . increase the odds of criminal choices."[12] So, too, I would argue does this culture make individual wrongdoing more likely against the organization.

This may be particularly true when the language of the organization operates to mask the true nature of given acts. Authors Hochstetler and Copes have theorized that euphemisms and codes and doubletalk may be invoked to make the unpleasant more acceptable and the illegal less onerous when organizational members are breaking the law in the commission of a crime to benefit the organization. They see these mechanisms as contributing to what they call a "criminogenic organizational culture," which operates to deny responsibility, deny the fact of injury being inflicted, minimize the existence of any true victims, condemn the condemners when actions are challenged, and serve higher loyalties such as the betterment of the company by virtue of the very acts undertaken.[13] If such mental representations allow the individual to pursue misdeeds on behalf of the company, we need not think too strenuously to conceive of how at least some of these rationalizations could be bent to justify acts against the company as well.

James Coleman, for example, has not only cited the need for additional research into the causes of white-collar crime, but has also opined on how rationalizations and the "everybody is doing it" mentality can operate to neutralize what would otherwise be the stigma of white-collar crime.[14] He further notes that due to the intricacies of cultural determinants within an organization, "work-related subcultures are often able to maintain a definition of certain criminal activities as acceptable or even required behavior; when they are clearly condemned by society as a whole."[15] Again, although Coleman is speaking of corporate crime, it is but a small step to see these mechanisms justifying occupational fraud as well. Yet, even in the face of such apparent vulnerabilities, the issue of the cost of prevention and detection remains.

In my experience, I believe most occupational fraud cases can be solved. Whether they can be solved in a cost-effective manner, where the cost of the inquiry is less than "X" percent of the possible loss, is another question entirely. This is a significant concern to most organizations, and is one of the major reasons more workplace frauds are not resolved. Some organizations and executives, a minority to be sure, take the position that any fraud against them is intolerable and will be pursued vigorously regardless of the cost relative to the loss. Their theory is based on, as best I can ascertain, one of two elements, or perhaps some combination of the two: (1) a personal "Don't mess with me, pal" attitude, and (2) sending a message that if you are thinking about trying something in this organization, you better realize you will be pursued. It would be interesting to see research on the long-term economic efficacy of these tactics.

The third rationale cited by Thompson is that willful blindness may come into play. A company oriented to production or building schedules may have a "get it done on time" attitude that pushes controls and investigation of anomalies out of sight. A powerful CEO with a scheduled press conference to announce the opening of the new plant or project can provide some pretty powerful incentive to the person in charge of construction. If they let a few problems get in the way of hitting that completion date, they might as well mail in their resignation and spare the boss the trouble of firing them. Persons inclined to commit fraud, whether inside or outside the organization may be venal, but they are normally not stupid. They realize what is going on and that in the rush to complete things controls are not going to get the normal amount of attention, even assuming in normal times that level of attention was high to begin with. Thus do some frauds occur and never get looked at.[16]

Schon refers to varieties of such behavior as "dynamic conservatism," that is, the expenditure of significant organizational time, energy, and resources to try to stay the same.[17] He recounts a story told by historian Elting Morison in his book, *Men, Machines and Modern Times* about how innovation met opposition in the United States Navy as an example of this process at work. It seems a young lieutenant came up with an improved sighting mechanism for naval guns but had it rejected numerous times by Naval brass, even though the system was simpler and more accurate. He finally succeeded when he got the ear of President Theodore Roosevelt. The Navy, Morison concluded, was more interested in protecting the social bonding among gun crews than it was in a simple system that required no teamwork or great skill.[18]

Morison and Schon are speaking here of the powerful cohesion of social systems; organizations, among other things, are social systems. Bratton has commented on the tendency of organizations to drive work routines that seem to have little practical effect, and we shall later hear the observations of Lardner and Repetto as to how culture is passed down in police departments.

There is a famous scene in the movie *The Sand Pebbles* in which actor Steve McQueen plays a new arrival on a Navy ship stationed in China at the time of the Boxer Rebellion. On his first morning aboard, McQueen's character starts to shave when a Chinese servant runs up and offers to shave him. McQueen brusquely dismisses the servant. He is then confronted by another crewman, who asks why he will not let the man shave him. Mc Queen replies to the effect, "I can do it myself," to which the older crewman replies, "It's his rice bowl." McQueen relents, and allows himself to be shaved, since this service justifies the Chinese man's job on board.

So, too, with organizations. There is much invested, psychologically, socially, and financially, in the way things are. Structure and processes justify jobs, careers, and organizational status. Change may threaten all of these things, so it is natural to expect resistance. The issue is not resistance, but how to overcome it.

Lipsky, in his Introduction to Edelman's book, *Political Language*, refers to this phenomenon as "caused inaction." We can experience the lack of activity, but we can at best, absent research, only speculate as to its causation and rationale.[19] Lipsky goes on to speculate as to the forces that create "caused inaction," and concludes there is often a lot of effort and energy that goes into keeping things as they are. In this regard, he is conceptually similar to Schon in his thoughts about "dynamic conservatism." What may appear at first glance or after surface-level inquiry to be a solid mass may actually be an active collection of molecules and processes all working actively to keep things in stasis.

Edelman has observed that organizational realities are often the reflections of their creators' perceptions, objective data notwithstanding:

> What is appearance and what is reality? ... public policies rest on the beliefs and perceptions of those who help make them, whether or not those cognitions are accurate. ... research reflects the prevailing cognitions of respondents and researchers and, therefore, the dominant contemporary ideology; for it reproduces whatever people have been socialized to perceive and believe, rather than analyzing the range of alternative symbolic evocations.[20]

That these perceptions may be evinced and acted on by their holders with a high degree of certitude may speak, in Edelman's quoting of Neitzsche, to "the dogma of immaculate perception."[21] That is, the firm belief that I can observe reality unimpeded by my thoughts, beliefs, or perceptions, and that such observations are, therefore, untainted in their fundamental accuracy or utility for formulating appropriate courses of action.

Edelman also comments on the utility, and dysfunctionality, of benchmarks within organizations.[22] The establishment of a benchmark portrays a necessarily arbitrary definition of reality, which can then operate to subtly limit the ranges of organizational problem resolution. The idea, which can be objectively based on the ACFE's *Report to the Nation*, that 6 percent of revenue is what most organizations apparently lose to occupational fraud, can operate to become an unintentional benchmark that suggests that if my organization is only losing 6 percent, I am normal. Additional courses of action may, therefore, be foreclosed by my acceptance of a benchmark as an accurate representation of an organizational reality I may, or may not, accept and endorse based on my personal experience and organizational goals.

As we saw with regard to law enforcement, we must be wary of a mentality of regulation of occupational fraud, for this is a de facto acceptance of the "root cause" philosophy that dominated law enforcement in the United States for a good part of the twentieth century. In a perverse way, "root cause" perceptions and benchmarks work to reinforce each other, with the result that regulation of the problem toward the benchmark number becomes an acceptable response.

So, too, should we be careful about crises. Again, in the law enforcement experience, the occasional crisis, properly responded to and addressed, allows us the unintended consequence of returning to the comfort of our benchmark (read, normal) level of organizational dysfunction. This is not to suggest that the only acceptable measure of organizational success regarding occupational fraud is zero. We have seen, through the prism of law enforcement activities and policies of social regulation, the perverse consequences of zero tolerance campaigns. Enough five-year-old children being suspended from kindergarten for kissing other five-year-old children has perhaps awakened us to how rigid and unfeeling a number zero really is.

Yet, at the same time, does this mean that 6 percent is our ultimate goal, primarily because it is the only number we have? I think not, unless we are willing as a society to accept that the groundbreaking work done by the ACFE is as far as we need to go in looking at a $600 billion annual problem.

Such tacit acceptance of reality may be reinforced by the motives of many actors with a stake in the outcomes, not totally unlike the operation of political theory or, perhaps more accurately, political theology. Yuval Levin, in his review of *Heaven on Earth*, by Joshua Muravchik, a critique of the course of socialist theory around the world, notes that while socialism frequently resulted in poor economic performance and resultant poverty for hundreds of millions of people, it prospered as a political theory. Indeed, by 1985 almost two-thirds of the world's population in 70 countries lived under such regimes, often because of the appeal of its "Marxist" origins or the sheer ruthlessness of certain political leaders.[23]

The concept of political theory and its ability to serve the needs of some in the face of its failures for the many is indeed high drama when compared to the more mundane concerns of occupational fraud, but such observations can be instructive in understanding that much operating theory can not only survive, but prosper, in the face of objective failure.

I believe much of the resistance we encounter is because we routinely offer more of the same. Like our colleagues in law enforcement, we can argue, usually with quantitative support, that more of us equals more cases, investigations, recoveries, and so on, but, in an era of corporate and organizational downsizing, meeting analysts' expectations, and focus on quarterly earnings, we are talking ones and twos when the big guys are focused on tens and twenties. Ten more investigators or auditors may pay for themselves in the first year, with a little luck, but their impact on the revered bottom line is negligible. To get attention, we need to put before them the so-called magic bullet, the item that is going to improve the bottom line by that magic 3 percent.

Can this be done? I do not know, but I strongly believe it cannot be achieved through our present efforts, no matter how noble and strenuous they may be.[24] We cannot offer more of the same and expect any different reception than we have experienced several hundred times in the past.

As a child in the late 1940s and early 1950s, the scourge of my childhood was polio. It was a lurking evil monster that snatched victims away without rhyme or mercy and caused many parents sleepless nights. The medical community responded. Doctors and nurses and technicians tended those stricken and iron lungs were featured on posters and stamps as the best modern technology could offer to those afflicted. Yet the answer to this plague did not come in the form of more doctors and nurses, or in the form of an improved iron lung. It came, instead, from the hands and mind of Dr. Jonas Salk, who produced a vaccine that made the disease ineffective in attacking its human targets.

If we, as a profession, are to achieve breakthroughs of this magnitude we, too, must look toward the laboratories and not the wards. The wards, like our case folders, are full of battles already lost. We can and should deal with them, but the answers do not lie there. The answers, if there are answers, will be found in our collective experience and our willingness to look outside the normal scope of our everyday activities. Dr. James D. Watson, the co-founder of the double-helix theory of DNA research, has observed that intuition, conjecture, and experience have useful and appropriate roles in the development of even scientific theories, noting in an interview: "I think you have to speculate. If I have a good idea, I tend to believe it's true. An idea is better than no idea . . . that's the way good science works. An idea can be tested, whereas if you have no idea, nothing can be tested and you don't understand anything."[25]

I suggest we at least begin our search in the related field of law enforcement. There are no guarantees, and one can argue powerfully that there are worlds of difference in the law enforcement function and that of the forensic professional. Yet, I would counter, there may be bits of gold in those distant hills and, as a profession, it is our responsibility to explore them. Law enforcement must deal with the population at large: the young, old, infirm, deranged, previously convicted, aliens, substance abusers, and those acting in a moment of spontaneous rage. We should have a huge initial advantage. None of our co-workers is a sullen 15-year-old with a knife, a jealous lover spurned once too often, or a three-time loser out on parole. We may have issues of workplace violence close to us, but they are not our concern. We are forensic professionals. Of all the multitude of humankind's sins and woes, we need only concern ourselves with fraud. We can leave murder, substance abuse, and breaking and entering to our colleagues with the badges and guns or to corporate security.

The existence of such organizational issues that are the purview of other units and departments can actually work to our advantage. At first blush we may see them as competitors for scarce resources, but they may actually be partners-in-the-making. *Workplace violence*, for example, was a term little known or used 20 or 30 years ago, yet a study released in 2002 by the Bureau of Justice Statistics reports that between 1993 to 1999 there were an average of 1.7 million incidents of workplace violence in the United States each year! Workplace violence accounted for an average of 900 homicides each year, and all workplace violence, fatal and nonfatal, accounted for 18 percent of all violent crime in the United States.

Perhaps the most amazing thing about these shocking statistics is that they are actually down by 44 percent! They fell from 16 incidents per 1,000 workers to 9 incidents per 1,000 workers.[26] One of the reasons for this is that workplace violence was being publicized. It is likely you will see a report on the latest outrage in the workplace on television within several days of reading this paragraph. Because of such coverage awareness developed, and with awareness by shareholders, executives, managers, workers, and human resources and corporate security professionals came action. The problem still exists, but progress is being made. Is it possible that some of the techniques being applied to the reduction of workplace violence have applicability for our purposes? It is an area worthy of exploration.

But even addressing a more narrow scope of concern, our task may be long and difficult. At this writing, players for both the New York Yankees and the New Orleans Saints have been dismissed for theft of personal items from their teammates. Both had million dollar contracts.[27] Why do people do such apparently irrational things?

So, too, the military. A news story about misuse of government credit cards makes the following observation:

More than 700 military officers have walked away from debts on their government-issued credit cards, and one Navy employee who charged thousands in personal expenses has been promoted to the office that oversees Army finances.[28]

A later report indicated these 700 officers had amassed $1.1 million in debts on these cards.[29]

Why do people in trusted positions, even with security clearances, do such things? And why do their employers, in this case the U.S. government, handle them the way they do?

We have many questions and few answers. I suggest we begin the search.

CHAPTER 7

WHAT CAN WE LEARN?

We have seen that law enforcement had, for many decades, problems highly similar to ours. They were faced with high incidence rates, an often-unsupportive body politic, a public insistent on action and answers, and few magic bullets in their cognitive guns. There were many false starts and more than a few blind alleys. Yet, after decades of trying, they appear to have found a couple of things that work. Is there anything in their apparent success that offers the forensic profession any hope? Can these ideas that appear to have worked in the large and tumultuous environment of society at large be somehow translated into the much more confined walls of the organization with similar positive results? If modifications are required, so be it, but how, when, and where do we start?

To begin this process of exploration, let us start with an attempt to understand what seems to have made these concepts work. The first is community, a theme that seems to run strongly throughout all of the theories examined and one with both simple definitions and maddening nuances. We are all familiar with the term *community*; most of us live in one. It implies, by definition, lines of demarcation—an element of separateness from what is nearest to it. But we often use the term in other ways as well, as when we refer to the forensic community, implying a commonality brought about not by physical proximity as by shared interests, similar backgrounds, or like areas of endeavor.

Since this work is oriented toward those who practice in organizations, the obvious question is "Can the organization be conceptualized as a community?" I think the answer, although difficult in spots, is "yes." I have put forth the proposition earlier that community need not be defined solely by its most common characteristic, physical proximity. The community of Times Square is a large, unruly, and changeful thing yet, when viewed from the perspective of the law enforcement concepts discussed in this book, it seems to behave as a community with common interests, needs, and objectives.

Most organizations today operate in multiple venues, especially if they are large. Yet, there are powerful financial, psychological, and social themes that meld them into a community of self-interest, regardless of location. We hear much of the company family and our team that does not ground itself in geographic determinants. We are all ultimately paid from the same pot and have a common interest in its security. We all look to the quasi-parental figures of corporate or organizational leadership not only as custodians of hierarchical power, but also as embodiments of what we stand for. As of this writing, much news space is being devoted to one corporate parent (Enron) that apparently was abusive toward the children, most of us do not accept or expect such behavior as the norm.

Authors Argyris and Schon have noted that, at a minimum, the factors that differentiate the organization from the actions of a mob are the ability to make decisions on behalf of the collectivity, delegation of power to act for the collectivity, and setting of boundaries between the collectivity and the rest of the world.[1] Roger Harrison tells us that such an entity will have an ideology that specifies goals and values toward which the organization will be directed and by which its success will be measured; it will prescribe relationships between individuals and the organization, so that each has expectations of the other; it will indicate how behavior will be controlled within the organization; it will define which qualities and characteristics of members will be accepted or rejected; it will define the manner in which members will interact and treat each other; and it will establish methods of dealing with its external environment.[2]

Every organization I have been a part of, from the U.S. Army through the Federal Government to my present employer, easily meets these standards, and I suspect the vast majority of readers' organizational homes will, as well.

We next come to the issue of *reconceptualization*. As we saw in each law enforcement initiative examined, it was a basic set of reconceptualizations, repeated as needed, that drove the transformation process. Reconceptualization is a de facto rejection of theories of "root cause" causation, since the very act of reconceptualizing would be unnecessary if they were true. Reconceptualization is an affirmative action that states, both explicitly and tacitly, that something can be done. It is an attempt to understand what the real problems are, to study how we have dealt with them in the past, and to see how we can deal with them better in the future. Our attempt to begin to see elements of community in the organization is, in and of itself, a reconceptualization.

Gareth Morgan, many years ago, offered useful thoughts about the power, utility, and inherent limitations of paradigm and metaphor in thinking about organizations. He noted, for example, that we may refer to a boxer as a "tiger" in the ring and in so doing conjure up an image of one possessed of power, speed, stealth, and fierce aggression when facing their opponent. At the same time, we understand that unlike the boxer, the tiger has four legs, black stripes on an orange background, claws, and fangs, things the boxer certainly does not. Thus the metaphor has descriptive power only because it is incomplete. Were we to describe the boxer as "man," the metaphor is more whole, but lacking in meaning, since all boxers are by definition "men." Likewise, to describe the boxer as "saucepan" is meaningless, since the boxer and the pan have few attributes in common. It is only when we achieve a necessary degree of overlap between the object we seek to describe and the metaphor applied to it that useful meaning is created and transmitted. As Morgan notes, "Metaphor is thus based upon but partial truth; it requires of its user a somewhat one-sided abstraction in which certain features are emphasized and others suppressed in a selective comparison."[3]

The significance of such imagery is, to Morgan, that we routinely think, or perhaps do not even bother to think, about the paradigms and metaphors we both accept and apply to organizational action and our role(s) in that action. Referring to a story put forth by Mannheim about a peasant boy, raised in a remote village, having to adjust his worldview and mode of thinking to life in the city, he observes that both theorists and scientists not only have such "taken-for-granted" assumptions, but tend to have them reconfirmed by interactions with their peers and colleagues, to the point they assume a form of subconscious life of their own. It is only when some person or event challenges these "posits" can significant change even be contemplated, much less begun.[4]

In thinking about the transformations many law enforcement institutions began in the 1970s one can seek reference points from four paradigms of organization theory and analysis Morgan puts forth:[5]

1. *Functionalist.* Sees society as an "ordered and regulated" place where people function in roles and social context.

2. *Interpretive.* Sees society as a work in progress, where the meaning of any given situation is defined by the participants.

3. *Radical structuralist.* Sees society as filled with tension and contention between elements, leading to change being radical when it occurs.

4. *Radical humanist.* While it sees society as socially created and sustained, it questions the factors that may create self-formed traps that alienate people from their true nature and potential. It is particularly critical of such constraints in industrialized societies.

It would seem that the law enforcement transformations discussed thus far mesh most closely with the radical humanist critique of purposefully redefining the system(s) and structure(s) we have helped create and sustain. The police prior to the 1970s were certainly functioning in an industrial society and, to some degree, saw themselves (their metaphor, if you will) as being part of a production process (arrests) that could be tinkered with to achieve greater efficiency. Only when they began the conscious redefinition of that conception were they able to move away from the repetitive treating of symptoms and begin to think about addressing causes.

We, too, must also think about how we can reconceptualize ourselves, our mission, and our identity. Are we part of the control structure of the organization? Is this part of, or called, the audit function? Are we investigators? Or, are we more properly thought of as risk managers? These questions are more than a sterile discussion of titles, for our self-conceptualization has powerful implications for what we do, how we do it, how others see and react to us, and how success and failure are defined.[6] The first reconceptualization recounted in this book, that following the publication of Goldstein's article in 1963 (see Chapter 2, note 3), must have seemed astounding to those officers involved almost 40 years ago.

The next stop on our round of examination involves the issue of partnerships. As we have seen in our law enforcement examples, there are partnerships both within the community and also with other agencies and entities. Let us be both accurate and harsh. Partnerships are admissions of failure, weakness, or incompleteness. If we could do it all ourselves, we would not need to partner, but most persons with a modicum of organizational experience understand well that collaborative teaming is a reality in almost all effective organizational actions. Certainly, there is pride in oneness and self-sufficiency, not to mention pleasing benefits to be had in protecting turf, controlling decisions, defining problems, gaining resources, and standing alone on the stage when prizes are awarded for success. The only problem is that our trips to the stage are infrequent and even then are for first downs, not touchdowns. We may crack the big case or effect the sizable recovery, but usually we have had a minimal impact on the underlying causation. Were this not the case, we should be slowly going out of business if the problems were being eradicated by our successes. But, as a profession we appear to be getting larger. We seem by our own numbers to be making an excellent argument for our own ineffectiveness.[7]

Now, as to intelligence, the capability to become aware of what is going on in our pertinent environments (communities, if you will): We admit we basically have no idea how big fraud is, much less where it comes from and where it is going. Even the omnipotent federal government, the FBI, various Inspector Generals who are the watchdogs over public funds, Congress, or the all-seeing General Accounting Office reply with estimates.

Our organizational intelligence usually stinks. As a result of fragmentation, inadequate resources, lack of reporting systems (much less standardized reporting systems), fear of embarrassment, filtering negative information, incompatibility in reporting formats, varying definitions, and pure inattention, most organizations do not know if they have a problem, much less how big the problem may be. There may be a mouse or an elephant out there—arm yourselves accordingly.[8]

It may be instructive to offer a point of reference. Pfizer, Inc., the health care giant, concluded a megamerger with the Warner-Lambert Company in 2000. The new combined company has nine medicines in its portfolio that are number one in sales in their class, and eight of these earn in excess of $1 billion each year. The merger made Pfizer the world's largest privately funded biomedical research organization, with some 12,000 scientists around the world. Pfizer is estimated to spend $5 billion each year on research.[9]

Let us think of those numbers—$5 billion and 12,000 scientists. Those are huge. Certainly, we can argue that biomedical research is inherently risky and costly, and recognize that for every successful drug, hundreds or thousands fail. We can also recognize that patents and licenses expire and that the search to eliminate side effects is ongoing, even for effective drugs. We can recognize all of these factors and still look with wonder at the potential size of the occupational fraud problem— perhaps $600 billion? Then we can begin to search for our 12,000 scientists and $5 billion research budget. I doubt we shall have much success.

Incidentally, the research budget for the entire pharmaceutical industry is estimated to be about $31 billion.[10] A truly impressive number—probably less than one month's worth of fraud in the workplace, but impressive nonetheless.

If we add together all the FBI and law enforcement personnel who spend all or part of their time putting together the Uniform Crime Report (which, ironically, does not even treat fraud as a priority crime), all the forensic professionals engaged in research, all those affiliated with professional organizations, all those with an academic interest in the field, I doubt we hit 10 percent of Pfizer's total. If there are 1,200 persons funded at $500 million doing fraud research, I will be amazed. There are many times those numbers of people and funds conducting fraud investigations, but research is another matter altogether. Certainly, the occupational fraud problem is scattered throughout thousands and thousands of organizations, great and small, in every industry we can think of. This dispersion and complexity creates a problem in beginning to apprehend the size of the problem, much less the cure, but $600 billion is still $600 billion. Where, please, is our research?

For example, why is white-collar crime in general, and occupational fraud in particular, apparently such an underreported event? We have seen the opinion of the President's Commission on Law Enforcement and the Administration of Justice that in 1968 white-collar crime was believed to be viewed indifferently by the public and some even had sympathy for the perpetrators. More recently, our Canadian colleagues seem to have found that the number of persons who say they will report such acts is significantly higher than those who say they did make such reports. *The National Public Survey on White Collar Crime* by the National White Collar Crime Center found that significantly more persons say they will report such events, when they have been a victim, than actually do. The NWCCC goes on to state its belief that less than one in ten such episodes is ever reported to a law enforcement agency. Why is this?

In my private-sector forensic career I have seen few organizations that have a firm grasp on the size and components of their fraud problems. Usually they rely on incidental reports and, in turn, generate incremental responses. Jeffrey Seglin, writing of the tendency of some organizations to operate from a "close the barn door after the horses are out" mindset, takes particular note of the efforts being made by Harvard Business School Publishing to write a code of ethics after one of the editors of its publication, the *Harvard Business Review*, had a highly publicized affair with the subject of one of her stories. He quotes Michael Rion, a business ethics consultant as follows on this phenomenon: "The biggest mistake people make... is trying to rewrite policies to solve last month's problem."[11]

So, too, do many organizations, in my experience, rush to fix the last crisis in an effort to show appropriate concern, demonstrate resolve, send messages to employees and customers, and, most important of all, bring closure to the event. What tends to operate is a sort of organizational algebra that says, Problem A = Rule B. Once the rule is in place, the problem is deemed unfortunate, but appropriately dealt with, allowing the organization to move on. The significance here is not only the limited utility of such a posture, but also the fact that there is frequently no conscious or consistent effort to understand the dimensions of misbehavior in the organization. Rather, the tacit philosophy is a bit like the children's game where the furry creature pops out of one hole, is hit by a rubber mallet, and then pops up in another hole. In many organizations the game is the same, only the names are different. The organization hums along, doing whatever it does for a living, until the fraud or ethics problem pops up. The problem is hit with a new rule and goes away until it pops up again somewhere else. The process is then repeated.

Organizations may also attempt to apply best practice criteria to the formulation of an antifraud program, hoping this will suffice. Such efforts are verified by their designation as best in class, world class, or best practice. Such labels can operate as a sort of pacifier or body armor, depending on the dynamics of the situation. As a pacifier they allow the purchaser, the client, to relax, since their search for answers is effectively over—they just purchased a world-class solution. There is none better. Or, if under attack from above, they can hold up the policy and point to its best practices description (and price tag) and deflect incoming fire by arguing that they bought the best and most expensive model available and are, therefore, not to blame for any problems or incidents. This is not unlike the traditional police practice of ratios of officers to citizens. This was the best practice of the time, and if the proper ratios were in place, the problem was believed to be adequately addressed. Besides, who could argue with a best practice?

Hollinger and Clark, in their research of almost 20 years ago, also spoke to matters of organizational intelligence and its role in affecting behavior. They observed that one of the elements they believed key to reducing fraud was an understanding of theft behavior. Within our organizations we seem woefully ignorant of the extent of fraudulent behavior, much less of what is motivating it. Perhaps this weakness can be addressed by improved data collection and analysis, both from organizational information systems and human interaction.

Professionally prepared employee surveys may be one answer; we perhaps should recognize that even the police, one of the most hide-bound of professions, seem more than willing to avail themselves of this useful resource.

Research into the profiles of employees involved in fraudulent activities may reveal patterns worthy of consideration. The lowly exit interview form may be capable of being modified to ask departing employees for their thoughts on the organization's fraud environment, its informal norms and traditions, and the effectiveness of controls. Hollinger and Clark also spoke to the importance of these behavioral motivators, as did Leuci. While employees depart for a myriad of reasons and some are unlikely to be cooperative, a certain percentage will cooperate, and these interviews may yield useful data and insights. This is particularly true if one accepts the proposition that a departing employee is more likely to be candid and forthcoming. The objective should be made clear that the departing employee is not being asked to become a snitch on a nonconforming fellow co-worker. Rather, they are being asked to provide general thoughts and observations in an effort to improve the organization's performance.

Hotlines may be of use, not only in detecting ongoing fraud, but also in providing data for pattern and trend analysis. Their frequency appears to be increasing. The ACFE conducted an electronic poll of its members in January 2002. Of those responding, 31 percent said their organization had one in an investigative unit, 9 percent said there was a hotline in the internal audit unit, 3 percent said human resources had one, and 2 percent said the hotline was located in the legal unit. An additional 17 percent said their organization subscribed to a hotline through a vendor, 18 percent did not have hotlines in their organization but were considering such a step, and 16 percent said there was no need for such a mechanism in their organization.[12]

Finally, change ends our list. All of the above discussion is about change—in how we see our organizational homes; in our concept of ourselves, our roles, and our objectives; in if we partner, who we partner with, why we do it, how we do it, and what we hope to accomplish; and in our understanding of our environment. It cannot, should not, and must not be change for the sake of change, for if it is, it is doomed from the start because the means becomes the objective. If the objective is to change, then once we change we are successful.

This is the great weakness in much of the literature in organizational development—that once change is effected, success is achieved. That this approach is a tautology seems to go unnoticed, except for thoughtful observers such as the noted writer-philosopher-commentator George F. Will, who once opined that the great foolishness of our age is the mindless worship of change.

One is reminded of the adage of the hungry man and the fish, adapted for our purposes to "If you change a thing, you have changed a thing. But if you change a process, it goes on forever." The noted theorist T. Barr Greenfield stated this much more eloquently and thoughtfully. An editor writing the introduction to Greenfield's superb article, "Organizations as Social Inventions: Rethinking

Assumptions about Change" noted that for many years we have tried to change the environment for people in organizations by changing the structure and processes that drive them. Greenfield, the editor notes, operates from a perspective more in keeping with the works of the noted theorist Max Weber, seeing the organization as really little more than the sum of the people in it. He concludes:

> ...The task of changing organizations depends, first, upon the varieties of reality which individuals see in existing organizations, and second, upon their acceptance of new ideas of what can or should be achieved through social action.[13]

Unless we are willing to accept the "root causes" argument discussed by Kelling, and become case processors, there is only one set of answers that makes any sense and will make any difference. Collectively, we perhaps can bring the lessons of law enforcement, and many other fields, to ours in a productive and effective fashion. It will take much effort and many initiatives in many places. Most of them will fail; those in law enforcement certainly did. And, it will not happen quickly; those in law enforcement did not. Time, wind, and weather will wear us down. Remember Kelling's concerns about the need for continuity at the top. We, too, must be mindful of that, although our existence as a profession may guarantee that we have many tops (i.e., seedbeds of experimentation in many organizations that can be moving simultaneously toward solutions that can then be shared). We can learn from our failures as well as from our successes, and we should be prolific in sharing both. We should become, in the words of one of my old graduate professors, "a learning community." Professor Peter Senge of the Massachusetts Institute of Technology has written of such organizations in his book *The Fifth Discipline: The Art and Practice of the Learning Organization.* Murray, in describing how he applied Senge's concepts to his organization, noted they have five elements: personal mastery, shared vision, mental models, team learning, and systems thinking.[14]

We may wish to look to Senge and others for guidance on how such constructs operate. Being in a learning organization may be a new experience for many of us, but for those who have experienced them, they bring a new richness and sense of adventure and discovery to work. One does not go to the office every day for more of the same. Certainly, the organization's work must get done, and these efforts are not a form of endless brainstorming sessions or advanced stargazing. They are hard and serious work that needs to get done while the routine business continues. In this regard, they can be demanding. The reward comes in not only peeling back the onion to see what the next layer looks like, but also in gaining an enhanced understanding of what the mission of the organization is all about. In that regard, it is the most efficient form of organization when great things need to get done, and it can also be a lot of fun, personally and professionally.

CHAPTER 8

INTERNAL CONTROLS

Controls are, in many ways, the bedrock infrastructure of the organization's defensive system against fraud and other types of business risk. They have been described in this role as follows:

> Internal controls are the first line of defense against fraud within any organization. A comprehensive, fully implemented, and regularly monitored system of controls is essential to the prevention and detection of losses that arise from fraud. Internal auditors who understand the various types of fraud and their relative rates of occurrence will be more likely to recognize any red flags and be better prepared to fight the high organizational cost of corruption.[1]

The *Fraud Examiners Manual* of the ACFE has a chart that breaks down the three main categories of occupational fraud: corruption, asset misappropriation, and fraudulent statements. The chart then subdivides these broad categories into eight major classifications of fraudulent activity, and further segments these into more than 40 subclassifications.[2] Suffice it to say that each of these areas has various financial controls that surround it. Some of these controls are unique to the organization, and others are specified by the Generally Accepted Accounting Principles (GAAP) of the American Institute of Certified Public Accountants (AICPA).

The emphasis of this book has not been on organizational control programs and techniques, although they play a significant part in the future of the forensic profession. There are two reasons for this approach. The first is simple volume. A hierarchy of GAAP pronouncements alone has five levels, containing 20 sources of accounting guidance, from Financial Accounting Standards Board (FASB) Statements of Financial Accounting Standards to AICPA Practice Bulletins. Several books of this size could easily be written about technical issues in any of these areas.

The second reason is even more basic: A very common reason many occupational frauds occur is not because there was some defect in the content of the written controls. Often, they are fine. The problems typically occur because there are no controls at all, or the ones in place are not being followed. Almost all occupational frauds involve a failure of controls, but this failure is often one of absence or application, and not content. This is a subtle, but significant, distinction. Now we involve humans, and humans can do terrible things to controls, even if they are not intent on committing fraud or facilitating it. Inexperience, laziness, ego, impatience, inadequate staffing, and pure sloppiness can come into play. For example, it is not unusual to encounter the scenario wherein the star performer, highly visible and lauded frequently by management, has an attitude that "controls do not apply to me." In this context a star performer can be a person, unit, office, or even corporate division. They are often successful in deflecting attempts to subject their activities to controls procedures, for they have their success to shield them.

A reader of *Internal Auditor* magazine reflects this view in a letter to the editor that appeared in the April 2002 edition. Barry Lipton, CPA and DABFA, wrote:

> After 35 years in the field of internal auditing, I am of the opinion that systems are generally in place. My experience tells me business failures and incidents of financial statement fraud occur because existing controls were not operating, not because they were improperly designed and installed. Often, internal auditors are not permitted to do their jobs. Serious audit results impact executives, and many executives are resistant to change or feel threatened. Consequently, those who can make a difference are stifled.[3]

Steve Albrecht, the noted theorist and practitioner in the occupational fraud field, some of whose contributions we have examined in thinking about theories of fraud, has commented on this phenomenon as follows:

> Fraud occurs when pressure, opportunity, and rationalization come together. Most people have pressures. Everyone rationalizes. When internal controls are absent or overridden, everyone also has an opportunity to commit fraud.
>
> Internal control is comprised of the control environment, the accounting system, and control procedures. Common control fraud symptoms include a poor control environment, lack of segregation of duties, lack of physical safeguards, lack of independent checks, lack of proper authorizations, lack of proper documents and records, the overriding of existing controls, and an inadequate accounting system.
>
> Many studies have shown that the most common element of employee fraud is the overriding of existing internal controls.[4]

KPMG, in its *1998 Fraud Survey*, was reported to have come to a slightly different conclusion based on the observations of respondents. They reported that when their organizations experienced occupational fraud, poor internal controls were cited 58 percent of the time, and management override of controls was mentioned in 36 percent of incidents. Various forms of collusion were also mentioned frequently: 31 percent of respondents cited collusion between employees and outside third parties, and 19 percent cited collusion among employees or management. Other causal factors mentioned were directors' lack of control over management (11 percent) and a poor or nonexistent corporate ethics policy (8 percent).[5] From the structure of the responses, it is evident that more than one causal factor could be cited for a given incident or series of incidents.

When I have been involved in reviews of controls programs, such as anti–money laundering controls, I like to employ a three-stage approach. First, I meet with key professionals in the controls and compliance programs to learn how their programs were developed, staffed, and implemented. I also learn how they are administered. More times than not, the programs are well written, comprehensive, and perhaps even draconian in tone. Second, I spend some amount of time checking documentation regarding training, monitoring, and follow-up. Last, I cheat. I saunter down to human resources and ask to see the data for the last year or so for persons sanctioned or terminated for violating these controls. Invariably, I get a blank stare. I usually follow up by advising that I do not need to see all of these employee folders, just a few of the recent ones. The stare gets blanker.

Then, I mosey back up to the compliance people to congratulate them. They are an organization—say, if it is a financial institution—that has a couple of million customer accounts and a couple of thousand account representatives and, evidently, no one has broken any of these rules in the last year or so. That is impressive. It is also usually the sign of a compliance program that is not being very actively or comprehensively enforced.

It is not unusual to investigate a significant occupational fraud and see that the organization has fine controls—on paper. They just have not been followed or were overtaken by events. Control systems can age and become out of alignment with the new shape of the organization or its current operations and interests.

A brief look at several current financial controversies may offer instructive guidance:

Allied Irish Banks PLC suffered losses of $691 million at the hands of rogue trader John Rusnak. While initial reports indicated Rusnak had concocted some incredibly sophisticated scheme to pull this off, other reports indicate that lapses in more basic control procedures may have had a role.[6]

It would seem at this stage there were a number of factors responsible for the problems at Allfirst, but apparently high among them were issues of controls adequacy. Likewise, at Lehman Brothers, where broker executive Frank Gruttadauria is accused of defrauding customers of $125 million over a 15-year period, *The Wall Street Journal* wrote: "The star stockbroker in the Cleveland office of Lehman Brothers who allegedly cheated clients out of millions of dollars also supervised the office-compliance executive whose job it was to help police the office's brokers, according to people familiar with the matter."[7]

Yet, many organizations utilize their controls effectively. Controls can take many forms—many that are not immediately obvious to us. The ubiquitous automated voice on the telephone informing us "This call may be monitored for training and quality assurance purposes" is a form of controls. Likewise, the unseen video camera somewhere in the ceiling above every dealer in almost every casino is a form of controls. The state inspection sticker on the windshield of your automobile is a form of control the state uses to promote highway safety.

A survey of 500 executives that appeared in *Sales & Marketing Management* magazine reported that 27 percent of companies had terminated employees as a result of some sort of monitoring. The three primary reasons cited for conducting such monitoring were to ascertain quality interaction with clients, productivity, and to spot criminal or illegal activity.[8] It seems that the quality or rigor of the controls, while important, is not as crucial as the fact that they are in place and are being properly utilized.

Controls programs are the bedrock of most compliance efforts and, while often basic in their nature (e.g., segregation of duties), they will surely benefit from future development and refinement. In thinking about controls, I am prone to recall Leuci's observation about people in organizations: 5 percent are clean, 5 percent are dirty, and 90 percent are "waiting to see what happens." In discussing Leuci previously, I mentioned him in the context of organizational socialization processes and informal cultures. I think it is also possible to think of his observation in terms of controls as well.

Carpenter and Mahoney likewise cite the Institute of Management and Administration/Institute of Internal Auditors *1999 Business Fraud Survey* on this issue:

> Similarly, communication of the organization's ethics and fraud program to the workforce would seem to be an obvious component of an effective fraud detection program. However, 34 percent of the respondents noted that their program was "well-intentioned but meaningless to employees," while an additional 21 percent stated that no such program existed. When asked how their fraud detection programs could be enhanced, 63 percent of survey participants recommended requiring strict monitoring of basic internal controls.[9]

In this regard, it appears that Campbell, in his thoughts on building a successful security function at Fidelity Investments, was insightful in his emphasis on the need for effective communication of program objectives as being crucial. We shall later examine Campbell's accomplishments in more detail.

Controls are ubiquitous. They are probably unnecessary for 5 percent of employees, and are seen as an obstacle to be evaded by another 5 percent, but it is the remaining 90 percent that interests me. The 5 percent who do not need controls must accept them as the cost of doing business. The 5 percent that may try to evade them must be identified and dealt with in an appropriate manner. For the remaining 90 percent, controls are certainly constraints on their behavior but also, I would hope, instructive in explaining the organization's view of how one is expected to comport one's self. They are designed and in place as a ready reference guide, to be consulted when uncertainty or temptation appears.

Perhaps Leuci has done us a great service in suggesting we resist the temptation to focus on the anomalies—the good and the evil—and pay most attention to the middle.

When thinking about the law enforcement concepts we have discussed, especially in New York City, one is tempted to think about numbers. Numbers, indeed, may impede an effective controls program. One may be persuaded that while the NYPD was able to effect some impressive innovations and reduce crime by a significant amount, they are also a huge organization. Much bigger than any internal audit function of which I am aware.

There is substance to this argument, but we must not let it oversimplify our thinking. Certainly, a three-person audit shop in an organization with 50,000 employees is going to have its hands full and, in that instance, staffing levels may be a legitimate issue on the way to an improved compliance climate. But, let us again think of New York City. The NYPD has, for sake of argument, about 38,000 cops to police a city of roughly 8.5 million. That is a ratio of about 224 to one. Now, to take our mythical organization with 50,000 employees; we would need an audit capability of about 223 people to maintain parity with the cops. Is this likely? In my experience, no. Most organizations of that size would be unusual if they had an audit capability of one quarter that size, or 50 people. So, how do we try to be more effective when we may be seriously understaffed?

For gross understaffing, there is probably no magic answer. It is tough to get five pounds out of a one-pound bag. But, lest we be blinded by pure numbers, we should remember three things:

1. The cops in New York City also have a few more things on their plate than we do, like murder, robbery, rape, drug use, speeding, gang warfare, gambling, prostitution, underage drinking, organized crime, crowd control, guarding VIPs, protection of transit systems, and terrorism, to name but a few. We are dealing with only occupational fraud, although granted, it can occur in a lot of places and in a variety of formats.

2. Policing is a 24/7 type of business. Even though big-city police departments may have an impressive number of officers, they also have to deploy them through three shifts each day, cover holidays and weekends, and also devote substantial numbers to crowd and traffic control at sporting events, concerts, and demonstrations.

3. We must remember that it was the "throw numbers at numbers" mentality prior to the 1970s that had the cops wrapped around their own axles. If production of arrests is the answer to crime, then more and more cops are needed to make more and more arrests. They started to make progress when they got away from that mentality.

We must be prepared to pay heed to what well may be some disturbing trends in the internal audit profession, as well. The 2002 Institute of Internal Auditors survey of the profession in the United States indicates that only 15.7 percent of internal audit directors expected their audit function to increase in size, while 5.7 percent expected a decrease. The vast majority, 78.6 percent, expected no change. The survey also reported significant levels of turnover, particularly among younger internal audit staff. Of those with three to four years of experience, 42.3 percent departed, as did 24.1 percent of those with five to six years of experience. Such numbers do not bode well for building experienced staffs to handle more complex internal audit responsibilities, much less issues of occupational fraud. The survey indicated that only 5.3 percent of internal audit staff time is devoted to fraud investigations.[10] Such findings are also consistent with those reported by the IOMA/IIA in their 1999 survey.

Such conditions are also reported by our cousins in the world of corporate security. The 2002 Pinkerton study, *Top Security Threats and Management Issues Facing Corporate America*, reports that among corporate security directors surveyed, three of their top five challenges were tight or reduced budgets, the need to justify the effectiveness of their programs, and staffing issues. Perhaps not surprisingly, the top two factors they believed influenced their departmental budgets were the prevailing perception of risk and the ability to tie expenditures to bottom-line savings.[11]

With 84.3 percent of internal audit staffs either remaining at their existing staffing levels or actually decreasing in size, and with 66.4 percent turnover in the three- to six-year experience range, it may be difficult for most internal audit functions to adequately address occupational fraud. That only 5.3 percent of internal audit staff time is directed to fraud investigations may be interpreted several ways: perhaps there is little occupational fraud work to be performed; perhaps other duties are considered to be higher priority; perhaps fraud inquiries are conducted only on an incremental basis as issues are discovered; or, perhaps, there is simply no one qualified to perform this work.

The latter instance can be remedied by calling in outside forensic professionals and, while this option can work well, it tends to present two problems: (1) it is an unscheduled expense and, therefore, may be subject to several levels of internal review, thereby ensuring that the matter is not addressed in a timely manner, and (2) it is inherently a reactive posture. It does not affirm to employees, customers, shareholders, or board members that the organization believes it has significant fraud exposure and has staffed appropriately to address it. It also means, absent fortuitous discoveries, that the frauds will have reached sizable proportions before receiving the attention they deserve.

Courtenay Thompson has done an excellent job of summarizing the implications of such metrics for the average internal audit department as it faces what appears to be a growing occupational fraud threat:[12]

- Most auditors pass through the department within three years. Does their lack of experience reduce the likelihood that they will know the fraud exposures and symptoms for the areas they audit?

- How does the short-term auditor's interest in securing a job after auditing impact his or her professional skepticism and handling of findings, particularly when dealing with prospective bosses?

- Can we do a better job of building fraud detection into routine audits? If so, how?

- How can we use technology to detect fraud, either through ongoing or periodic monitoring, or as part of our regular audits?

- How can we be more effective in fraud detection without going too far and becoming "gotcha" auditors?

- Some audit departments devote significant resources to contract auditing, resulting in major cost recoveries and other findings. What contract auditing can we be doing?

  Problems are in the details. Are we testing enough at the detail level, or are we limiting our work to big-picture-control reviews, perhaps guaranteeing that there will be no findings?

  Some audit departments look for risks, but rarely look for incidents or occurrences. Should we look for occurrences more than opportunities?

  How can we mobilize management to be part of the fraud solution?

Thompson's points are well taken. As we design and build controls and programs, we would be well advised to be mindful that there are two players in every game of occupational fraud—the employee and the organization. Joseph Wells and the pioneering researchers who came before him were instrumental in setting forth insightful and useful characteristics of those prone to commit occupational fraud, and Jack Bologna and others have also performed a useful service in highlighting the characteristics that seem to make organizations more prone to occupational fraud than they need be. The wise organization would be well served to keep both elements in mind as it designs, implements, and operates its control procedures.

We should also be sensitive to the fact that controls should be part of a larger plan for mitigating risk to the organization and not an end unto themselves. Michael J. Corcoran, Chief Executive Officer of HarborView Partners LLC, offered his thoughts on this issue in a letter to *Internal Auditor* magazine in April 2002 as follows:

> I agree... regarding the lack of an architect for a system of internal control. I would add that the front end to a control model is a risk model. In providing risk and control services to companies over the past five years, I've found that very few chief executive officers, chief financial officers, board members, or U.S. Congressional leaders "get it" or spend time thinking about the issue.[13]

I would also offer a cautionary note: Controls for the sake of controls can be stifling. There is a saying that many organizations apply the thud test when evaluating their controls programs. The controls manual is held chest-high. The arms are extended and the manual is dropped. The louder the thud when it hits the floor, the better the controls program is judged to be.[14]

Rules can be the bane of any organization, as anyone who spent considerable time in one can attest. They can also at times be terribly dysfunctional. There is a law in New York State that prohibits public employees from striking during a labor dispute. There are two common ways around this, as used from time to time by the officers of the NYPD. The first is the so-called blue flu, when large numbers of officers call in sick for a given shift. The department does not have the resources to examine such a large number of people in a short period to determine if they are, in fact, sick.

The other tactic is called work to rule. It is a simple, yet highly effective, technique that strangles the organization on its own rules. Let us say there is a roll call, and officers are dispatched to their cars to begin their shifts. Many NYPD vehicles have their share of dings and dents from near-constant use in congested city streets. There is probably a rule, somewhere, that says a police vehicle cannot have a cracked taillight. The technique is simple: look at the car, find a rule violation, and return to the station house to inform the Sergeant that you are forbidden by department rules from operating an unsafe vehicle. Multiply this by hundreds of officers, and this approach effectively shuts down the department.

So, too, in all organizations. The unwritten yet understood axiom in most organizations is that the work comes first. The rules are there, and are there for a reason, but slavish devotion to them often gets in the way of organizational efficiency and effectiveness. There is also an issue of fairness, or at least the perception of it, which is probably even more important. If there are 10,000 rules and 20,000 employees, some rule is probably being broken every second. To call someone to task for an infraction in such an environment is often perceived by the offender as unfair and arbitrary, when others to their left and to their right go unpunished.

I have often had this debate with my good friend, ethicist and educator Dr. Ed Delattre of Boston University. Ed, who has written extensively in the area of police ethics, is a believer in the slippery slope theory of ethics (i.e., deal with small infractions before they become commonplace and lead to even bigger ones). Ed illustrates his position by examining one of the more common things in law enforcement—the free cup of coffee from the restaurant:

> The free coffee may not cause the vulnerability, but it may, by indulging in it, lead to worse things. . . . Accordingly, departmental policy should treat all gratuities as unacceptable. They undermine public respect and cause resentment —costs that police in general must pay. In this sense, the free coffee is much too expensive. Young officers should take nothing except their compensation, rather than be faced with questions about how far to go. Once that becomes the issue, the matter has gone too far.[15]

In this stance, which he argues with great effectiveness from his commanding knowledge of both modern and ancient scholarship in the field, he is conceptually similar to those police theorists who believe that dealing with small crimes effectively reduces the incidence of more serious offenses.

Mike White is a career law enforcement officer who in 1997 became the chief of a small police department. Of note was the fact that he was the first chief who had not come up through the ranks of the department—he was an outsider. One of the first tasks White undertook was to enunciate his policy with regard to gratuities. In recounting this experience some years later, he sets forth the following observations of the considerations he took into account when crafting his policy:[16]

The arguments for and against gratuities are

- *Allowing Gratuities*
    - They help create a friendly bond between officers and the public, thus fostering community-policing goals.
    - They represent a nonwritten form of appreciation and usually are given with no expectation of anything in return.
    - Most gratuities are too small to be a significant motivator of actions.
    - The practice is so deeply entrenched that efforts to root it out will be ineffective and cause unnecessary violations of the rules.
    - A complete ban makes officers appear as though they cannot distinguish between a friendly gesture and a bribe.
    - Some businesses and restaurants insist on the practice.

- *Banning Gratuities*
    - The acceptance violates most departments' policies and the law enforcement code of ethics.
    - Even the smallest gifts create a sense of obligation.
    - Even if nothing is expected in return, the gratuity may create an

appearance of impropriety.

- Although most officers can discern between friendly gestures and bribes, some may not.

- They create an unfair distribution of services to those who can afford gratuities, voluntary taxing, or private funding of a public service.

- It is unprofessional.

To this day, White reports, police departments across the country vary widely in their stance on this long-standing and controversial activity.

I do not disagree with the logic of Ed's argument—I cannot, for he is right, both conceptually and morally. My concern, like that of Chief White, is not in the rules, but in their implementation. During my career, I have had jobs where I had hundreds of people working for me. One of my concerns, say, with having 100 rules was that we did not actively enforce 30 of them, at least not consistently. It was just not practical, but there the rules were, sitting on the books. I always worried that this position could cause employees to begin to wonder if we were serious about the other 70 rules, as well. This concern probably speaks much more directly to the need to think seriously before we put rules on the books and to actively review and discard those that have become outdated, nonsensical, or unimportant. We saw the staying power of rules in Bratton's patrol cars endlessly responding to the same street corner, with little practical effect. The ACFE also has recommended that small businesses, which seem particularly susceptible to occupational fraud, strike a balance between trust and openness and a reasonable level of controls.

Even Ed, as stalwart and vigorous a champion of ethical behavior as can be found, recognizes that slippery slope issues must be viewed in context. He is on the record as stating that the proposition that a law enforcement officer who takes a free cup of coffee is certainly going to take even larger liberties in the future is nonsense. He notes that the most important issue on such matters is a "sense of proportion." In a police department where there are large or widespread issues of brutality or corruption, to focus on issues like free cups of coffee is to lack a sense of proportion and to waste precious political and organizational capital. The answer, he notes, is to address the issue of small-scale gratuities in light of the circumstances and history of the department, or in our case, the organization.[17]

That such a balance is vital to the organization finds support with many people now involved in examining the problems of Wall Street. David Wessel, in an article in *The Wall Street Journal*, quotes two sources who have seen the issues in question firsthand, noting that one mutual fund manager sees problems coming largely from two groups—those who are morally bankrupt and confirmed crooks, and others who push the envelope as a matter of routine until they forget where the lines are. Treasury Secretary Paul O'Neill concurs in this assessment, noting that small indiscretions seem to always grow larger with time.[18]

Authors Koontz and O'Donnell, in their work *Principles of Management: An Analysis of Managerial Functions,* are even more harsh in their appraisal of incomplete or inconsistent application of organizational codes, and their observations may have meaning for issues about controls, as well. They note:

> Most so-called ethical codes are, at best, a stopgap and, at worst, deceptions. As a stopgap, they are employed as a means of trying to provide some assurance of ethical conduct on the part of a membership. In this sense they may be making a contribution if only in pointing up the critical need for development and teaching of a science of ethics. As a deception, they easily give the appearance of restricting the behavior of members to some recognized standard, but in fact they are incapable of so doing, In this sense they are notoriously misleading, especially to the customer, patient, consumer, and voter.[19]

Most organizations, in my experience, operate on a system of slack resources, when it comes to internal controls. They just assume they are there. In reality, it is an abrogation of responsibility from the top to the bottom. I mean that literally. If headquarters is not going to make decisions as to what will and will not be done, it is going to be decided at the most junior levels of the organization. If there are not slack resources in the system, then each manager or entity is going to make an independent decision as to what they will stop doing so they can do something new. I am told we call this management.

There is a saying to the effect that the only thing worse than your enemies are your friends. I thought Jim Murphy was my friend. Jim, a former NYPD officer before he joined the FBI, had been one of my colleagues on the bank robbery squad in New York, and we spent the better part of five years chasing bank robbers and terrorists together. Jim, also on his first tour at FBI Headquarters, was assigned to the Office of Program Evaluation, a sort of research and special studies unit. The FBI at that time had 40 years' worth of manuals that told you how to do everything (e.g., format a letter, investigate a kidnapping, or display the American flag in the reception area).

Jim had been tasked with reviewing and reformatting these manuals and had been empowered to seek out volunteers. I should have been smarter, especially since Murph assured me the entire project would take about three weeks.

For five months we labored in a barren room in the basement of FBI Headquarters, with copies of these many manuals spread over a sea of gray metal government-issue desks. We took each manual and physically chopped it into paragraphs. Yes, paragraphs. We then tried to track the paragraph back to the headquarters unit that had produced it so many years ago. Of course, many of the people who had been in those units were long gone, but if we could track it, then the unit was responsible for determining if the rule was still viable, needed to be updated, or could be deleted. Some were easy—a rule about the proper procedures for investigating a bank robbery went to the bank robbery unit, even if the rule in question had been written 20 years ago.

Others were more difficult. Some we resolved and found their owners. Others, we did not. When the process was through, we were unable—in a big organization that keeps track of everything—to locate where 30 percent of the rules had come from. Such is how organizational rules accumulate. We need to be mindful of this situation when we start writing new ones. We should be mindful also of the "bop the weasel" tendency of many organizations—the idea that when one is hit with a problem or an incident it is solved by writing a new rule. As with the FBI and its manuals, rules, like junk in the garage, have a tendency to build up over time. Going through them is interesting archeology—Why did you ever buy that metal detector on the beach trip 16 years ago?—but promotes sloppy or inconsistent management. Rules create clutter, just like 1,300 calls for service at a street corner in Boston many years ago, and can obscure what is truly important.

I offer such observations because I believe they are important to any consideration of organizational controls. We must have such controls, but we should develop them with thought and wisdom and, once they are in place, we should apply them consistently and fairly. There will always be discretion and judgment calls, just as there are with patrol officers observing those drivers going but a few miles over the speed limit. To do otherwise, I believe, seriously weakens and dilutes our message and our efforts.

It is probably fitting to conclude our discussion on controls with a reference to law enforcement, for to some degree they function in a highly similar manner. Most people do not appreciate the subtleties of law enforcement and how misleading some of the terminology is if taken literally.

When we see a uniformed police officer, we may rightfully think of him or her as a law enforcement officer. While that is technically true, and these officers do enforce the law, their primary function is crime prevention. To some degree, of course, this is accomplished by writing tickets and making arrests; however, the bulk of their mission is accomplished through their presence and visibility. That is one of the reasons, police sartorial instincts aside, that they try to wear highly visible and distinctive uniforms. There is a logic to those large badges, Sam Browne belts, and Smokey the Bear hats. The theory is that by their very visibility, crime is prevented.

Detectives, on the other hand, try to dress much like civilians, but do not really detect crime; they investigate it after it has already occurred. What they are trying to detect is not the crime itself—that is already known. They are trying to detect who committed the crime. Even sworn law enforcement officers are affected by the existence of rules, or perhaps more accurately, the proliferation of rules. Authors Robertson and Simpson have cited a survey by the Traffic Injury Research Foundation in which 2,700 police officers in 16 states were queried regarding their views on the DWI violation arrest process. Referring to the study, Robertson and Simpson note:

> Virtually no other criminal charge requires as much documentation as DWI. These arrests may take many officers an average of two to three hours to complete and much of this time is consumed by filling out a multitude of forms. Many police agencies have 10-15 separate forms that officers must complete. Sixty percent of officers report that extensive paperwork discourages them from making a DWI arrest. In light of this, it is not surprising survey results show that, on average, only 50 percent of investigations result in an actual arrest.[20]

In thinking about controls and their role in occupational fraud, we may conclude they operate much like the uniformed police. Their presence is meant to deter fraud. Their track record in detecting it is more problematic. Statistics from the ACFE may be useful in assessing their efficacy in this regard. In August 2001 the ACFE posted an online poll of its 25,000 members, asking the following question: How is fraud most frequently discovered in your organization?
The results, published the following month, were as follows:[21]

Other tips by employees	56.6%
Audits	22.6%
Management review	5.4%
Hotline tips	4.7%
Lifestyle changes	1%
Other	9.5%

If we take "Other tips by employees" and add "Hotline tips," which are really the same thing delivered through a different medium, we see that almost two-thirds of frauds discovered (61.3%) were probably surfaced by co-workers.

Such findings are also reflected in the ACFE's *2002 Report to the Nation*. This survey reported that data from 532 respondents indicated that internal controls surfaced only 15.4 percent of frauds reported and internal audits identified only 18.6 percent. The report advised that 46.2 percent of frauds covered were brought to light by tips from employees, customers, vendors, or anonymous sources.[22]

Such statistics may be seen by some as an argument against the effectiveness of internal controls, but that would be contrary to the sentiments of the people offering the assessments. In the same survey, *The Report to the Nation* asked respondents what they believed, from their professional experience, to be the most effective antifraud strategies and measures. Participants were asked to rate eight measures on a scale of 1 (most effective) to 8 (least effective).[23] The winner, by far, was "internal controls":

Strong internal controls	1.62
Background checks on new employees	3.70
Regular fraud audits	3.97
Established fraud policies	4.08

Even though the controls in place in these victim organizations did not prevent these frauds from occurring, the report offers data that suggests that the presence of controls appears to have a tempering effect on fraud losses. In organizations that did not perform preemployment background checks of employees, the median fraud loss was $130,000, versus $90,000 for organizations that did perform such checks. In organizations that had in place an anonymous reporting mechanism, such as a hotline, the median fraud loss was $77,500, versus $150,000 for organizations without such a capability. Likewise, organizations that had periodic internal audits or fraud surveys had median fraud losses of $87,500, while organizations without such processes had median losses of $153,000. Finally, organizations with external audits had median fraud losses of $100,000, while those without external audits had median losses of $140,000.[24]

The professional services firm of KPMG Peat Marwick has reported survey findings that seem both to contradict and support some of the data reported by the ACFE. In a survey released in 1999, KPMG reported that it surveyed 2,000 large companies that had experienced fraud. These frauds were discovered in the following manners (percentages may add to more than 100 because some respondents experienced more than one fraud and some frauds were discovered through a combination of factors):[25]

Internal controls	59 %
Internal auditors	47 %
Notification by customers	38 %
Accident	32 %
Anonymous letter	28 %
Notification by supplier	13 %
Notification by police	12 %
Notification by employee	10 %
Notification by government	10 %
External auditor	3 %

It seems reasonable to infer two findings from these data: (1) the presence of one or more control mechanisms either tended to restrain the size of the fraud loss or, remembering the issue of the length of time schemes were reported to have been committed, caught it earlier; (2) we may presume, I would argue, that an organization with some element of control structure in place has announced to its employees its position on financial integrity and occupational fraud. Given that the teacher is watching, the classroom may not become as loud or rowdy.

As intriguing as these data are, it would be interesting to attempt to tease even more information out of them. For example, can we show a proportionality between levels of organizational controls effort and reduction of fraud incidence and loss? That is, does the organization with two controls mechanisms in place have lower losses than an entity with but one, and are three controls mechanisms even more effective? Until we can avail ourselves of further and more detailed research, we can only speculate.

It is not surprising that the respondents to the survey opined that controls were the primary issues in the vast majority of frauds these organizations experienced: 46.2 percent cited "Insufficient Controls" as the reason the fraud(s) took place, while 39.9 percent advised that controls had been ignored. Only 10.8 percent of respondents believed that the fraud would not have been prevented regardless of the controls in place.[26] Again, Leuci's diagnosis seems to be borne out. A certain small percentage of the population seems to see controls as a challenge to be overcome. In this regard, they appear to be behaving in much the same manner as predicted in Gottfredson and Hirschi's general theory of crime. Most people, however, seem to respond appropriately to controls, at least insofar as we may reasonably infer from the data available in the report. Also, per the report, the victim organizations seem to learn from their mistakes; 72.8% of respondents reported that the control deficiencies that permitted the fraud to occur in the first place had been addressed.[27]

I return to my earlier comment about internal controls. Often, they are fine. The organizations that get into trouble either do not have them in any meaningful sense, or more likely, do not enforce them consistently and rigorously. All too often, this is a simple matter of resources. Far too many organizations are penny wise and pound foolish in their approach to internal controls staffing and monitoring, but seem willing to pay the almost inevitable price when problems occur, then bemoan the lack of ethical values in the employee population. As Leuci would probably argue, in an environment where no one ever checks, even the decent are tempted. The dishonest are free to run wild, while the upright are perplexed and frustrated as to why their organization allows this sort of thing to go on. Indeed, a survey co-sponsored by Walker Information and the Hudson Institute of 3,000 employees found that 55 percent of employees stated that the ethical dimensions of their workplace were important to them in terms of their loyalty and willingness to continue working there. On the negative side, only 42 percent said that the ethical or compliance problems were dealt with fairly or completely, only 56 percent said the ethical issues of the organization had been communicated to them effectively, and only one-third advised that they would be comfortable reporting internal misconduct.[28]

Such findings suggest that employees, whether vocal about it or not, are watching and are sensitive to how their employing organization handles issues of misconduct. Unfortunately, at least some portion of them seem to be saying, "If you don't take these things seriously, why should I?" If such is the case, problems are sure to follow. As William Boni, the chief information security director of Motorola Information Protection Services, has noted with regard to digital intellectual property; "One of the best ways to help newly hired staff learn how to handle sensitive information is to indoctrinate them before they develop bad habits."[29]

Some organizations have adopted more proactive approaches, such as performing periodic analyses of vendor, invoice, and other data to determine if there are patterns that may be indicative of employee fraud.[30] Such efforts are laudable but can still only detect what has already occurred. In the experience of many forensic practitioners, even these programs are the exception and not the norm in most organizations.

In thinking about controls, we may benefit from envisioning them spatially. In terms of the amount of time and resources put into controls versus other fraud prevention techniques, it might look like the representation in Exhibit 8.1.

Exhibit 8.1 Relative Reliance upon Techniques in Occupational Fraud Prevention

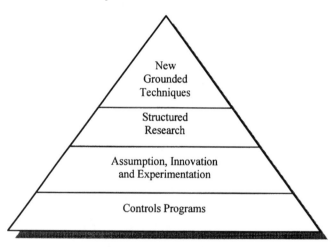

In this case, the base of the pyramid represents the broad spectrum of time, effort, and resources that go into creating, maintaining, and improving traditional controls techniques. This is well and good but may represent more of a problem than we acknowledge at first glance. If the ACFE's estimates, produced by the cumulative input of its responding members (a sort of Delphi technique), are accurate, then for a five-year period, 1997 through 2002, occupational fraud seems to be holding steady at about 6 percent of organizational revenue. That this number remains unchanged may be a function of the consistency of the respondents' estimates, a result of economic conditions, the percentage of the employee population inclined to commit occupational fraud remaining steady, or perhaps the natural limit of what current controls can maintain.

Herein lies an area ripe for further inquiry. The ACFE's 6 percent figure is a median number, with half of reporting persons having estimates both above and below that figure. It would be intriguing to know the characteristics of the controls in organizations significantly higher and lower than the 6 percent level. Joseph Wells has informed us that smaller organizations seem more prone to occupational fraud, but is this because their controls are also smaller and less robust, or is it a function of size and trust? In either event, there are probably a number of bewildering amalgamations of controls profiles: old controls in place for many years; old controls recently updated; new controls yet to be fully ingrained into the organization's operational schema; good controls administered with adequate staffing and resources; good controls with inadequate operational support behind them; or many other combinations of controls and resources.

Given these possibilities, it would be useful to have structured studies done to determine if given rates of occupational fraud and given controls profiles exhibit any sort of causal relationship. I fear little has been done in this regard, but it is a promising—indeed, a vital—area for future research.

Thinking about our existing controls efforts in this light will lead us to the next level of the pyramid—Assumption, Innovation, and Experimentation. As we begin to more formally and rigorously study controls' efficacy, we will invariably be drawn toward opportunities to experiment—to see if what works in "X" environment has applicability in "Y" setting. This was the original premise of this book, when I began to think about the possibility that law enforcement techniques might be adaptable to the control of occupational fraud. While my concept is a more pronounced departure from normal controls thinking, much can be done within the confines of controls methodology to advance our understanding of their internal logic, effectiveness, and transportability. George Campbell, in discussing his work in building a corporate security function at Fidelity Investments, has performed a highly useful service for both the security and forensic professions by setting forth his ideas about what has helped make his program successful. We shall examine in more detail the workings of Campbell's program in Chapter 12.

We should note, however, that the pyramid begins to dramatically narrow at this point, since we are talking here of the amount of time and resources devoted to each area. Controls, as we have discussed, are ubiquitous. Some work better than others, some are applied more consistently than others, but every organization has them. Unfortunately, articles such as Campbell's are not that common yet.

The third level of the pyramid is Research. As I have discussed, many fields appear promising, from neuroscience to game theory. To more fully develop as a profession, we must begin to explore mutual research opportunities with practitioners in these fields to more formally determine their utility to the task we have at hand. Here the pyramid, with its descending surface, may be unintentionally misleading. The implication of Research being in a more narrow position is not to imply that there is a dearth of work being done in fields as broadly spread as sociology, psychology, game theory, neuroscience, criminology, and the like; the reverse is true. There is so much research of possible utility available that we must begin to think creatively of how best to access and analyze it for our purposes. This is what I believe is not being done in any significant measure; thus the location of Research toward the top of the pyramid.

Finally, the apex of the pyramid is New Grounded Techniques. I use the word *grounded* advisedly, since I mean to refer to new techniques in occupational fraud prevention that spring from targeted research. Given that there is a dearth of research directed or reoriented toward occupational fraud prevention, it holds that there is even less in the way of new techniques built on the findings of such research. As we move up from the base of the pyramid, we see increasingly scarce resources being brought to bear on the issues we need to address.

Now, let us build another pyramid using the same blocks but reversing the order (see Exhibit 8.2).

Exhibit 8.2 Efficacy in Controlling Occupational Fraud

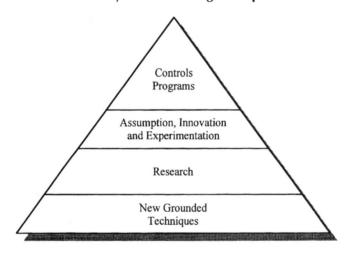

Now, we can reverse the order of significance. Beginning at the top, we can, I will argue, expect additional resources put into the development of new and improved controls programs to have diminishing returns. Certainly, automation and more focused analysis will pay benefits, but I do not believe these will be as effective as other opportunities in making significant improvements in our occupational fraud prevention posture. There may be, à la the ACFE's 6 percent figure, a hard limit to how far we can go with traditional systems of controls, even if we accept that their primary function is prophylactic (preventing occupational fraud), as opposed to diagnostic (detecting occupational fraud).

Yet, in the next five years, I venture to say this is where most of our time, money, and resources will be spent. In this regard, we are not unlike the cops, who spent much time, for example, developing a better nightstick, while pursuing their decades-old patrol patterns. Nightsticks, like traditional controls programs, are important, but we must seriously consider if as a profession they offer us our best return on investment.

As we drop down to Assumption, Innovation, and Experimentation, our base of influence begins to broaden. Efforts like Campbell's are, I am sure, out there, but we need to become more aggressive and proficient in discovering and publicizing them. This will permit those in organizations great and small to begin the process of in situ experimentation that will provide valuable data to the profession. Absent a central, funded, and directed research capability, this may be the logical first step to be taken in a quest for improvement. We need not only proceed in this arena when we are sure we are onto something. Watson, the co-founder of DNA research, has commented that only an idea, a hunch, is necessary to begin the research process, noting that having an idea at least promulgates something that can be tested. Those without ideas have no research to do.

When we reach the level of research, our opportunities to exert influence on occupational fraud rates becomes immeasurably broader. The world is a big place, and there are hundreds of thousands of gifted and dedicated professionals working in all of the fields we have discussed and many that we have not. We simply do not know where an exciting discovery or revelation may come from, especially if we are not inclined individually or as a profession to speculate and investigate. One can rest assured that as the 1970s began, and law enforcement initiated its process of exploration and discovery, there were few people in the United States who drew any linkage between architecture and policing. Yet, today the use of Crime Prevention through Environmental Design concepts is not only accepted as being effective, but it is also commonplace. Our problem is not that there is not very likely much profitable information that we can glean from the work and research of others; our issue is that this undertaking is so vast that we must begin to think about how best to organize it.

Finally, Controls Programs have moved from the base of our pyramid to its apex. This is in no way meant to denigrate their role or necessity; they have been with us for hundreds of years and will stay with us for the next couple of hundred. It is meant to suggest that there are probably natural limits, given their inherent characteristics, of how much they can be improved. Certainly, they can be refined and developed, and we can learn much from their successes and failures, but we must look carefully at them as we continue to allocate time, energy, and resources in search of more effective solutions to our occupational fraud issues. We must be mindful that their utility appears to lie much more in prevention than detection.

In thinking about controls and our two pyramids, the observation of sports commentator Mike Francesa of radio station WFAN in New York City comes to mind. Once, several years back, he was commenting during one of his shows on the rationale of baseball and some of its immutable laws. He noted that in a given season the worst team in baseball will win about one-third of its games. In the same year, the best team in baseball will lose about one-third of its games. It is how teams deal with the middle third that will determine success or failure over the course of a season.

It may be useful to think of controls in the same fashion. Even an organization with poor controls will prevent some degree of occupational fraud, and even the organization with excellent controls will experience some degree of occupational fraud. It is the middle that may offer us the ability to more effectively and significantly affect the rates of occupational fraud.

Controls may, finally, offer one additional benefit: they are neutral. We shall examine the issue of profiling and its potential utility in deterring occupational fraud in Chapter 11. Profiling is a concept that has strong proponents and some statistical support to attest to its efficacy. At the same time, it is a concept that must be applied carefully, as it has been at the heart of some highly contentious social disputes in the past.

Controls, on the other hand, are directed toward things—numbers, systems, procedures—and not people. Writing of techniques used in the war on terrorism, Ashton B. Carter, Professor of Science and International Affairs at Harvard University's John F. Kennedy School of Government, notes: "Surveillance of the means that terrorists employ is potentially more important than surveillance of persons, and raises far fewer civil liberties issues."[31]

Controls certainly fill this requirement. For the person intent on committing occupational fraud, the will to commit the act is only a piece of the equation. In some fashion they must also overcome the internal controls in place to consummate their deed, and organizations have all the leeway in the world to craft and monitor these controls in any way they see fit.

CHAPTER 9

COMPLIANCE PROGRAMS

Compliance programs have been with us throughout most of recorded history, if we accept the position that religious teachings and dogma are forms of compliance instruction and monitoring. On a secular organizational level in the United States they also have a fairly lengthy history as codes of conduct or ethical codes of various groups and vocations. The first adoption of a code of ethics by public school teachers took place in Georgia in 1896.[1] A survey conducted in 1924 found 133 different codes of business ethics in existence, in industries ranging from accounting to the manufacture of ice. By 1933–1934, more than 500 businesses had adopted codes of ethics in keeping with the aims of the National Recovery Act.[2]

One of the finer distinctions in thinking about compliance programs is how they are similar to or differ from controls programs. Karen J. Stensgaard, of PricewaterhouseCoopers, has defined them as follows in an article in *Internal Auditor* magazine:

> Compliance functions provide business management and the board with comfort that services and products comply with regulatory issues, business practices, and internal mandates. . . . Ultimately, however, business management and staff are the first line of defense for the organization when a compliance problem occurs. . . . the mission of the compliance function can very often be aligned directly with a business process and kept totally separate from other compliance mechanisms in place across the organization.[3]

In many ways, the compliance function is very similar to internal auditing. Both monitor business units to promote compliance with regulations, policies, and guidelines. In addition, both . . . report exceptions to management. . . . compliance staff align themselves more closely with the business and may also be more sympathetic to its needs and any control deficiencies. Internal auditing, of course, is an independent function, and its role in the organization is more broadly defined.[4]

To many persons, compliance programs, corporate codes of ethics, and corporate governance are synonymous. While to some degree they overlap and can have mutually supporting objectives, there are important distinctions. Compliance programs are set in place by the organization to effect its goals for operating in an ethical manner. They also, however, can be mandated by legislative or regulatory bodies on an industrywide basis, in the form of programs such as Equal Employment Opportunity, the Americans with Disabilities Act, the Clean Air Act, or Occupational Safety and Health Administration requirements. In other situations they may be put into place as part of an agreement between the organization and the government because of organizational misdeeds that took place in the past. In some industries, such as health care, these arrangements are referred to as corporate integrity agreements (CIAs).

In the latter situations, there is normally a requirement that the organization hire a compliance officer, often a former government regulator, prosecutor, or investigator. The compliance officer is then charged with (1) training the organization's executives, managers, and employees on the requirements of the agreement; (2) setting in place mechanisms to detect and report potential violations, such as hotlines; (3) investigating possible violations; and (4) developing and implementing a reporting mechanism from the organization to the regulatory body in question.

A variation of these arrangements, particularly in the Northeast United States where the concept was developed, is the Independent Private Sector Inspector General (IPSIG). Conceived in the 1970s to 1980s, these are also referred to as monitors. They have become particularly common in organizations or industries that have had traditional problems with organized crime involvement or control. Usually following an investigation and prosecution, the organization, as a condition of being allowed to continue in business, must agree to hire and pay for an IPSIG or monitor. While a monitor, much like the compliance officer, can be a former government prosecutor or investigator (and, in some instances, even a judge), the IPSIG is often an organization—a law firm, a professional services firm, or the like. Like the compliance officer, there is a line of reporting back to a regulatory or enforcement agency, or perhaps a sitting judge who is charged with overseeing the entity on an ongoing basis.

The primary objective of the IPSIG or monitor is to ensure that the organization does not slip back into its old ways of doing business or permit persons with unsatisfactory backgrounds or associates to become associated with it.

Corporate codes of ethics normally come from one of three sources. The first is the internal adoption of the code as an organizational statement of "who we are and how we operate." As such, it can have just as much impact as a mandated program, but it has primarily an internal audience. That audience may be the executive leadership of the organization, its board of directors, or its customers. Many customer service functions in organizations exist not only to resolve customer complaints in an effort to promote loyalty, but also as a sensing mechanism to determine if the organization is living up to its stated intentions and ideals.

The second source of many corporate codes is associational in nature. To be a member of the XYZ association of independent yak dealers, for example, it may be required that each individual member organization adopt and enforce the association code. More active and vigilant associations may even have some form of inspection activity to police compliance with the code. The National Collegiate Athletic Association (NCAA) is one of the better-known examples of such an associational code group. Educational institutions who are members agree to follow certain practices, file compliance reports, may be inspected, and in the event of a potential violation, may be investigated and sanctioned by the parent group.

The third source is statutory in nature, emanating from requirements such as those set forth in the Sentencing Guidelines of the U.S. Sentencing Commission.

Corporate governance is a more generic term that refers to the broad scope of responsibilities the board of directors and senior executives have to see that the organization functions in a legal and ethical manner. In this regard, corporate governance can refer to some or all of the organization's legal, regulatory, financial, and ethical responsibilities. Lal Balkaran has referred to these responsibilities as crucial to fighting corruption within the organization, noting: "Good corporate governance, appropriate tone at the top, and sound controls are the three main tools at management's disposal for accomplishing this goal."[5]

While such frameworks are valuable in setting the appropriate tone for the organization and its operations, there will always be crucial issues of judgment involved. Kreuze, Luqmani, and Luqmani have commented on these considerations as follows:

> Well-developed corporate codes of ethics help organizations foster ethical environments, deter unethical behavior, and cope with problems and ethical dilemmas. The codes establish the ground rules by which the organization operates and evaluates.
>
> By its very nature, however, the zone of business ethics can be amorphous. It can be pervaded by many shades of gray, even in environments that are quite similar. When the environments are clearly diverse, boilerplate codes of ethics will not be relevant or effective.[6]

Perhaps the only thing worse than not having an ethical framework that operates to guide the organization, its operations, and employees, is to have a paper program (i.e., a program that looks fine on the outside but has either no meaning in the daily life of the organization or is limited to only misdeeds by those at the bottom). Such programs are troublesome for a couple of reasons. First, they are inherently unfair, telling employees what they cannot do in the name of organizational integrity, and then permitting higher-ups to do as they please. Employees are neither blind nor stupid and will quickly see through such an arrangement. Some will then be tempted to evade such guidance, or in their minds be justified in making their own decisions about which rules they will and will not follow in conducting their affairs.

Second, since the program is well crafted and often well publicized to both internal and external audiences, it may create a false impression of soundness when in reality it is anything but. Such appearances can be deceiving when relied on by customers, investors, or prospective employees who are evaluating their decisions to become associated with the entity. Stephen Burns takes an aggressive tack when he sets forth an anonymous but true account of one such organization and the consequences that flowed from following a paper program orientation:

> If only on paper, corporate business ethics programs exist in most large international companies. Unfortunately, many of these efforts would have to be regarded as meaningless.
>
> A real-world scenario reinforces this point: Every four years...employees gathered to hear canned speeches about the importance of ethical behavior. For 99 percent of those listening, the message was limited to "Don't cheat on your expense account." At the same time that the employees were receiving their every-fourth-year ethics lesson, top management was operating as it pleased, often at the expense of the stockholders. The corporation was eventually assessed two of the heaviest penalties ever levied by the U.S. federal government, one for tax evasion, and another for pollution.[7]

Many in the compliance community would take issue with Burns' characterization that "many" large international companies have "meaningless" compliance or ethics programs, at least as of this writing five years after his article. Most organizations have sensed that it is in their best interests to have such programs, and many have made a good-faith effort to move in this direction. For example, the Ethics Officer Association (EOA) is devoted solely to supporting and improving the state of organizational ethics in the United States. Founded in 1992 by about one dozen ethics officers, the organization today has almost 800 members, including ethics officers from more than half of the Fortune 100. Other members include representatives from nonprofits and governmental entities. Foreign members are also welcome, and the EOA estimates that its members and the firms and organizations they represent affect the conduct of business to some degree in over 160 countries.

The EOA maintains relationships with the U.S. Sentencing Commission, the World Bank Group/World Bank Institute, the Ethics Resource Center, and the Center for Business Ethics at Bentley College, among others.[8] Among its other activities, the EOA is exploring the development of a business conduct management system standard (MSS) through the International Organization for Standardization (ISO) process. This effort is being made in such a manner as to be consistent with the management system standards ISO 9000 for quality and ISO 14000 for the environment. In commenting about the history behind this effort, Lee Essrig notes that since the 1980s actions by the U.S. government have encouraged such activities, as did the promulgation of the Federal sentencing guidelines in 1991. In addition, a number of associations, industry groups, and non-governmental entities have joined in this activity. Some of these efforts are directed toward issues of corporate social responsibility, and not all have been enthusiastically embraced, since they often lack a management or business process focus. Other complaints have been that the third-party certification often required is costly.[9]

As Essrig notes, much of the impetus for such programs came from the work of the U.S. Sentencing Commission in 1991, but this was not the sole source of movement on compliance programs. Authors Fiorelli and Rooney have noted that:[10]

In 1987 the Treadway Commission recommended to the SEC that the management reports of all public companies include an acknowledgement of responsibility for internal controls and an assessment of the effectiveness in meeting those responsibilities. The Committee of Sponsoring Organizations was formed to support the implementation of the Treadway Commission's recommendations. The Committee released Internal Control—Integrated Framework in September of 1992, and an addendum was published in May of 1994.

COSO provides the following definition of internal control: Internal control is broadly defined as a process, effected by an entity's board of directors, management, and other personnel, designed to provide reasonable assurance regarding the achievement of objectives in the following three categories:

1. Effectiveness and efficiency of operations
2. Reliability of financial reporting
3. Compliance with applicable laws and regulations

COSO considers these three categories to be overlapping, yet distinct. The effectiveness of an internal control system is measured by the capacity of the system established to provide reasonable assurance to the board of directors and management that these three objectives have been met.

In addition to these goals, COSO identified five interrelated components of internal control:

1. Control environment
2. Risk assessment

3. Control activities

4. Information and communication

5. Monitoring

These components combine to form an integrated system of controls.

While COSO set forth five elements of an integrated control environment, the Federal Sentencing Guidelines set forth seven:[11]

1. The organization has in place a system that is "reasonably capable" of deterring criminal conduct.

2. High-level individuals within the organization are specifically charged with overseeing the operation of the program.

3. The organization does not delegate program responsibilities to any person known to have criminal tendencies.

4. The organization has in place mechanisms to communicate policies and procedures to employees and other interested persons.

5. The organization has controls in place to monitor compliance and also to permit reporting of possible or suspected violations without fear of retaliation.

6. Consistent enforcement and appropriate disciplinary mechanisms and actions.

7. Evidence the organization has taken steps required to prevent reoccurrences in the future, to include modifying the program.

In the opinion of most compliance professionals, there is little problem in integrating the more specific requirements of the guidelines into the broader scope of procedures recommended by COSO. Together, these two sets of requirements form the basis for most organizational ethics and compliance programs, noting that the individual organization or an associational membership may add still additional requirements.

COSO continues to be a watchdog on organizational behavior, especially that of public companies. In 1996 it published its report, "Fraudulent Financial Reporting: 1987–1997, An Analysis of U.S. Public Companies." The report dealt with approximately 200 companies, alleged to have been involved in instances of fraudulent financial reporting, that were investigated by the SEC during that 10-year span.[12]

In addition to COSO and guidelines guidance and requirements, the federal government had earlier weighed in when it promulgated and enacted the Foreign Corrupt Practices Act of 1977. Kreuze, Luqmani, and Luqmani describe its impact and that of related regulations as follows:

This legislation makes it a crime for U.S. based multinationals to make "sensitive payments" or bribes, to officials of foreign governments. The act implies that U.S. ethical standards should apply to business activities both inside and outside its boundaries, thereby establishing a clear example of moral absolutism, where one universally acceptable set of moral views and behavior is defined. Additionally, the Organization for Economic Co-operation and Development's Convention on Combating Bribery of Foreign Public Officials in International Business Transactions, obliges signatories to adopt national legislation that makes it a crime to bribe foreign public officials.[13]

Anthony Green, writing in the Spring 2002 edition of *Chief Legal Officer* magazine, lays out an even more stark rationale for compliance programs—civil liability. He cites a study, "D&O Current Developments," by Arter and Hadden, that indicates that since mid-1999 the size of settlements in director and officer litigation has risen dramatically. There have been more than a dozen settlements or judgments in excess of $100 million, and one-third of these were in excess of $200 million. He also notes that Jury Verdict Research reports that from 1994 to 1999 median jury awards in business negligence cases have risen 128 percent, and that the plaintiffs' bar that pursues such matters is now larger, better funded, and more aggressive. Further, he advises that Robert Hartwig, PhD., a senior vice president and chief economist at the Insurance Information Institute, revealed in a recent interview that today one in five jury awards is $1 million or more, versus one in four in 1994, and that one business in 10 has had a liability loss of more than $5 million in the last 10 years.[14]

One of the effects of this environment, he notes, is increased emphasis on, and cost for, insurance. He reports that a recent survey of 2,400 U.S. firms by March Inc., reported in *Investor's Daily*, indicated that firms with more than $5 billion in sales raised their liability coverage an average of 5.4 percent, to $314 million, and firms with less than $500 million in sales reduced their liability coverage by 8.8 percent, to $52 million.[15]

Compliance programs can be seen as having a number of sources and an even greater number of nuances. They may be affected by how the organization envisions itself and what codes it sets for its own conduct; they can be influenced by the associational relationships the organization has or desires to establish; they may be mandated by instances of past conduct on the organization's part; or they may be set by the nature of the organization's business, such as being in foreign trade. For this reason, while all compliance programs are to some degree the same, it is unlikely any two are identical.

In the event an organization runs afoul of the law and comes under the purview of the Federal Sentencing Guidelines, the existence of a competent compliance program meeting the seven criteria of the guidelines can have a significant mitigating effect on punishment the organization may face.[16] Such consideration is mandated by the guidelines in a formula to be used by the sentencing judge.

Although without the direct, and by definition criminal, impact of the U.S. Federal Sentencing Guidelines, somewhat similar standards for risk management are already in effect in a number of other countries. David McNamee cites the following examples:

> Several authoritative bodies have addressed the need for more guidance on risk management. The Australian/New Zealand Joint Standards Committee was the first to codify standards of risk management, with its release of AS/NZS 4360 Risk Management in 1996. The Canadian Standards Board followed in 1998 by releasing CAN/CSA-Q850/97 Risk Management: Guideline for Decision Makers, which provides a framework that decision-makers can use to assess and communicate risks. In addition, BS 6079-3 Guide to the Management of Business-Related Project Risk, which was published by the British Standards Institution in January 2000, presents a risk-assessment framework with special emphasis on project management.[17]

In thinking about compliance programs, it may be useful to try to conceptualize how they relate to issues of deterrence of occupational fraud. As can be seen from the various sources of guidance, many of them have little or no relevance, other than to set a tone of general and ongoing compliance within the organization. Others, such as those established by the Federal Sentencing Guidelines, are much closer in intent, but may also include things such as illegal environmental dumping, trade practices, or the paying of bribes to gain additional business. As we have seen in our discussion of definitions, many of these acts would meet one or more definitions of white-collar crime or economic crime, but they are not directly on point with controlling or detecting fraud in the workplace.

David Crawford, in discussing how his organization, the University of Texas System Audit Office, went about implementing the requirements of COSO's Internal Control—Integrated Framework, addressed the issuance of redundancy between compliance audits and controls audits. He notes:

> As we searched for a way to define the roles of the two assurance functions, we were concerned initially that internal auditing and compliance were both going to audit the same items in the same way. This practice seemed unproductive, and we knew that it would be unexplainable to both management and auditors.
>
> Our deliberations led us to the conclusion that all control functions operate in a three-dimensional environment:[18]
>
> 1. *Time.* How close is the control to the execution of the event or transactions?
>
> 2. *Involvement.* How involved are the executors of the control in the process that generates the event or transaction?

3. *Items affected.* How many of the events or transactions are operated on by the control?

Based on this analysis, Crawford and his team developed a four-tiered process of monitoring that addressed the following areas: operating, monitoring, oversight, and internal auditing. He goes on to detail the unique characteristics of each area, noting that operating controls are embedded in a process and are provided by those workers involved in the process. Monitoring controls are usually executed within the process by first-line supervisors and take place immediately after the process is complete. Oversight controls are performed by higher levels of line management outside of the process, but on a frequent and regular basis. Finally, internal audit controls take place outside of the line management hierarchy and assess both the overall existence and effectiveness of the controls environment.[19] Based on this approach, he believes the University of Texas System can perform both compliance and controls audits without creating confusion between the two functions, without putting undue burdens on line management, and without sacrificing the needs of either system.

In structuring such an approach, Crawford has not only managed to avoid issues of redundancy and confusion, but has also established a system where compliance and controls work to cross-support each other in a positive fashion. In this formulation, he is close to the observation with which Kreuze, Luqmani, and Luqmani conclude their article, when they note:

Effective codes of ethics are vital to organizations at many levels. At a practical level, they can also dramatically affect internal audit practice. In situations where unethical behavior is suspected, the lack of a code of ethics multiplies the internal auditors' required tests and significantly lessens the validity of any assurances rendered.

In their evaluations, internal auditors must acknowledge, assess, and consider jointly all the elements that act as powerful incentives and impediments in guiding corporate ethical behavior. Auditors must differentiate among the shades of gray and recognize that "one size fits all" cannot be applied to corporate codes of ethics.[20]

Burns, likewise, believes in the power of organizational codes when clearly stated and consistently enforced. In discussing his experiences, particularly when operating in foreign venues, he also believes there is value in making a visible point about exceptions. In this regard he is highly similar to Kellings' thoughts about policing and how making a fuss about the little things can help keep the bigger things in check. Burns notes:

As an expatriate manager, I know that every decision I make and enforce is observed and analyzed. Many players are likely to test the waters, to assess my tolerance level. I often act aggressively in small situations, hoping thereby to avoid the occurrence of large ones. My recommendation is zero tolerance. For example, I took the stance of holding a service supplier responsible for a small misdeed perpetrated by one of his subcontractors. From a purely legal stand-point, the supplier was perfectly innocent. However, the message I sent was clearly received by all concerned.[21]

Lest we think that compliance programs are benign things greeted by all with great exuberance, we should note the comments of Samantha Linsley. Speaking at a conference on "Managing for Fraud Prevention," sponsored by the Royal Institute for International Affairs, she observed that with the advent of such pro-grams, many organizations adopted a new position—the Compliance Officer.[22] Usually operating out of the Office of the General Counsel, these officials are typ-ically charged with oversight of compliance programs, education, training, monitoring, and exception inquiries. They operate much like those positions dis-cussed previously in health care organizations operating under a Corporate Integrity Agreement.

As Linsley noted, however, in some organizations they quickly became known as Business Prevention Officers. They were viewed by some as just another impediment to getting the job done or the business sold. Frustrated salespeople would often point in exasperation to competitors who seemed to operate in a free and unconstrained manner, and therefore had an unfair competitive advantage.

In my professional experience, such complaints are not uncommon, although with the maturity of such programs and their acceptance by more and more organizations, such negative reactions tend to fade, though rarely disappear altogether. This is tempered also by the tendency for the free and easy organiza-tions to sooner or later pay the piper, when their loose methods of operation cause them a significant problem in the marketplace or with regulators. At that point, having the Business Prevention Officer seems like a wise move in the long run.

It is perhaps most useful to view such complaints as a form of dynamic tension within the organization, not unlike many other instances where two organiza-tional elements, charged with important responsibilities, come into legitimate conflict as they go about their work. I recall an engagement I performed some years back for a major credit card issuer. My task was to review their antifraud controls, and I spent a fair amount of time with the company's compliance and security officers. The organization had a fairly sophisticated set of antifraud screens built into its application and acceptance processes, and these were auto-mated experiential systems that could be updated as the fraud schemes in the marketplace evolved and changed. Such screens operated to the ultimate bene-fit of everyone, since the security people were rated on their success in helping hold down bad debt and fraud losses. Even the operational people had an ele-ment of bad debt writeoff built into their performance rating metrics. The key word, however, is *element*.

The highly competent, but frustrated, security officer spent some time explaining to me that much of his professional life was spent battling the people in marketing. Their mandate was to build business, and you did that by "putting cards on the street," that is, into the hands of potential customers who would use them, build up balances, and pay interest on their accounts. Certainly, bad debt writeoffs were an element of their performance evaluation, but a much smaller element than total new accounts. Thus the dynamic tension—the salespeople resisting any new requirement that would disqualify potential customers or make the application process more time-consuming or cumbersome. On the other side was the security officer, arguing that analysis of loss and fraud patterns indicated that just requiring one more piece of data on the application or adding one more screen to the automated rating program could reduce fraud and bad debt losses by "X" percent.

It is a situation where there is probably very little black or white and an awful lot of gray. I suspect such discussions will go on for many years in most organizations. Some calls are easy: illegal acts are illegal acts and should be condemned. Other forms of compliance—really a form of risk management in the case of the credit card company—are more judgmental and, therefore, dynamic.

CHAPTER 10

COMMUNITY, CORPORATE CITIZENSHIP, AND QUALITY OF LIFE

We have seen, in every tactic that law enforcement developed to better control crime, the consistent element of community. Whether teaming with the community to develop innovative solutions to issues or defining what was really important, community appears time and again.

The central issue before us is whether the organization can be conceptualized as community to see if we can make some of law enforcement's techniques work for us. In at least one police department, we can see firsthand the effects of such thinking. Stephen Doherty is the Chief of Police in Wakefield, Massachusetts. In an article titled, "How Can Workplace Violence Be Deterred?" he recounts his reconceptualization of this issue following a rampage in which a disgruntled individual took a cache of weapons to work and killed seven people:

> As a law enforcement professional, I was aware of how the community polic-ing model had been successfully applied to the problem of domestic violence. It occurred to me that those principles could probably be successfully applied to the problem of workplace violence.... Companies tend to treat these situa-tions internally—just as domestic violence was once treated as private.[1]

Doherty goes on to recount how his department became involved with a local Fortune 500 company that was experiencing parking lot thefts and internal loss of goods and equipment. After working with the company to design and imple-ment deterrence strategies, the loss rates dropped and other areas of mutual interest were discovered. The company, for example, was faced with the need to lay off a number of employees and worked closely with the police to determine how best to do this without encountering instances of violence or retribution. As a result of the initial partnership, Doherty now has a similar relationship with another company in town and is working with Northeastern University's School of Criminal Justice to further study whether community policing techniques can be expanded in this arena.[2]

Howard Hallman, writing about the benefits to be gained from infusing a sense of community into governmental structures or, in some instances, in lieu of governmental structures, defines the term as follows:

> Community is a feeling, an attitude of the mind, built upon common purpose and shared values. True community does not mean submerging individuals and groups into one dominating cultural pattern but rather recognizes cultural pluralism and enhances it. Community is not a passive state. It is characterized by action directed toward mutual goals. We achieve community by doing things together. If we disagree on some things, as is both inevitable and proper, we should keep in view the larger good.... The sense of community broadens life and strengthens social relations.[3]

In discussing his conceptualization of community and its import for improved civic functioning in the modern state, Hallman traces its antecedents to the thoughts of Rousseau and other theorists concerned with the welfare and rights of the individual in the face of overwhelming state power and authority.[4]

For our needs, while Hallman's definition and cognitive history are useful, we need not be so commanding or sweeping in either our formulations or our ultimate objectives. We seek a narrower frame of reference and more limited goals. As we approach the concept of the organization as community, what reference points do we have in our cognitive framework to suggest that this exercise may in fact bear fruit? I offer the following observations on organizational characteristics as potential anchors for such a formulation:

- *Most organizations, like proximate neighborhoods, are concentrated.* Some organizations may be in one building, some may be in many; some in one town, others in many countries. Still there is, for most, a sense of proximity that in many ways parallels that of the common political and sociological concept of community.

- *Organizations tend to comprise relatively homogeneous populations.* Certainly there are significant differences in age, experience, race, gender, ethnic background, and many other factors; however, most organizations do not encompass teenagers, those in grade school, or the elderly. Likewise, they usually do not include those severely stricken with mental or physical disabilities, habitual criminals, or persons without some level of formal education or training. Neighborhood communities are much more inclusive.

- *Organizations are inherently voluntary associations.* People are members of them because they chose to do so. Certainly, there may be powerful economic, sociological, or psychological factors that promote or hinder membership in a given organization, but for most organizational members, their presence and participation are voluntary.

- *Organizations have a sense of mission, while even many communities do not.* We may think of the regular patrons of a park as a community, and in many ways they are. Their sense of mission, however, is much more diffuse. Some come for recreation, others to have a place to walk the dog, many to watch children at play, and so on. While people join organizations for a substantial variety of reasons—from making money to a sense of belonging to a dedication to organizational goals and objectives—there is an overriding sense of mission to most organizations. Even those formed for purely economic reasons usually have, or at least seek to have, a mission, often dressed up in a formal declaration of purpose. To be the best frozen ice cream packaging company east of the Mississippi is a mission.

- *For many people, organizations are one of, if not the primary, source of recognition and rewards.* These rewards may be financial, psychological, sociological, or represent some other dimension of their being and psyche. Human beings are complex and multifaceted beings and have numerous associations and reward and recognition structures, but their primarily organizational membership will likely always play a significant, if not dominant, role in their reward and recognition matrix.

- *To the degree that numerous needs tend to be met by a person's primary organizational membership, organizations can be important in providing a sense of self.* While the days of the 30-year career and the gold watch are apparently gone forever for most of us, even a temporary or transitory employment-oriented organizational membership is still a powerful definer of one's societal and psychic standing in even larger communities.

- *We have seen in the work of other theorists that organizations are inherently about boundaries.* That this is so approaches a tautology. To be a member of an organization is to have crossed a boundary, from nonmember or member of the general public to status as an organizational member. Often, achieving this status may take strenuous clearance of hurdles, be they competitive, educational, professional, or of some other nature. To be a member of an organization is to be set apart from those who are not members, regardless of what other organizations they may be a part of. Certainly, multiple organizational memberships are not only possible, but are likely the norm. Still, one's primary organizational affiliation sets them apart from those who are not members and, presumably, creates a level of bonding or identification with fellow members.

- *To be a member of an organization implies, if not requires, that one adopt, embrace, accept, or at a minimum tolerate, a system of ethical perspective.* Each organization, knowingly or implicitly, creates, promotes, nurtures, and lives a system of ethical rules and goals. Some of these may be intentional, largely unitary, and, hopefully, operate in a functional manner to advance the interests of the organization and its members in a manner acceptable to the larger society of which it is a part. Others believe they espouse and promote one set of ethical constructs but permit or allow one or more others to operate. Remember, if you will, Leuci's comments about what he saw and experienced in the NYPD of the 1970s. One need not envision a system of tyrannical psychological lock-step to acknowledge that within most organizations, while there may be differences of opinion and competing schools of thought, there tends to be an overriding ethical flavor that reflects what the organization is, or hopes to be, about.

- *Organizations typically share a common language with their members, be it technical, trade, or field based.* One need only sample the breadth of organizational archetypes to quickly learn that the language of employees in one construction company will have much more in common with another construction company across the country than it will with an insurance company that may be in the next building. So, too, do individual organizations often seek to create a language that is unique to them, even against competitors in the same field. Disney, for example, may refer to employees as "cast," even though they are not in the direct entertainment part of that business. Vanguard, the huge investment and financial services company located outside of Philadelphia, names its buildings after famous ships and refers to its employees as "crew" to advance the nautical motive it has adopted to differentiate itself. So, too, do most organizations, consciously or otherwise, tend to develop a language that is in some way unique to them.

- *Organizations are about power and politics.* For many, this is one of the more unpleasant aspects of organizational life, but it is a reality nonetheless. One need not only think of the petty bickering, backstabbing, and one-upsmanship when considering the role of politics and power in organizational life. Like neighborhoods, organizations are groupings of social control with many facets important to their members. Milton Kotler, in discussing the motivations for the student takeovers of some colleges and universities in the 1960s and 1970s has observed that these young people had developed a sense of neighborhood and community in the brief space of the several years they were in school. They therefore came to believe they had a legitimate voice in the governance of their community. Kotler makes the significant point that the power of one's group need not be controlling or absolute to be real. A group can have power even though it is in a subservient position to another organization or entity.[5] To see that such is true, one need look no further than the example of prisoner of war camps or modern prisons to observe the group power of those under extreme conditions of control by others.

- *While industries, trades, and organizations come and go with technology, tastes, and the times, organizations are one of the few things we routinely encounter that do not die because of the imperatives of biology.* Many great organizations have passed from view, due to failure or merger, but many still remain alive after decades of existence. With this longevity comes history and culture. When one enters an organization, there is usually some effort to inculcate at least a modicum of this heritage, the intent usually being to imbue some sense of mission and pride in the new arrival and to act as a sort of a bonding mechanism to link the past to the present, and the new employee to the more senior.

When we think of the power and persistence of such attributes or organizations, be they great or small, one is struck by how many elements of community seem to be already present. The typical organization would seem to be farther down the road toward a sense of community than even some urban neighborhoods defined by lines drawn on a map. It may be, then, that we should seriously consider the rationale for exploring the concept of organization as community when thinking about the success of law enforcement crime control techniques. In so doing, one is struck by one element all organizations, by definition, have in common—membership, and what the membership process is all about.

Since, as organizations, we self-select our fellow citizens, are there elements of the human resources function we need to become more knowledgeable about? We probably meet these people at the end of investigations, when employees are being let go. Do we partner with them on the front end of the process and try to develop fair and legal guidelines as to who we accept for citizenship? We should remember that one of the controls Hollinger and Clark identified as being potentially effective in their study some 30 years ago was selection of new employees.

Most of us are members of several organizations, perhaps dozens, be they professional, vocational, avocational, religious, fraternal, or social. Two of the defining characteristics of each are that they have boundaries—members and nonmembers—and they have entrance criteria, be they high or low. It may be fairly easy to join the local garden club and quite another matter to be accepted as a Fellow of a professional society. Nevertheless, the function of entrance criteria is the same—to ensure than certain minimum standards are maintained, usually to admit only persons of good character and some degree of competence, and to advance the purposes of the organization.

So, too, with organizations that have financial resources and are potentially subject to the ravages of occupational fraud. But, given that these forms of organizational membership are usually about employee status, there come into play an elaborate and changing set of additional criteria coming primarily from case law having to do with fairness in the hiring process and the elimination of various forms of discrimination.

Confining our thoughts to issues of occupational fraud and the role of selection criteria, we need not look far to see numerous thoughts and comments on the issue. Barry Leithhead, writing in the magazine *Internal Auditor*, has noted that the Competency Framework for Internal Auditing will expand the role of the internal auditor into new areas of risk management for the organization, to include the human resources arena. The tone of his article is mainly positive, emphasizing the role that internal audit, from a risk perspective, can play to ensure that the organization's human resources function is operating effectively and efficiently to adequately meet the organization's needs.[6]

Others are more direct as to issue of selection and fraud risk. Mark Cisz, in his review of the book, *Are Your Employees Stealing You Blind?*, by Edwin C. Bliss and Isamu S. Aoki, notes that the authors contend that nearly 75 percent of employees steal at least once and half go on to be repeat offenders. They further contend that nearly one of three small business failures can be tied to internal theft.[7]

Lal Balkaran expresses similar concerns, also writing in *Internal Auditor*, when he notes:

> Because employees can make or break a system, it is essential to ensure that the organization hires suitably qualified people. Auditors should make sure their companies are performing thorough background checks on candidates for employment. In addition, auditors can verify that employers are validating information such as qualifications and work experience stated on resumes, as well as checking references. The company should hire individuals with a history of integrity and honesty and avoid putting square pegs in round holes. By hiring appropriately qualified employees, management has taken one important step toward eliminating corruption.[8]

Survey results tend to confirm these fears. *Fraud: The Unmanaged Risk*, a 2000 international survey of 700 organizations in 15 countries by Ernst & Young found that 82 percent of organizations responding had experienced fraud, and nearly 40 percent thought it possible a significant fraud could occur within their organization. Further, the survey revealed that employees are the probable perpetrators of these incidents. Unlike the predictions of Gottfredson and Hirschi's general theory, they are usually not the new kids. The survey found that employees were involved in 82 percent of the frauds reported, and one-third of these frauds were carried out by persons in management positions. The survey reported that most of these persons had been with their organization for more than five years, and almost 25 percent had been in place for more than ten years.[9]

Such concerns for selection criteria need not be couched only in negative terms. Miller has reported that Walker Information and the Hudson Institute have found that over half of employees surveyed want to work in an ethical environment and that the presence of such an environment is a factor in their continued loyalty to the organization. Further, only 56 percent of employees responding to the survey believed their organization was doing a good job of communicating with them on ethical issues in the workplace. While many of the concerns addressed in the survey were for the ethical behavior of the organization, as opposed to the individual members, it is likely that persons concerned about their organization's ethical dimensions would have similar feelings about the activities of their peers as well. As Steve Walker, President and Chief Executive Officer of Walker Information, put it: "This study shows that having good ethics within an organization is good business."[10]

Michael Stamler recommends a fairly straightforward approach to handling pre-employment issues. These can be terribly important for several reasons:

- There is a moral and legal responsibility to treat all applicants in a fair and uniform manner.

- A hasty, incomplete, or improperly done background investigation that raises false-positive (nonissues that appear to be issues) may deny the organization a promising employee, create legal liability, and hurt the reputation of the organization.

- An application process that has not been thought through can waste a lot of time, cause desirable applicants to give up and go elsewhere, and cause needless expense.

- The procedure must meet the requirements of federal, state, and even local ordinances.

Stamler recommends the following steps:[11]

1. Inform candidates in advance of the recruiting steps.

2. Require candidates to complete an application form that includes all relevant information and have them sign it to attest to its accuracy and completeness.

3. Follow up with a telephone call to the applicant to resolve any unclear or contradictory information on the application.

4. Ask the right questions. Skilled human resources professionals are quite adept at spotting inconsistencies and gaps in work and educational histories or incomplete answers to sensitive questions.

5. Conduct a competent background investigation.

While the time and resources required might seem to be a minor consideration, they can become costly, particularly in a large organization or in one that experiences fairly high turnover.

We have seen, from several sources, the suggested importance of preemployment background investigations. I supervised these programs in the FBI in both the field and at headquarters, to include the always popular White House Background Investigations program (top Cabinet officials and Federal judges). There is good news and bad news.

The good news is there is no more effective and, in the long run, efficient process to select employees than through the use of a professional, fair, well-designed, and well-run background and selection programs. It is a lot easier to avoid hiring problem personnel than it is to live with them and have to go through the troublesome and potentially expensive process of terminating them. There are excellent background investigation firms throughout the country that, depending on volume, can do basic background inquiries for about $50 per person. This is so because an increasing number of pertinent records are available online, so the days of someone walking around asking questions about every piece of an applicant's history are long gone. That may still have to be done, and it can be more expensive, but most basic applicant information is probably available online, if the proper releases and authorizations have been provided by the applicant.

There are also companies and vendors who will sell or design software programs that permit an organization's own human resources (HR) department to do these checks themselves. I have had no personal experience with these systems, but based on my work in the field I would suggest a careful evaluation. A competent, professional HR department can probably do fairly well with one of these systems, especially if the hires are local and the requirements are minimal (e.g., most employees come from the immediate town or county and the requirements are fairly basic: high school graduate? valid driver's license? any arrest record in this town or county?)

If, however, the candidate has three degrees from colleges in other states or countries, has worked for seven previous employers, and has lived in six towns in four states and two countries, it may be a different matter altogether. Records systems vary from town to town, state to state, college to college, employer to employer, and country to country. Unless you have a top-flight HR department with a lot of experience in doing these things, it might be better to farm this work out. This is particularly true if your HR department is old Charlie, who is also the payroll clerk, shipping clerk, and assistant fire warden.

Examples of vendors, among many, providing such services are The United States Mutual Association, which is an association of 700 retailers who jointly maintain a database of millions of fraud cases in which both employees and nonemployees have been involved. Many of these cases never made it to a court proceeding, so they are unavailable through criminal records checks. The Association, based in Chicago, charges a per-inquiry fee for this service. Due Diligence is another provider that provides access to civil and criminal records in 30 states for a fee and claims that about one in ten searches uncovers a criminal record. KnowX is a provider that for a fee will provide information on lawsuits, business records, liens, bankruptcies, and outstanding warrants. Credit agencies are, of course, a mainstay of many business-rating systems. The three primary agencies in the United States are Experian, Equifax, and Trans Union. Searches of these sources are regulated by the provisions of the Fair Credit Reporting Act. In addition, while not a vendor, the Social Security Administration allows online searches of social security numbers. A potential problem employee will often adopt the number of someone else, perhaps deceased, to increase the chances of gaining employment.[12]

Errors in background searches can occur in two directions, and neither one of them is good: (1) bad information may be missed, with the result that you hire a problem employee; (2) in some ways worse, the inexperienced person running the background may see false positives—information that looks bad enough to be disqualifying, were it accurate. This may come from any number of sources: an arrest that did not involve a conviction; a judgment that was later satisfied or withdrawn; an address that does not appear to check out when in fact it is valid. The possibilities are endless and many of them are caused by simple confusion. If you want to verify this, just run yourself in one of the many credit or data services, even with an identifying number such as your Social Security Account Number or date of birth, and see what you get back. There will probably be names and addresses associated with you that may be keying errors by some clerk several years back, the name of a child or ex-spouse that is still linked to your credit history, or information that shows you apparently living in two places at the same time. Throw in factors like being a Junior when your Father was the Senior, or having a common name, and it only gets worse. False positives can lengthen and confuse the hiring process, but their greatest risk is legal liability. When you reject an otherwise qualified applicant on the basis of a false positive, there may be potential liability.

Having said all that, preemployment background investigations are worth the time and expense. There are, however, some practical issues that have to be dealt with. The first is that this cannot be done by the seat of your pants. Competent professionals, be they attorneys or HR professionals, should be involved in the design of the background investigation process for the simple fact that by federal and state law there are some questions you cannot ask. There are other issues as well. The items we are about to examine may highlight some of the practicalities of the preemployment background investigation process.

First of all, there may be resistance. In the period immediately after the terrorist attacks of September 11th, a number of companies, particularly ones in industries believed to be sensitive in a terrorism environment, decided on their own or were Congressionally mandated to initiate background checks of both new and existing employees. Several unions representing airline employees have filed suit to challenge these procedures, since they contend they go beyond the intent of Congress in mandating such checks. First, they contend that these checks include data older than the 10-year look-back window mandated by Congress and also pick up offenses other than the 28 serious offenses specified in the authority. The suits note that the FBI's criminal data files may well reflect arrests, but at least half of the time disposition data is not included. Such data would indicate whether the arrest resulted in a conviction, acquittal, dismissal of charges, or other diversion from the judicial system. (It is noted the FBI files contain only information provided to it by other criminal agencies and courts, be they federal, state, or local.)

Other airline employee concerns involved companies, such as Southwest Airlines, that are looking into employee offenses, big or small, that they never before knew about. A representative for Southwest confirmed that that company was conducting fact-finding interviews and believed it had a responsibility to do so when such information surfaced. Other employees in the industry have raised other issues about preserving the ability of an employee to demonstrate their security worthiness following a revelation that they had a heretofore-unknown brush with the law many years ago.[13]

In response to such issues and suits, Northwest Airlines announced one month later that it would no longer use FBI criminal background data to dismiss workers for previously unknown offenses. Rather, the company indicated it would use such data only to bar these workers from sensitive areas of airport facilities. Employee groups had cited a provision of the enabling statute that said the FBI data could be used only for "security access" purposes.[14] Prior to this decision Northwest, like many federal agencies in the past, was evidently taking the position that since a security clearance and freedom of movement at airport facilities was a valid job requirement, not being able to maintain a security clearance because of a prior criminal conviction meant being unable to perform the job, and was therefore grounds for dismissal.

The post-9/11 demand for security checks is also causing headaches for law enforcement agencies and delays for employers and applicants awaiting results. Some agencies report increases of as much as 100 percent in background check volume in systems that were already under resource strain. Terrorism concerns have only exacerbated the tendency over the last two decades to require licensing and background checks in various occupations, ranging from hairdressers and day care workers to truck drivers. The Pennsylvania State Police report that when they initiated background checks in 1983, they got fewer than 24,000. In 2001, they received 732,000, an increase of 3,050 percent in just 19 years.[15]

Testing of various types is also often thought of as part of the selection process and can be useful, if utilized properly. When the courts find that tests were improperly constructed or utilized, the results can be unpleasant. Target Stores in 1993 agreed to pay more than $1 million to a class of approximately 2,500 security officer applicants when a California court held that the test used violated the California Constitution's right to privacy and provisions of California statutes prohibiting religious and sexual orientation discrimination. One employment law attorney, Condon McGlothen, provides the following suggestions when thinking about the use of testing tools:[16]

- Counsel should inventory and review what tests are contemplated or are used.

- Employers should assess whether tests are necessary to achieve a business purpose.

- Experts recommend using tests as a factor, but only a factor, in making employment decisions.

- Tests should be customized to measure the job in question or the issue at hand, and not be an off-the-shelf item.

- Tests should be validated in accordance with the Equal Employment Opportunity Commission's Uniform Guidelines on Employee Selection Procedures.

In thinking about selection systems and issues of organizational membership, we may be tempted to move toward the extremes, but I counsel against it. We may be concerned about the complexity, the time and expense, the potential liabilities, and adopt a fatalistic attitude: "If it's going to happen, it's going to happen; we'll get through it." Others may tend toward the other end of the spectrum and decide that they are going to have a world-class, ultra-sophisticated, bulletproof selection system that will screen out all evildoers, thus eliminating all risk. I think both positions are wrong.

The first is an invitation to disaster—you might as well leave your front door open when you go on vacation and leave the keys in the car ignition so you will always know where they are. It is unfortunate, but in life the vulnerable tend to get victimized. The second position is more realistic, to the point of being unrealistic. It is impossible, and terribly expensive, to try to eliminate all risk. Sensitive governmental agencies with vast powers (e.g., the Central Intelligence Agency, the Federal Bureau of Investigation, and the National Security Agency) have employees go bad. It is doubtful the average organization can throw up more effective entry screens than they can. The point I am driving at is that security and risk mitigation are relative things.

No matter how many alarm systems you put on your house, a skilled thief can defeat them. The point is not to be impenetrable—it is expensive and usually a waste of time. The point is to be harder than the average target. People who are intent on committing occupational fraud usually have nothing personal against you or your organization; they just want to steal money. If it is harder to do that at your organization, they have one of two choices: keep trying and see where they get or go somewhere else where the controls are weaker. That, in my view, is a balanced and rational perspective on security, financial controls, and selection systems. Should you be inclined to accept all or at least part of Gottfredson and Hirschi's general theory of crime, they contend that it is simple and opportunistic. Making the commission of workplace fraud more difficult in your organization removes it from the category of simple and, thus, reduces the opportunity. You can never eliminate it entirely (please remember Leuci's notorious 5 percent), but you can reduce its incidence.

We must also examine the concept of quality of life within the context of the organization. My co-worker who leaves the lunchroom a mess certainly affects my quality of life, but does the co-worker who routinely pads his or her expense account? Must the transgression be so large as to affect the financial health of my employer for it to have meaning to me, or will another standard suffice? If so, how do we determine what it is? If I, too, believe the organization has done me wrong, do I have a higher tolerance for those who decide fraud is an appropriate response in their case?

Law enforcement may offer a stark example to issues we wish to deal with regarding quality of life in an organizational setting, but William Bratton's recounting of his experiences as Commissioner of the New York Transit Police may be instructive. Shortly after becoming Commissioner of the Transit Police, he initiated a campaign to deal with fare-beaters—those who entered the subways without paying a fare, at the time $1.15. It was estimated there were 170,000 instances of this per day, these actions alone costing the city in excess of $80 million per year, much less the crime and mayhem such persons caused once on the trains.

One of the tactics Bratton installed was a "Bust Bus," a specially refitted city bus that was essentially a courtroom and holding pen on wheels. Parked in front of subway stops, handcuffed prisoners were led there to be processed, fingerprinted, and booked. This attention to a problem that had been a continuing source of irritation to millions of New Yorkers did not go unnoticed. Bratton recounts the experience as follows:

The sidewalk was cordoned off, as the arrest-processing activity continued. Civilians know what's up when they turn the corner and all these cops are standing around; they're both drawn to it and kept away. The more assertive ones saunter over. "What's going on?" It was clearly a crime scene. Prisoners in handcuffs snaked in a long line from the nearby station onto the bus. An officer stood on each side of the door.

An old woman pulling a wire shopping cart read the lettering on the bus: Arrest Processing Center. "A jail on wheels!" she exclaimed. "Why don't you bring that on up to my neighborhood? You can lock 'em up all day!"

And so crime, disorder and fare evasion began to go down.... We had reduced fare evasion, motivated the cops, streamlined the arrest process, and increased police productivity; we had involved the public, increased their attention, and won their approval; we had controlled disorder and achieved a decrease in crime. All for arresting people for a buck-fifteen crime. We were proving the Broken Windows theory.[17]

Sarah Glazer, writing of the New York City experience with subways, notes that some senior commanders had their own theories as to the collateral benefits that came from the fare-beating arrests. She observes that one, Deputy Police Commissioner Michael Farrell, noted that these arrests permitted the police to not only check for outstanding felony warrants but also to search for weapons. One in seven persons so arrested had either an outstanding warrant or a concealed weapon. As the word of these tactics got out on the street, people were less inclined to carry concealed weapons onto the subway. Farrell speculated that since many homicides were evidently caused by spontaneous disputes and resolved by a handy weapon, the mere fact of removing the ready availability of weapons had a positive impact on the homicide rates. What could have become a murder was essentially reduced to a fistfight or a shoving match.

Glazer also cites Kelling on the subject of squeegeemen, hyper-aggressive panhandlers who would offer to wash the car of a motorist stopped at a red light. If accepted, the wash job was normally perfunctory and imperfect; if refused, the motorist could expect curses, threats, and even damage to the vehicle. Many motorists paid a dollar or two just to get the person to move on to the next car in line. Glazer notes Kelling's position that when the police actively started arresting these people, the phenomenon quickly disappeared. Also, he contends, about half of the squeegeemen had previous arrests for serious felonies and almost half had arrests for drug-related offenses.[18]

We should note that the experience of the squeegeemen and the fare-beating program seems to support the general theory of crime advanced by Gottfredson and Hirschi. That is, those with low levels of self-control will tend to seize on an opportunity that appears to offer immediate gratification with little regard for long-term consequences. The fare-beaters appear to operate in this manner, whether it be evading a fare of a dollar or so, or settling a real or perceived insult with a handy weapon. The squeegeemen appear to be using this profitable gambit as just another in their long string of brushes with the law.

I do not wish to suggest that we must parade those who commit occupational fraud in handcuffs through the hallways of our organizations to a "Bust Bus" outside the building to achieve an impact. But, we may wish to give some thought to how we, as organizations, do send messages to our honest, law-abiding employees, that we do care and are doing something about issues that may be important to them. From data presented in the *2002 Report to the Nation*, it appears we may infer that most organizations do not fully subscribe to these tenets.

The report noted that 75.4 percent of victim organizations reported their losses to law enforcement, but the median loss for these events was $125,000. Conversely, 24.6 percent of victim organizations did not make a law enforcement referral. The median loss in these events was $75,000.[19] Several things seem to be inferred here. The first is that the larger losses tended to get reported, while the smaller ones did not (noting that a median of $75,000 is hardly small in the eyes of most people). While this logic may be evident, it is precisely the wrong signal to send from a "broken windows" perspective, since it appears to some to say that small incidents will be tolerated as long as they do not become large incidents. From the perspective of the "broken windows" theorist, this logic makes no sense. They would probably argue that few people commit a major offense their first time out. Usually, they start small and build up their repertoire. Even Gottfredson and Hirsch might agree that the 15-year-old who attempts to rob a gas station probably started with smaller crimes such as shoplifting, even though they would argue neither the robbery or the shoplifting required any notable amount of planning or skill. Few eight-year-olds, one would suspect, attempt armed robbery, but some percentage of them certainly shoplift.

If this is also true for the organizational behavior of adults, remembering that occupational fraud tends to go up with age until about age 50, should more attention be paid to the smaller offenses? "Broken windows" theory probably says it should.

How organizations deal with such issues can be a tricky and complicated business. They often tend to err on the side of keeping the matter quiet. The *2002 Report to the Nation* indicates that respondents cited the following reasons most frequently as to why a fraud incident had not prompted legal action by the victim organization:[20]

Fear of bad publicity	30.6%
Private settlement reached	26.6%
Victim wanted closure	25.8%

Several other rationales were covered in the survey, and more than one reason for nonreferral could be cited for a given fraud event, but these figures tend to support the view that many organizations seem to be making a deal with the devil, knowingly or not. For the benefit of avoiding unpleasant publicity, they are willing to trade greater potential exposure to workplace fraud. While this is certainly true from the theoretical perspective of "broken windows" concepts, it has a commonsense logic to it as well. If Mary sees John get caught red-handed and be allowed to quietly resign, is she more or less likely to fear arrest and exposure if she gets caught in a similar workplace fraud? Gottfredson and Hirschi would argue that such cost-benefits analysis is unlikely to enter into the equation, since they do not see the causation of criminal behavior coming from a rational or economic model. I am not sure I agree with them on this point.

When the offending employee is allowed to resign for so-called personal reasons or to pursue other interests, many believe such tactics have several adverse consequences. Among these are the fact that most employees know informally who left voluntarily and who was fired and, in the absence of hard information from management, may be inventive in speculating as to the reason for the departure. The need to avoid legal liability is often cited for the organizational wall of silence, but others see such silence as being dysfunctional. To some degree, a "bad penny" is being passed from organization to organization, if all pursue such policies. Also, the sanction imposed represents no clear message from management as to the organization's values. In those cases where a key employee or executive does, in fact, leave to pursue other interests there may be adverse implications drawn from clients, investors, and analysts, since this phrase is presumed to be a shorthand code for something bad.[21] In the absence of such messages, both positive and negative, employees are left to try to intuit and interpret what the organization stands for—a point Leuci was trying to make when he cited the troublesome 90 percent in the middle "waiting to see what happens."

One of the techniques Bratton used to achieve positive change in the New York City Transit System was to force senior commanders to become personally involved. The subway was often referred to as "the hole" or "the rat hole" by transit cops and transit police brass alike; it was a place to be avoided. Bratton told his subordinate commanders that they, too, should get down in the "hole," see what was going on, and begin to fix it.[22] When the brass began to show up, the cops paid more attention. Would the lunchroom stay messy if even some of the corporate brass ate there once a week?

As we consider issues of community, corporate citizenship, and quality of life, we may be tempted to see these as three related, but distinct, attributes of orga- nizational membership. They need not necessarily be so construed. At least one theorist has put forth a powerful argument that holds that these issues may in reality be nothing more than reflections of each other. In 1995, Robert D. Putnam published a significant and much-discussed essay, "Bowling Alone: America's Declining Social Capital." Following the wide reception that piece received, Putnam followed that effort in 2000 with a book, *Bowling Alone: The Collapse and Revival of American Community*.

Putnam notes that since the publication of Alexis de Tocqueviile's *Democracy in America*, following his visit to this country in the 1830s, America has been regarded as one of the prime examples of the linkage between democracy and civil society. In this regard *civil* does not mean cordial or polite, but having to do with civic involvement on the part of citizens. De Tocqueville noted that one of the facets of American life that struck him most powerfully was the tendency for ordinary citizens to be involved in a wide variety of civic associations, be they religious, social, local, or national. He saw great promise in these groupings of "intellectual and moral" associations.

Putnam observed that a wide variety of social scientists have unearthed evi- dence in a variety of fields that seems to support the view that the level of involvement in groups and civic activities tends to equate well with charitable giving, assisting one's neighbors, and caring about one's community.[23] Putnam notes that his own research into the workings of local and municipal govern- ments in Italy also bears this out. Things, he noted, such as civic involvement, voter turnout, newspaper readership, and even support for local sports teams were the hallmarks of a successful region. He rejects contentions that such phenomena are the result of a region's success, arguing instead that they are a precondition for such success.

In discussing these phenomena, Putnam refers to this as *social capital*, and likens it to the more common concepts of physical capital and human capital, noting the term "refers to features of social organization such as networks, norms, and social trust that facilitate coordination and cooperation for mutual benefit." When such social capital is present, he sees a variety of benefits ensuing: generalized reciprocity, social trust, improved coordination and communication, better resolution of dilemmas and disputes, increased equity in political and economic negotiation, an enhanced sense of "self" for the individual, and the embodiment of past successes as templates for resolution of future problems.[24]

As powerful and utilitarian as Putnam believes these attributes to be, and as inherent in the American psyche as de Tocqueville found them almost two centuries ago, they may now be waning. Putnam cites a broad range of research and statistics that suggests that Americans are not as civic as they once were, or at least are not so in the traditional manner. He notes, for example, that membership in a wide variety of organizations, from the American Association of University Women to the Parent-Teacher Association and from B'Nai B'rith to the American Bar Association are down significantly. Most of these groups tended to peak around the middle of the century, roughly from the early 1950s through the late 1970s.[25]

At the same time, he cites research that indicates that in those states with higher relative levels of social capital there are impressive benefits to be realized: kids are better off, by any number of measures; schools work better; kids watch less television; violent crime is rarer; mortality is lower; and health is better.[26]

In thinking about these figures, Putnam speculates that perhaps they represent the influence of four primary factors. First, he notes, is the pressure of time and money, most frequently thought of as the two-income household that has little energy for other involvements. Second, he believes, is commuting and the sprawl of the suburbs, which have pulled us further apart spatially. Third, he opines, is the impact of the various forms of electronic entertainment that allow us to do alone what previously we would have done in groups. Finally, he concludes, we are experiencing the passing of a generation of "joiners" whose children and grandchildren do not tend to form the bonds of yesteryear.[27]

Even the ubiquitous small group may not be the exact functional equivalent of traditional civic associations in building the base of social capital. Putnam quotes Wuthnow to this effect, noting his work that showed that about 40 percent of Americans belonged to small groups that met regularly to provide mutual support to members. While nearly half of these groups are based on religious affiliation, a fair number are organizations like Alcoholics Anonymous, groups for retarded citizens, garden clubs, book clubs, and hobby clubs. Unlike the large and more formal organizations, these organizations are believed to provide significant bases of support for their members in what Wuthnow describes as a more "fluid" way.[28]

In thinking about how the United States can begin to recapture some of the social capital that once characterized much of its civic life, Putnam offers the following suggestions. First, he counsels, begins with the education and socialization of children by their families. Second, is to make the workplace a more "family-friendly" environment, that will permit the time and resources to explore social capital opportunities. Third, that the design of communities and public spaces will be oriented more to integrated and pedestrian modes of transportation with less reliance on the ever-present, and alienating, automobile. Fourth, he cites a need for a spiritual "community of meaning," that can bind together, while respecting diversity and differences. Fifth, he calls for modes of entertainment, even those that are electronic, that are more integrating than solitary. Sixth, he believes that the arts can be a ready forum to bring people together in groups, rather than be passive by-standers. Seventh, he believes we should encourage more civic involvement in the political process, in matters both great and small.[29]

As we explore organizations for elements of community, we would be well advised to keep Putnam's thoughts and observations in mind. Clearly, the associational nature and inclinations of most Americans have changed. Whether we believe that change is bad or good is beyond the point; it is both present and persistent. The issue is perhaps best considered from the perspective of what is present, rather than what has passed from the scene. People still socialize, they just do it in different ways. People still join, they just do it less often and in different ways. People still care about issues, they just articulate that caring in a different arena. Most of all, people still have healthy portions of self-interest in their psychological make-ups.

If we look at some of the organizations that prospered during an era of associational decline, one is struck by the presence of self-interest. The National Organization for Women is, among other things, about equity and equality in the workplace, the courts, and society. The American Association of Retired Persons is, along with other issues, about health, finances, and vocational opportunities. Perhaps this is what the cops saw when they began to put together community policing projects in noncommunities, like Times Square. Perhaps they encountered not the traditional community of close neighbors and white picket fences, but a community of self-interest. Evidently, that was enough community for their purposes and for their projects to work.

We, too, may have similar issues in organizations as we seek to explore community. We have one hurdle out of the way already. Unlike the Red Cross or the Boy Scouts, we already have our membership in place—they are our employees, and I have speculated earlier on the many forms of glue that operate to hold them together. Perhaps our greatest challenge is to educate them as to why occupational fraud is in their self-interest, and is not just a management issue.

CHAPTER 11

WHAT'S NEW?

Theories of Social Deviance

Some recent research in the area of social control suggests there may be powerful evolutionary traits in the human psyche that not only motivate altruistic and selfless behavior, such as that seen in disasters and accidents, but may also provide motivation to punish cheating, even if it is not directly threatening. Writing of this research, conducted by Dr. Ernst Fehr of the University of Zurich and Dr. Simon Gachter of the University of St. Gallen in Switzerland, one observer commented that new avenues of social science research may indicate that there is a tendency among people to punish those who cheat, even when the cheating in question does not affect them personally.[1] Such research is worthy of further investigation if we are to better understand the motivations and perceptions of our organizational peers in our search for better fraud deterrence strategies.

The concepts of punishment and their efficacy in affecting human behavior in organizational and community settings are also worthy of further exploration and analysis. Kelling has offered his view that enforcing small penalties may help prevent the commission of more serious offenses. This may be particularly pertinent to our efforts to deter fraud if we accept the intuitive proposition that most occupational frauds start small (testing the waters) and become bigger with time, confidence, and lack of discovery. Hollinger and Clark have noted, from their research, a belief that employee perception of the likelihood of discovery may have a deterrent effect and, recalling our discussion of sexual harassment, it appears that at least some "root cause" behaviors are capable of being reduced by a combination of enforcement and education/counseling. (In fairness to "root cause" theorists, we should note that at least some of the successes recognized in the Excellence in Problem-Oriented Policing awards came about because police and other agencies began to deal with what many would call "root cause" issues. Among these, for example, would be the poverty and drug habits of prostitutes in Buffalo.)

It appears that the bulk of research exploring the deterrent value of punishment has been done around the most serious of crimes and the most serious of penalties—murder and capital punishment. As one might imagine, such issues stir powerful passions, and there are studies and statistics flying in all directions. It is not my intent to even begin to try to do justice to this volume of work, but one writer, Paul H. Rubin, has performed a valuable service in capturing the flavor of the complexities of this debate:

> The question of deterrence has long been at the forefront of the debate on capital punishment. Theoretical arguments exist on both sides. Those arguing against deterrence claim that murders are not sufficiently rational to calculate probabilities or respond to incentives, or that murders are committed in the heat of passion and murderers do not consider the consequences. Those making the opposite argument claim that humans are generally rational and respond to incentives, and that criminals are not fundamentally different from others in such qualities. Among the major proponents of the latter view is Gary Becker, the Nobel Laureate in economics who, in a famous article published in 1968, argued that criminals respond to changes in conditions in about the same way as everyone else.
>
> Because theory cannot definitively answer the question of the existence of deterrence, analysts have turned to empirical or statistical methods.[2]

Such analysis would appear to offer some level of comfort since, by definition, numbers are numbers. But, Rubin cautions against so simplistic an approach, citing state-to-state comparisons often seen in newspapers as an example. These, he contends, are misleading because many factors may intervene: murder rates differ by income, age, racial composition, population density, and other factors; and probability of arrest also differs and obviously affects rates and subsequent punishment. Another factor often overlooked is that causality can go either way. A given state may have a capital punishment statute precisely because it has a higher murder rate. As Rubin notes, "In such a case, observing capital punishment and a high murder rate says nothing about causality, and the deterrence argument is that rates would be even higher if there were no capital punishment."[3]

Such observations may initially be disheartening when one thinks of the much broader, more frequent, and less serious issue of occupational fraud. If the best and brightest cannot achieve any consensus around the meaning of statistics relating to murder and capital punishment, what earthly chance do we have with occupational fraud?

Upon reflection, however, we may have a few advantages as we think about research concerning punishment and deterrence:

- Murder is committed for a wide variety of reasons—passion, hatred, money, flight, psychosis, pride, or simply to cover the commission of another crime by leaving no witnesses. Fraud is committed for only one reason—greed. I am mindful here of Cressey's finding that some frauds are committed to try to save a dying business, perhaps implying some sort of altruistic behavior, but I do not believe these are so common that they befoul the causal definition. If greed is the common motivator behind most frauds, we have a much cleaner analytical landscape on which to think about research directed toward deterrent strategies.

- Murders are committed in a wide variety of locations, from cornfields to highrise apartment buildings. Frauds are committed in the workplaces we call home. We have much tighter control over what is by definition a much more limited arena of activity.

- Murderers flee. Only the insane or the emotionally immobile remain at the scene of the crime. Those committing occupational fraud return to the scene of their crime time and time again, often for many years.

- Fraud tends to be accumulative. When one commits a murder, there is usually no driving imperative to commit two the next time and four the next. Fraud, on the other hand, usually tends to get bigger with time.

- Murderers are usually anonymous. We have the whole world to look at for suspects. Occupational fraud perpetrators are within the confines of our organizations: they wear the same employee badges we do and eat in the same cafeterias. They also have the same human resources files, full of potentially useful information about who they are, where they came from, how well educated they are, how many kids they have, and where they live.

- While there are occasionally witnesses to a murder, the victim can provide no information as to who committed the crime or why. While the exceptionally rare fraud may result in murder, we almost always have a victim available, usually with detailed knowledge about the perpetrator(s), the technique(s) utilized, and, perhaps, the motive(s).

- Since the penalties are less for fraud, the possibilities for cooperation are increased. Plea bargains in murder cases are the stuff of noisy headlines and stern editorials, but they still occur. The implicated fraud perpetrator is not facing death by lethal injection and we, the investigator/victim organization, may decide that in exchange for valuable information about the incident(s) we are willing to bargain.

We probably think we know more about the efficacy of deterrence than we do. Perhaps giving the white-collar criminal 30 years instead of 30 months will have a deterrent effect on others, but I would hazard that this proposition is built more on intuition and emotional investment than it is on empirical research. We have seen the complexities that abound around the issue of deterrence of so simple a crime as murder, and these may tend to dissuade us from further research. If we choose this course, however, we continue to fight an important battle with our theoretical framework rooted solidly in little more than intuition and emotion.

I have suggested on several occasions the desirability, if not the need, for the forensic profession to look beyond its traditional boundaries if it is going to become capable of offering new answers to old questions about occupational fraud. I am also mindful of Bratton's observation that the law enforcement field benefited greatly once it swallowed its fear and allowed the pointy-headed academics into the inner sanctum. There are many possibilities. In the arena of deviance and social control, one partner we may wish to consider is the American Society of Criminology. The organization describes itself as an international entity interested in research into the causes of crime and delinquency, as well as strategies for its prevention and control. It embraces students, scholars, and practitioners, and is also interested in issues of measurement and detection.[4]

Available through the Society's Web site are abstracts of papers written under the Society's auspices for the past 15 years or so. A review of the most recent five years' works (1997–2001) is instructive. A cursory examination of these papers revealed 176 submitted during this period. Among some of the more interesting to the forensic professional are:

- "Snakes and Ladders: Upper-Middle Class Male Offenders Talk about Economic Crime," by Sara Willott, Christine Griffin, and Mark Torrance (2001)

- "The Role of Public Social Control in Urban Neighborhoods: A Multilevel Analysis of Victimization Risk," by Maria B. Velez (2001)

- "Social Altruism and Crime," by Mitchell R. Chamlin and John K. Cochran (1997)

Such works and many others may be useful, or may be blind alleys of little benefit to what we are about. I believe we, as a profession, must begin to look at such materials broadly and consider involving independent researchers more deeply in our organizations and our profession if we are to grow and mature. There are many interesting questions to be answered. For example, we can recall the March 2002 poll conducted by the ACFE. It found, in the latest internal fraud incidents investigated by its members, that fully 27 percent involved 3 to 10 people and an astounding 9 percent involved more than 10 persons. Why do such group violations occur? Why did no one report them? One would think that if more than 10 persons were involved in the commission of the same fraud, many more were recruited but declined to participate. Did any of these persons come forward? If not, why? Could we be dealing with a Leuci situation where the vast majority of employees are "waiting to see what happens"?

If the theories of Doctors Fehr and Gachter have validity with regard to the control of social deviance, under which sets of conditions do they tend to operate and under what other conditions can these apparently basic human instincts be muted or overridden? Until we are able to begin to formulate answers to such basic questions, our goal of deterring fraud in the workplace will continue to be a formidable one.

Profiling

This term has gained a substantial measure of negative baggage in recent years, to the point where it has become almost a buzzword, conveying volumes of information and sentiment by its utterance. Much of this comes from a series of confrontational law enforcement cases and practices that in some instances involved arrests, shootings, and even deaths. Several of these incidents resulted in long and highly publicized trials of police officers, for the base allegation was that minority members of the community had been targeted for investigation or enforcement actions solely, or largely, on the basis of their race.

Other bases for concern in the use of the practice come from studies that tend to show the disparate racial impact of profiling even in the light of protestations that such is not its intent. *The Law Enforcement News* recently ran an article that recounted some recent examples:[5]

- A survey by *The Tulsa World* in May, which found more than one-third of people stopped in 11 Oklahoma counties that were heavily patrolled for drugs were black or Hispanic, although the populations there were over-whelming white.

- Members of Michigan's Arab-American community are often detained at airports and at the Canadian border, according to a report released in May by the Michigan Advisory Committee to the U.S. Commission on Civil Rights.

- A report using data collected from law enforcement agencies throughout Rhode Island from January 15 through the end of March found that blacks were twice as likely to be searched and released as whites during a routine traffic stop, and three times as likely as whites to be searched and arrested.

- According to the third report by an independent monitor appointed under a 1999 consent decree between the Justice Department and the state of New Jersey, the percentage of blacks and Hispanics arrested on the New Jersey Turnpike was back up to 1997 and 1998 levels—the same rate as before state police officials admitted to racial profiling.

Still other agencies, while emphasizing they never engaged in the practice, restated their concern that race not be used as the basis for any law enforcement action. *The New York Times* reported that Police Commissioner Raymond W. Kelly banned the use of racial profiling in enforcement activities, noting he had adopted a similar policy while U.S. Customs Commissioner.[6]

Concerns about profiling are also not limited to the law enforcement community, although many of them reside there. In a program aired in April 2002, the *Religion and Ethics Newsweekly* feature of The Public Broadcasting Stations devoted substantial time to private security organizations' use of surveillance cameras at major events and in public places. Note was made of the use of these devices at events such as the Super Bowl, when screening software was also utilized to match random faces in the crowd against a digitized database of known and suspected terrorists and criminals. While some welcomed the additional and ostensibly nonintrusive level of security this technique provided, others saw in it a disturbing element of Big Brother watching over innocent persons going about their business in a public place. Likewise, an increasing number of urban police departments use cameras to provide continuous real-time surveillance of high-traffic areas. While these departments insist they are looking only for signs of active criminal activity, the same privacy issues are voiced by others who worry about a permanent electronic record being maintained by the government of who was where when, who they were with, and what they were doing.[7] Such issues are sufficiently close to matters of profiling that we would be well served to keep them in mind as we examine these techniques.

Most of the public became aware of the positive uses of profiling in the hit movie, *The Silence of the Lambs.* This film, based on a composite of several serial sexual offenders, among them Ted Bundy, highlighted the work of the FBI's Behavioral Science Unit, which developed much of the basis for the studied use of profiling in law enforcement. Lest we think profiling is a radical departure for the forensic profession, we should remember that much of the work that Cressey, Albrecht, and Hollinger and Clark did were early attempts at profiling. In seeking to determine the causes and characteristics of fraud behavior, they were also trying to build a model that would have some measure of predictive or heuristic value. It is here that the problems with profiling usually arise.

If we were to conduct a study indicating that many arsons are committed by left-handed redheads, that is well and good—as far as it goes. It says nothing about any particular left-handed redhead and can in no way—and this point cannot be overemphasized—be the sole basis for an enforcement action. In police terms, this is called *probable cause.* As a patrol officer, I cannot pull over a vehicle on the pure basis that I am bored or because I believe people who drive red cars are up to something. That, simply, is not probable cause, and any resulting arrest (let us say, for the sake of argument, that 200 pounds of cocaine are found in the trunk), will properly be thrown out by the courts.

To discuss the many nuances of probable cause here is beyond the scope and intent of this work, but it is a crucial consideration in any discussion of profiling. If, then, profiles do not provide probable cause, of what use are they? To approach this question, it is useful to think of the early stages of the development of the technique.

Jack Douglas, an FBI Agent formerly assigned to the FBI's Behavioral Science Unit and a technical consultant on the movie *The Silence of the Lambs*, has recounted much of this developmental activity in his book, *Mindhunter*.[8] Douglas and other Special Agents assigned to this unit began their work from academic backgrounds in psychology and social science. They were assisted in this endeavor by several renowned detectives and investigators from police departments around the United States. The initial premise was simple: how one dresses says something about one's personality; how you decorate your house says something about your personality; and how you commit a crime says something about your personality. It is crucial to note here a subtle distinction. The issue is not whether you committed the crime, but how you committed it. The investigative value comes from studying the crime scene and being able to make some assumptions about the type of person who committed the act(s). This permits investigators to pay attention to a more limited range of suspects and better focus their investigation. Again, the subtleties are important. If, as in my example, an arson has been committed, this is not an injunctive to begin rounding up left-handed redheads. If, however, a left-handed redhead is among the suspects already developed on the basis of other evidence, then this person may warrant further attention.

Profiling in its developed form is not some variant of predestination theory that attempts to predict human behavior on the basis of cosmological factors or status. It is, rather, an attempt to infer, from thousands of hours of study and analysis, what the perpetrators of crime are telling us by how they committed it. In developing this body of work, Douglas and others devised a strategy brilliant in its simplicity: they asked the bad guys why and how they did it. The personnel of the Behavioral Science Unit fanned out over a period of several years and spent thousands of hours interviewing hundreds of the worst criminals imaginable. Often locked away for multiple life sentences, they were surprised to find these so-called worst of the worst willing, even eager, to talk. Part of this reaction they attributed to simple boredom, while others they believed were eager to brag about their exploits. Still others saw the interviewers as a challenge, to be bested in a game of forensic chess—the master criminal against the professional sleuth, not unlike several of the movie scenes between Dr. Hannibal Lecter and Special Agent Clarice Starling.[9]

From these interviews and other developmental work, the Behavioral Science Unit was able to formulate theories about the commission of these crimes that could be applied to future investigations and provide investigative value. Some of these theorems may seem simple to the layperson, but they can be of immense value to the investigator faced with a myriad of unknowns: Is it likely the perpetrator knew the victim? Was the act spontaneous or planned? Is it likely the perpetrator is familiar with the neighborhood? Does the act suggest some level of intimate sexual or psychological relationship with the victim? Does the perpetrator collect souvenirs of the crime? Is the perpetrator likely to escalate in the volume or violence of their acts?

Thankfully, the forensic professional does not have to deal with such revolting acts as serial murder or sadomasochistic sexual assault, but can we learn from these techniques? I think so, for we have several inherent advantages. First, we own the crime scene. While the crime scene of a murder or rape may be a rooftop, warehouse, or stretch of deserted highway, all of our crime scenes are within the organizations we call home. Certainly, business must go on, and we cannot shut down a given department because a fraud was committed there. At the same time, we have a substantial ability to gather important knowledge about how the act was committed without interference from wind, rain, snow, or passing traffic. We also have substantial knowledge of the perpetrator. Criminals, once they are identified, usually have rap sheets—official records of their past criminal acts, associates, and so on. We, however, have personnel files, perhaps pre-employment background investigations, maybe psychological tests, and always co-workers. We may wish to begin to think about how we can mine these valuable sources of intelligence to better prepare ourselves and our profession to investigate and even prevent such transgressions in the future.

We have been profiled many times over, usually with some degree of consent. We fill out forms, accept coupons, enter sweepstakes, drop a business card in the jar at the restaurant, or answer a quick telephone survey; these are all forms of profiling. Customer lists have long been considered valuable pieces of intellectual property by businesses. We hear in the media from time to time the latest flap about some organization selling its list to some other outfit. State Departments of Motor Vehicles have been doing this for years. This is profiling, if I am interested in the average age of the drivers of a given model car in a given locale because I want to target them in an advertising campaign.

The issue of one's personal profile and how willing you are to share it in exchange for convenience is now a major issue in American business circles. Quentin Hardy reports that the "digital identity" movement is well established and being hotly contested by many companies who want to be leaders in the field. "Digital identity," he advises, is the accumulation of personal data—name, address, Social Security account number, credit card data, medical information, and more—that you are willing to have assembled through the use of software so it can be provided to one or more vendors with whom you would like to do business. What you are trading off for this lack of privacy, Hardy explains, is the ability for that vendor to service your needs almost immediately and tailor products and services to your specifications. He notes that Tony Scott, the chief technology officer for General Motors, believes this ability to adjust to the customer's driving, service, and even accident history could help build lifetime relationships and, most important, repeat purchases. The On Star tracking system is an early step in that direction, he advises, since it automatically notifies the police whenever an air bag is deployed in a car equipped with it.[10]

Hardy further notes that some privacy advocates worry about how much personal information will migrate into corporate hands, but the On Star system provides a near-perfect example of the issues of personal profile tradeoffs. One is willing to let the machine tell the police where you are. The benefit is that if you are unconscious in a wrecked vehicle and in need of medical attention, the machine will come to your assistance. Proponents of the use of digital identity note there is an inherent safety valve around privacy issues—participation in systems such as On Star and other digital identity programs is voluntary.

Much profiling is done with our knowledge and at least tacit consent to help service providers protect us as consumers. Steven Scott has written of the use of Bayesian statistics to deter fraud against consumers, noting: "The idea behind Bayesian statistics is to create a probability distribution describing your subjective belief about some uncertain quantity. . . and to update the distribution using Bayes' rule as relevant data become known. It is the updating that makes Bayesian statistics a science."[11]

He goes on to note that AT&T, for example, uses such calculations to help prevent losses to long-distance fraud that are about $4 billion a year, on an industry basis. Using Bayesian statistics, AT&T can update a customer's calling patterns to spot calls that might be indicative of fraudulent activity by a third party. Thus the Bayesian profile of the customer's normal calls, updated and weighed in various sophisticated ways, becomes a fairly active indicator of when a number, account, or even switch has been taken over by persons intent on committing fraud. Such techniques are also used by credit card companies to prevent theft or fraud losses and by computer companies and organizations to detect hackers.[12]

Credit scores in general affect many of the everyday payments we make for mortgages, auto loans, and other forms of financing. Fair, Isaac and Company (FICO) scores are used to rate consumers as to their credit-worthiness and can have a significant impact on the interest rates charged. For example, as of April 2002, depending on one's credit score in the FICO system, the rates for a 60-month auto loan could vary from 5.59 to 10.95 percent, and the rates for a 30-year mortgage from 6.851 to 8.664 percent.[13]

We each profile one another dozens of times a day, sometimes for good or bad reasons, but it is one of the most common of human traits. Sociologists might call it stereotyping, but the hundreds of social interactions that occur in a typical day might be different and strange without it.

When used in law enforcement activities, the courts have recognized that the totality of the officer's observations and experience is the basis for a probable cause judgment, such as whether to stop a suspicious vehicle. Writing in *The Police Chief* magazine, Michael Whalen cited one recent case on this subject, *United States* v. *Arvizu*, noting: "The U.S. Supreme Court's recent ruling in *United States* v. *Arvizu* continues a series of decisions that recognize the inexact science of determining probable cause and reasonable suspicion and the importance of teaching officers to document all of the facts leading to their decision to make a stop or conduct a search."[14]

In this case, Stoddard, a Border Patrol Agent, learned of a vehicle driving on a little-used border road late at night, and knew this road had been used by drug smugglers in the past. He followed this vehicle, noting a man, woman, and several children who made a display of waving to him in an overly friendly manner. He then saw the vehicle turn onto another road not usually traveled by passenger vehicles. He stopped the vehicle and asked for permission to search it. During the course of the search, drugs were discovered. The issue became a classic probable cause hearing—whether he had sufficient basis to stop the vehicle in the first place. The U.S. District Court for the District of Arizona upheld the stop as reasonable, but the U.S. Court of Appeals for the Ninth Circuit overturned it, holding that each factor that went into the decision that there was reasonable suspicion had to be examined individually. If there was a possible innocent explanation for the single factor, it had to be discarded and could not be used as part of the overall rationale to justify the stop.

Whalen advises that the U.S. Supreme Court reversed the Ninth Circuit, noting:

The U.S. Supreme Court reversed the Ninth Circuit's decision, relying on the Supreme Court's past decisions that a finding of reasonable suspicion is based on the totality of the circumstances. These factors must be reviewed as a whole and are not subject to individual scrutiny. While the concept may be abstract, it "allows officers to draw on their own experience and specialized training to make inferences from and deductions about the cumulative information available to them that might elude the untrained person." The fact that an observation may have an innocent explanation does not preclude the behavior from consideration when determining reasonable suspicion.[15]

Thus have the federal courts held in a series of cases that individual pieces of information in the hands of a trained and experienced person, such as a law enforcement officer, can be sufficient to justify a law enforcement action such as a vehicle stop. While the position of the forensic professional is different in many ways from that of the law enforcement officer, such positions do support the fact that profiling in the hands of a competent, trained, reasonable, and thoughtful person may have considerable utility when addressing issues of fraud in the workplace.

Of late, the technology most states now use on drivers' licenses and the availability of fairly cheap scanners have combined to take this voluntary behavior to a new level. Jennifer Lee, writing in *The New York Times*[16], provides one example in noting the policy of a popular Boston bar to use scanners to check driver's licenses of patrons. Ostensibly done to :prevent underage drinking and to spot known troublemakers, the device also encodes useful data as to age, address, and date of visit. Such data is valuable in planning entertainment offerings, product promotions, and advertising campaigns.[17] All of this useful data comes under the canopy of profiling.

Many other companies and services also track our movements for the purposes of collecting business intelligence. Edward Ip, an Assistant Professor of Statistics, Information and Operations Management, notes that AT&T collects data on the 130 million calls it handles each day and that Amazon.com monitors "click stream data" from the 29 million customers who use its services. Such data are used to produce decision and product mix models to improve customer satisfaction, promote customer loyalty, and increase profits.[18]

Authors Taylor and Jerome note that we can also be profiled in areas extremely important to retailers—our buying and browsing decisions. They note, for example, that Microsoft's Windows Media Player creates a record of the DVDs you watch and the music you play. This information is then automatically relayed back to a corporate headquarters' database in Redmond, Washington. They also advise that Comcast used to track its customers' surfing habits, but dropped this policy after a Congressperson and privacy rights groups voiced complaints. Amazon.com goes about the same goal in a slightly different manner, they observe. This e-tailer asks customers to complete questionnaires rating various products according to their tastes. These data are then compared to peer group ratings, and from this data future product selections are recommended for purchase. In fairness, Taylor and Jerome note that most customers are happy to have Amazon provide this service, with the company acting as sort of a personal shopper on their behalf.[19]

Other companies, they note, are willing to trade with customers who are willing to provide them with important marketing information. They cite Proctor & Gamble, which sponsored a print and media campaign to promote a new product, Crest Whitestrips tooth-bleaching kit. The ads encouraged consumers to go to the company's Web site, where they could get coupons and discounts. As a result of this traffic, Proctor & Gamble learned that 80 percent of this product was purchased by women, and that half were between 35 and 54 years of age. Armed with this important information, the company adjusted its advertising campaign accordingly.[20]

Even *The New York Times*, which is not normally reticent in decrying perceived threats to civil liberties, recently endorsed increased funding to permit law enforcement agencies to use perhaps the ultimate form of profiling—DNA analysis. Noting that state and federal databanks held substantial numbers of DNA profiles of criminals and suspects, *The Times* argued that more widespread and timely use of such data, now hindered by budget constraints, would help capture sexual assailants and also free those wrongly accused or imprisoned.[21]

Wells, and the 1996 and 2002 *Reports to the Nation* on the size and characteristics of occupational fraud offer us a type of a profile of those who commit occupational frauds—a college-educated white male with no prior criminal record for fraud. That description fits a huge number of people, but it is a sort of a profile. We still, however, must deal with the sticky issue of predictive value. While profiling techniques may be useful in the solution of a crime (or a fraud), how can we use such information in the prevention of future acts without falling into the same pattern of problems law enforcement has encountered with racial enforcement? If we know left-handed redheads are more likely to commit fraud than others, is the answer to avoid hiring left-handed redheads in the future? I think not.

We may, for example, be able to learn of warning signs in our employee populations. Perceived financial hardship is a common element cited by every theorist who has studied occupational fraud. Would we be better served in the long run to make employees aware of professional resources available to them when they experience such events, and thereby perhaps reduce fraud occurrences? I believe such matters are worthy of greater consideration, especially when we expand the circle to include compulsive gambling, living beyond one's means, and credit card addiction.

Steve Albrecht, the noted fraud researcher and theorist has also commented on items we may wish to think about in this regard. Much like the previous FBI example, these items may be best suited for inclusion in management/supervisor awareness training:

> Research in psychology reveals that when a person, especially a first-time offender, commits a crime, he or she becomes engulfed by emotions of fear and guilt. Those emotions cause the individual to experience a significant amount of stress, and in order to cope with stress, the individual will exhibit unusual and recognizable behavior patterns. Some recognizable behavior patterns are insomnia; increase in drug and alcohol abuse and smoking habits; unusual irritability and suspiciousness; inability to relax; lack of pleasure in things usually enjoyed; fear of getting caught; inability to look people in the eye; visible embarrassment around friends and others; defensiveness or argumentativeness; unusual belligerence in stating opinions; unsolicited confessions; obsessive contemplation of possible consequences; constant development of excuses and identification of scapegoats; tendency to work standing up; and increased perspiration.
>
> It is not any particular behavior, but rather changes in behavior that signals fraud. People who are normally nice may become intimidating and belligerent; people who are normally belligerent may suddenly become nice.[22]

Albrecht also raises two issues frequently associated with occupational frauds. The first is lifestyle changes. Apparently, once perpetrators of workplace fraud get more comfortable with their new identity and activities, it is time to begin to enjoy the fruits of their labor. He notes that sometimes the fraud in question could have been detected because it was, to use the classic phrase, "too good to be true." Albrecht uses the experience of General Motors to make both points. In early 1992, it was discovered that John McNamara, a Long Island car dealer, had defrauded General Motors of approximately $436 million. While not technically an employee of General Motors, McNamara's relationship with that company was such that his activities exhibited all of the symptoms of a classic occupational fraud. The interesting thing is, General Motors thought of him as a star performer for most of the time the fraud was being committed. Albrecht describes the scheme as follows:

> Essentially, what McNamara did was to establish a phony van-assembly company, Kay Industries, in Indiana. Supposedly, McNamara Buick, a company owned by McNamara, paid Kay Industries for customized vehicles he claimed to be exporting overseas. At one point he was supposedly purchasing as many as 17,000 vans per month. Kay Industries would give McNamara Buick invoices stamped paid. McNamara Buick submitted the invoices to GMAC, which gave McNamara a 30-day loan of approximately $25,000 on each customized vehicle.
>
> McNamara Buick would then supposedly sell the vehicles to another McNamara-owned corporation, which in turn, claimed to be shipping them to a McNamara-owned buyer in Cyprus, Cydonia Trading CTD. McNamara Buick would then repay the loans within 30 days while, at the same time, borrowing additional funds from GMAC for the next shipment of vehicles. All but the last round of loans, totaling $436 million, were repaid. GMAC loaned McNamara $715 million in 1989, $1.88 billion in 1990 and $1.93 billion in 1991. The total loans made to McNamara over a four-year period exceeded the gross domestic product of the country of Panama.
>
> McNamara's fraud was possible because he always paid GMAC on time. He was a valued customer who consistently increased his line of credit. GMAC was obviously making a "profit" on his transactions at a time when the company was very hungry for sales. GMAC managers were under pressure to generate profits, and McNamara was an answer to their profit concerns. GMAC officials got raises and promotions based on the quantity of his loans.[23]

While the experience of General Motors and its commercial lending arm, GMAC, is a classic case of news that was too good to be true—17,000 vehicles per month is more than 565 vehicles a day!—Albrecht also goes on to point out some of the behavioral warning flags that might have been worthy of attention. Even an apparently successful dealer like McNamara might be hard-pressed to justify the following level of expenditure described by Albrecht:

> There were numerous symptoms that could have tipped internal auditors and others to the fraud. In terms of lifestyle changes, McNamara bought—over a short period of time—a private jet; an expensive airplane; considerable amounts of stocks, bonds, and notes; numerous real estate companies; two additional auto dealerships; a commodities brokerage; a $500,000 trust for his daughter; a $350,000 home for his ex-wife; a $500,000 personal home; more than 100 properties in New York, Maryland, Georgia, Florida, and the Middle East; 70

different corporations and partnerships; a limousine; two gold mines in Nevada; two seats on the New York Mercantile Exchange; a newspaper company; a Day's Inn motel; a pharmaceutical company; and a car loan company.[24]

In the 20/20 perspective of hindsight, these may seem to have been awfully big warning signs, both from the perspective of news too good to be true and lifestyle changes. They are, however, instructive when thinking about the potential that profiles built on the foundations of professional research and practitioner experience have to offer. Properly constructed and thoughtfully applied, they need not be overly onerous.

Speaking at a conference in New York City, "Israel's Security Industry: Technologies and Strategies for Homeland Defense and Counter-Terrorism," Jacob Perry, the former Director of Israel's General Security Services made the following points regarding profiling. The title of his talk was "Security and Civil Liberties," and he noted that Israel is rightfully famous for its strict security standards, especially around air travel safety. Profiling, he noted, is a necessary but highly effective measure, but one that is carefully applied to avoid being oppressive. Perry observed that even during states of high alert, 95 percent of passengers boarding flights in Israel go through only normal security and baggage checks, 4 percent received a heightened review of their baggage, and only 1 percent are questioned about their travel, destination, and documentation. This, he believes, is a fair balancing of Israel's significant security concerns and the rights and needs of travelers for personal freedom and dignity. He noted this was possible only because Israel had long placed emphasis on developing effective screening procedures and did not apply them in a blanket or haphazard fashion.[25]

The potential of profiling is demonstrated no more tellingly than by recent press accounts about the terrorist attacks of September 11th. Long after the fact, it now appears that nine of the nineteen terrorists involved in these attacks had been picked up by standard airport security profiling techniques and their luggage subjected to increased scrutiny. The failure of these checks to hamper or prevent the subsequent attacks was not the fault of the profiling filters utilized, but rather of the follow-up actions. In the wake of previous attacks, these procedures called for checking luggage for evidence of explosives. When none was found, the nine individuals were allowed to board their flights. The procedures, based on past events, did not envision a search for the small, sharp cutting instruments that were used to take control of the aircraft.[26]

Given that we may, by definition, engage in a form of screening and prevention, there are perhaps valuable lessons to be learned from such experiences and that of others, always with the caution that we tread a fine line between organizational effectiveness and personal liberties; but, it may be an area worthy of further exploration.

We need also to begin to think about profiling organizations. It is not as strange as it may seem at first blush. It is likely that the building you work in has been profiled at some point in the past, albeit for a somewhat different reason. Building management companies, insurers, rating agencies, risk managers, and others will often have a security or fire safety survey done of a given building, operation, or complex. Because of their criticality to many operations, data centers are also frequently profiled. These procedures may be done by in-house personnel or through the use of outside experts and are performed to assess policies, procedures, training, equipment, personnel, and redundancy. These surveys are useful tools for the organization to identify and address areas of weakness and plan remedial actions. The surveys may, among other purposes, also be used to establish or adjust insurance rates.

The Wall Street Journal, for example, recently had a special 16-page section entitled "On Guard—Protecting Employees and Facilities Is Suddenly a Top Priority. But How Should Companies Do It? And Will the Office Ever Be the Same?" The section contained articles on protecting buildings, mail, traveling employees, computer files, and safeguarding against future threats. Many of the articles offered tips and checklists for assessing security readiness. The section also featured advertisements from companies providing such assessment and protection services. These items represent, at base, forms of profiling or surveying organizations.[27]

Audit committees also have become more active in tending to the security risks facing their organizations. Writing in *Internal Auditor* magazine, Curtis C. Verschoor notes:

> Additionally, since Sept. 11th, audit committees have elevated in importance their need to spend more time overseeing the risks of physical and technical security, as well as to more closely monitor organizational processes for assessing, evaluating, mitigating and monitoring significant business risks. The Winter 2002 *AUDIT Committee Quarterly*, published by KPMG's Audit Committee Institute, reports feedback from participants in the institute's Fall 2001 series of audit committee roundtables. According to the feedback, 85 percent of audit committee participants said that risk-related issues would receive the most consideration at the board level due to the changes in risk since Sept. 11th. Thirty-five percent of those respondents chose enterprise risk management as the most important issue, while 27 percent said general security procedures were most important.[28]

For certain categories of risk, the decision about whether to conduct such organizational surveys, or profiles, is becoming less arbitrary. A recent article in *The National Law Journal* noted that the National Infrastructure Protection Center, created jointly by the Department of Justice and the FBI in 1998, has stressed the need for organizations to perform audits of their cybersecurity risks and put remediation plans into place. The article goes on to point out that not to do so may leave key corporate officials open to liability in the event of a security compromise. Citing a Pennsylvania case, *In re* Logue Mechanical Contracting Corporation, they note courts have been moving toward a more expansive and affirmative standard for officers and directors when addressing such risks.[29]

It is becoming more common for some organizations to have fraud risk assessments performed of their controls, procedures, systems, and operations. Sometimes this is done after a fraud incident, with the intent of discovering if other areas may also be at risk. More farsighted organizations do not wait for an event to trigger such an assessment, but perform them periodically as a form of risk management. Again, the assessments can be performed internally but are most often conducted by outside professionals. Some companies and organizations also perform assessments during and because of significant organization change, such as mergers, rapid expansion, acquisitions, and joint venturing. When such an assessment is conducted before a merger or acquisition, it is usually considered to be part of the due diligence process.

Yet, there still seems to be some level of organizational ambivalence about the use of surveys and their findings. In March 2002, Ernst & Young LLP released its *Global Information Security Survey 2002*. The survey, conducted with 459 Chief Information Officers, Information Technology Directors, and business executives in 17 regions and countries, found that 60 percent of respondents believed their systems would experience greater vulnerability in the future as connectivity increased. At the same time, in the face of these beliefs, their responses seemed out of step. Only 53 percent had a business continuity plan in place, only 40 percent were confident they would even detect an attack on their systems, and 40 percent did not even investigate security incidents. At the same time, they had a greater concern about externally based attacks (57 percent) than internal attacks (41 percent), even in the face of public data that indicates more than 75 percent of all attacks come from within.[30]

If we accept the fact that there may be fraud-prone individuals in our midst, we should also recognize that there may also be fraud-prone organizations. Jack Bologna and others have suggested several of the characteristics of such entities, based largely on their professional experience. As a field for potential academic research, it is an area of considerable promise. Ernst & Young LLP's internal fraud report, *The Unmanaged Risk: An International Survey of the Effect of Fraud on Business*, was released in May 2000. A survey of more than 10,000 international businesses and organizations, it had the following findings on the issue of such organizational profiling, as reported by Carpenter and Mahoney:

A focus that was unique to the Ernst & Young report was its emphasis on the value of fraud vulnerability reviews. The report revealed that organizations that had not performed fraud vulnerability reviews were almost two thirds more likely to have suffered a fraud within the previous 12 months. Furthermore, while more than 80 percent of the respondents expressed serious concerns regarding the likelihood of a significant fraud within their respective organizations, only 33 percent reported that a fraud vulnerability review had been recently performed. Additionally, nearly 40 percent of survey participants who thought that their organizations were vulnerable to fraud indicated that their organization lacked a specific policy with respect to reporting fraud.[31]

The tenor of such activities need not necessarily be negative. It is increasingly common for many organizations, especially those involved in Six Sigma and ISO 9000 activities, to engage in benchmarking exercises in which they measure themselves against best practices in industry or commerce. Certainly, it is possible to undertake such an endeavor with regard to occupational fraud, using either in-house professionals or with outside professional assistance.

Profiling of organizations appears to be a fairly benign issue; however, profiling persons, even given the extensive use made of the technique, may be a thornier issue for organizations to deal with as they seek to reduce the incidence of occupational fraud. On April 14, 2002, *The New York Times Magazine* ran a lengthy piece called "Silicon Valley's Spy Game," in which author Jeffrey Rosen discussed the potential for computing power to be able to coordinate and deliver vast amounts of potentially useful information to governmental agencies involved in the fight on terrorism. The Chief Executive Officer of Oracle, Larry Ellison, was quoted as noting that while Americans are afraid of an all-powerful government, perhaps using such comprehensive information to restrict civil liberties, he was of the opinion that, "It's our lives that are at risk, not our liberties."[32]

We must recognize that editors of magazines, newspapers, and news programs, while trying to be fair, also have tremendous discretionary judgment over what goes before the public and what does not. In a subsequent edition of the same magazine, five letters to the editor were published concerning the article in general and Ellison's comments in particular. All five were negative, generally taking the view that if computers permitted a government entity such all-seeing access to data about individuals, the terrorists had in fact won, since the United States had been forced to become a potentially repressive society in order to better defend itself.[33] We shall never know how representative these letters were of all those received concerning the article or Ellison's comments; however, such concerns will probably always be a factor in decisions on how, or if, to utilize profiling techniques on individuals.

Neuroscience

In the age of technology and cloning, it is perhaps inevitable that the issue of biology raises its head. Commenting on research recently reported by neuroscientists, writer Sandra Blakeslee observed that these scientists and researchers now believe there may be certain brain circuits that subtly influence what we commonly believe to be conscious choices. In this research, such apparently disparate activities as "Compulsive gambling, attendance at sporting events, vulnerability to telephone scams, and exuberant investing... may... have a common thread."[34] She goes on to note that these brain circuits are believed to be identical to those with which animals assess rewards, such as food and sex, that are important to their survival. One of the most pronounced findings of the research, she reported, is that these circuits appear to operate outside of conscious awareness and may be involved in the manner in which we "assess social awards as diverse as investment income and surprise home runs in the bottom of the ninth."

She notes that while such ideas have been around since Freud, modern researchers now suspect that the unconscious processing of information may be more important than thought. Dr. Gregory Berns, a psychiatrist at Emory University School of Medicine, has opined that most decisions are probably made with varying degrees of conscious awareness. A much smaller number may invoke full, conscious, attention.

Following the logic of this example, Blakeslee advises that while driving our familiar route to work, we may pay little attention to that which is routine—buildings, signs, traffic. Since all of these things are patterned into our brain circuits and, since things are where they should be, we can safely ignore them. This is much like our awareness that gravity causes objects to fall, buildings usually stay put in one place, and light at an angle will produce long shadows. These matters are taken for granted and arouse little curiosity; however, the car running a red light prompts an entirely different pattern of brain wave activity, since there is now an abrupt disconnect between what is expected and what is happening. Drawing on our databank of past experiences, we may hit the brake, swerve, or take other actions. Only after a second or two do we begin to consciously process the event that just occurred. Dr. P. Read Montague, a neuroscientist at Baylor College of Medicine, has estimated that as much as 90 percent of our daily activities are controlled by these unconscious subsystems that evolved to allow creatures, such as us, to survive. Like animals, we have become used to what we can safely ignore (the building that remains where it should be), what we need to pay attention to (the car running the red light), and what is worth learning more about.[35]

There are also reports on research that focuses on the two primary facets of advertising: attractiveness and resistance. Advertisements, it seems, can operate in one of two primary fashions: (1) they can assume a persuasive strategy and try to increase the attractiveness of an offer (referred to by researchers as "alpha" strategies), or (2) they can try to lower the level of resistance to the offer ("omega" strategies). Researchers report interesting findings regarding the apparent mechanisms by which these strategies operate, and suggest that resistance responses are perhaps hardwired in the developing human brain. There are also studies that suggest something perhaps akin to the findings of Montague. In one study a group of college students was put on the street to impersonate beggars.

Researchers found that they received money 44 percent of the time when they asked for it without specifying a sum. When they asked for a single-coin amount, a quarter for example, they received it 64 percent of the time. But when they asked for a randomly chosen odd amount, say 37 cents, they got it 75 percent of the time.[36] It seems that the more precise, and therefore unusual, the request the less people were able to resist it. Could it be, like Montague's car speeding through the red light, this is because the uniqueness of the request forced people to actually process it in a conscious manner, rather than tune it out like the passing scenery?

Blakeslee advises that people use these same animal circuits for a variety of more diverse activities because of our bigger brains and cultural development. Such activities may include enjoying food or asthetic activities, using intoxicants, or making financial decisions. Of the two primary circuits involved in such activity, researchers have discovered significant variations in the levels of a chemical called dopamine, which gives us a feeling of pleasure. One of the circuits studied is part of the frontal cortex called the anterior cingulate, one of whose tasks is picking up disruptions in information flow in other parts of the brain. Blakeslee notes that the amount of dopamine that reaches this area seems in experiments to be related to delight or disappointment in expected and unexpected rewards.[37]

She goes on to cite the work of Dr. Jonathan Cohen, a neuroscientist at Princeton, who has noted that both people and animals seem to adjust their behavior and expectations according to their reward "histories." Like parrots and crackers, they seem to "learn" what acts tend to produce rewards, with dopamine seeming to carry the messages.[38]

Some people, Blakeslee advises, appear to have "vulnerable" dopamine systems that can get "hijacked" by social rewards that can include money, sex, risk, or drugs. The first time such people "win," say at gambling, their systems seem to record the huge dopamine rush and seek repeatedly to recreate it, even though parts of their conscious brains may well understand that it is ultimately a losing proposition. The same may hold true for the unpredictability of sports (the winning home run in the bottom of the ninth) and many other activities. Older people, she advises, may have ailments that impair the functioning of the frontal cortex, which seems to leave them less adept at gambling activities but more prone to believe misleading advertising.[39]

Such are the complexities of the human brain, and we are just now beginning to share some of its secrets. Is there a rush in fraud? One would certainly assume so. Money, obviously, is involved. Risk is present. Money may easily lead, as time and experience have taught us, to other rewards, such as gambling, sex, and drugs. Are there biological predispositions to fraud? If so, what can and should we do about them? How do we factor such information into hiring, screening, prevention, and intervention strategies? Perhaps comedian Flip Wilson was onto something when one of his characters used to say, "The Devil made me do it!"

Some figures seem to offer support for the view that some fraud/risk behavior seems to have at least some psychological, if not a neurological basis. One article reports that shoplifting occurs in the United States an astonishing 800,000 times a day, costing retailers and merchants (and, ultimately, consumers) $13 billion per year. A significant percentage of this loss appears to be at the hands of store employees, teenagers, or persons supporting a narcotics habit. But, there still remain many thousands of persons for whom the motivation may be heavily psychological, among them accused celebrities such as actress Winona Ryder, actress Hedy Lamarr, Olympic gold medalist Olga Korbut, film critic Rex Reed, former Miss America Bess Myerson, and singer Jewel. The article recounts the particular story of Gretchen Grimm, who at age six in 1918 shoplifted a lipstick as a gift to her mother and continued shoplifting until 2001, when she ended her activities at age 83 with the help of psychotherapy and medication. During this time she also worked as a nurse at the University of Iowa and raised five children.[40]

Another aspect of neuroscience research may be worth reflecting on—the manner in which our brains are evidently wired to ignore the routine and pay close attention to the unusual. We speculated earlier on the role of strangeness in occupational fraud. We may be wary of the stranger but comfortable with the face we have seen down the hall for seven years; yet in all likelihood the latter may represent a greater threat from an occupational fraud perspective. Research is still ongoing, and again we tread an area full of ethical and privacy issues, but certainly more continuing attention is warranted to such promising findings. We may discover that delving into the world of neuroscience begins to bring us into contact with the advertising business.

Advertising, with the apparently simple objective of influencing consumer choice, has utilized a variety of research techniques over the years to help improve the effectiveness and efficiency of its messages. In the 1950s motivational research was the rage, with psychologists advising companies on how to tweak their packaging and messages to enhance subliminal content. Such techniques enjoyed considerable popularity until Vance Packard skewered them in his 1957 bestseller, *The Hidden Persuaders*, and compared them to George Orwell's Big Brother. A decade or two later, physiology was the rage, with researchers using a variety of instruments to measure subjects' physical reactions to varying advertisements and products. More recently, the preferred methodology involved the use of questionnaires and focus groups to test campaigns and messages.[41]

There is now developing a school of thought, based on research in neuroscience, that holds such measures are inherently flawed, since they involve the conscious mind. As Tom Brailsford, director of technological research at Hallmark, noted with regard to consumers, "It's not that consumers won't tell you what's on their minds. It's that they can't."[42]

Many of the advances in this approach are credited to Gerald Zaltman, a marketing professor at the Harvard Business School. One writer described Zaltman and his work, noting that he created the Zaltman Metaphor Elicitation Technique, which attempts to measure attitudes about products and services.There are many who belileve this is a superior measurement device, since many people do not consciously know what influences their opinions and decisions.[43]

Accordingly, Zaltman uses photos, visual depiction, and metaphor in his research to try to better understand the relationship between the consumer and the product or advertisement at issue. This approach may be worthy of consideration within the forensic profession. We are, to a degree, in the advertising business. Our message is usually some variant of "Fraud is a betrayal of trust, it hurts other people, it has negative consequences for you, we will find out about it—Don't do it." This is well and good, but do we know how fraud is perceived by the subconscious mind of an employee? Do we know how our antifraud message is perceived? Are we even doing it right? Perhaps neuroscience can help.

Game Theory

Another potential avenue of inquiry is suggested by the book *A Beautiful Mind*, by Sylvia Nasar, which spawned the popular and Academy Award–winning movie of the same name. These works deal with the life and work of Nobel Laureate and mathematician John Nash, who spent much of his academic and research careers in the field of game theory. The RAND Corporation was, for many years, involved with the U.S. government, especially the U.S. Air Force, in attempting to apply game theory to issues of military strategy and nuclear deterrence. Nash, for several years, was deeply involved in those projects.[44] At the risk of gross oversimplification, game theory is an attempt to understand human behavior, under certain assumptions, when something is at stake.

Hal R. Varian, writing in *The New York Times*, provides some context for the development of the field research leading up to Nash's work. He notes that the eminent mathematician, John von Neumann, laid much of the ground work for modern game theory as he sought to understand the basic logic behind strategic interactions. Later, teaming with economist Oscar Morgenstern, von Neumann began to develop mathematic formulations that could represent these situations in which two or more parties or players had opposing interests. Such scenarios, often referred to as "zero-sum" games could be fanciful in nature, such as sporting events or forms of gambling. Their name derives from the simple proposition that for one player to "win," every other player must "lose." They could also, however, be deadly earnest, like wars and international economic disputes. The point was not so much the size of the stakes involved as it was to attempt to understand and mathematically represent the logic brought to bear in such exchanges.[45]

Authors Hillier and Lieberman, in their book, *Introduction to Operations Research*, offer a somewhat more generic description of the field, when they note:

Life is full of conflict and competition. Numerous examples involving adversaries in conflict include parlor games, military battles, political campaigns, athletic competition, advertising and marketing campaigns by competing business firms, and so forth. A basic feature in many of these situations is that the final outcome depends primarily upon the combination of strategies selected by the adversaries. Game theory is a mathematical theory that deals with the general features of competitive situations like these in a formal, abstract way. It places particular emphasis on the decision-making processes of the adversaries.[46]

Nasar captures at least a portion of the complexity of this field when she notes:

More than a century earlier, the French economist Antoine-Augustin Cournot had pointed out that problems of economic choice were greatly simplified when either none or a large number of other agents were present. Alone on his island, Robinson Caruso doesn't have to worry about others whose actions might affect him. Neither, though, do Adam Smith's butchers and bakers. They live in a world with so many actors that their actions, in effect, cancel each other out. But when there is more than one agent but not so many that their influence may be safely ignored, strategic behavior raises a seemingly insoluble problem: "I think that he thinks that I think that he thinks," and so forth.[47]

It was such apparent imponderables that Nash and fellow researchers were trying to resolve, with the result that advances in the field became the basis for much military doctrine, economic research, and organizational decision making. Martin Gardner has commented on the sensitivity of such issues by noting, "Much of the research on learning machines has to do with computers that steadily improve their ability to play games. Some of the work is secret—war is a game."[48]

Varian provides a sense of Nash's contributions to the field:

What Mr. Nash recognized was . . . the best choice for any single player depends critically on his beliefs about what the other players might do. . . . we look for outcomes in which each player is making an optimal choice, given the choices the other players are making.[49]

Varian goes on to note that game theory typically assumes that a player is acting with full rationality, and often humans do not always behave in a fully rational manner. While this is undoubtedly true, Nash's equilibrium succeeds often enough to be useful in several fields, and it can come close to predicting reality in many other situations.

It may be useful for us to realize that combating fraud in the workplace is also a game. We are defending the organization's assets and the opponents—those intent on committing fraud—are attacking. What strategies will best serve us?

What do they think that we think that they think that we think? Lest we become dizzy with the possibilities, Nasar tells us that many great minds and much complex research have gone into these issues, factoring in considerations such as incomplete knowledge of others' intentions or their state of knowledge being the same or different than ours, opportunities for mutual cooperation that may appear and disappear, and so on. She notes that from the time Nash did his initial research, some 50 years ago, until now much progress has been made. At the very moment in 1994 that John Nash was in a taxi to Newark Airport on his way to Stockholm to receive his medal from the King of Sweden, Vice President Al Gore was announcing "the greatest auction ever." What Gore was referring to was a unique application of game theory to conduct the largest auction of public property ever held, in this case airwave spectrum allocations. When the auction was completed, more than $7 billion had been raised.[50]

Since the events of September 11, 2001 researchers and the insurance industry have become intrigued with the potential utility of game theory for their purposes—rating the likelihood of terrorist incidents when establishing premiums for a given piece of property. Writing in *The Wall Street Journal*, Christopher Oster observes that game theory has long been used in such situations, noting: "It tries to help explain how two or more adversaries would or should act during a conflict." Oster specifically cites the work of Dr. Gordon Woo, the author of the book, *The Mathematics of Natural Catastrophes*, and a consultant for insurance companies. He recounts Woo's interest as being to attempt to understand terrorist activities as a function of their organizational networks, much like the behavior of bees in a hive. Such understanding of the stucture that "drives" their behavior, he hopes, will enhance our ability to predict it, thus affecting insurance decisions.[51]

Game theory, while a powerful technique that has been used in helping address issues of huge financial dimensions, is not an automatic panacea. Hillier and Lieberman offer a typology of game theory and its approaches to various levels of complication in strategic or competitive environments. They note, for example, that game theory is most frequently thought of in two-person, constant-sum games, in which the payoff to the players is a fixed amount, regardless of the strategies employed. The familiar zero-sum games are a version of constant-sum games, with the difference that the constant in these games is zero. At a higher level of abstraction are n-person games, where more than two players are involved. Such games are more reflective of real life, since it is common to be in situations where more than one other player has an interest. They note that international diplomacy and most business situations are representative of these types of games. They also note that as of the date of their book, 1995, existing theory for such games was less-developed than that for two-person games.

Another level of abstraction is represented by non–zero-sum games, where the sum of the payoffs need not be zero or even constant. Again, such games may be even more representative of reality, since in many business situations there can be more than one winner, with various degrees of success. Such games may also have noncompetitive aspects that can contribute to the mutual advantage or disadvantage of all players. They cite the example of the advertising strategies of competing companies that can impact not only the market share of the individual company but also the size of the overall market. Because there is the possibility of mutual gain, non–zero-sum games can be further divided into noncooperative and cooperative games, based on the degree of preplay communication that is allowed by the situation. Labor–management negotiations and international trade negotiations can be thought of as examples of cooperative games, especially since players may have the ability to form coalitions to improve their positions.

Finally, Hillier and Lieberman cite infinite games, where players have an infinite number of strategies available to them. They describe such situations as those in which the players have a continuous decision variable. Examples of such games would be decisions as to how many resources to allocate to a given task or objective, or when to execute a given action or activity. They note, however, that the calculations necessary to try to address such games are "relatively complex."[52]

Adam M. Brandenburger of the Harvard Business School and Barry J. Nalebuff of the Yale School of Management have postulated, in their book *Co-opetition*, a theory of business management based on game theory. They see most business scenarios not as either war or peace, but as a mixture of competition and cooperation. Citing the work of von Neumann, Morgenstern, Nash, and others, they note that the concept of game theory had at least part of its roots in World War II, when British naval and air forces were attempting to improve their strategies for countering the offensive being waged by the German U-boat fleet. Addressing such issues helped give birth to the concept of game theory and improved the British success rates markedly. Following the publication of *Theory of Games and Economic Behavior*, by John von Neumann and economist Oscar Morgenstern in 1944, game theory came to be employed in fields as varied as computer science, economics, military strategy, law, and even evolutionary biology. Brandenburger and Nalebuff cite the following characteristics of game theory as central to its utility:[53]

- Game theory focuses directly on the most pressing issue of all: finding the right strategy and making the right decision
- Game theory is particularly effective when there are many interdependent factors and no decision can be made in isolation from a host of other decisions
- Game theory is an especially valuable tool to share with others in your organization
- Game theory is an approach you can expand and build on

Is game theory too esoteric for our purposes? It appears to be a matter of mutual self-discovery. Those in the forensic profession need to become more conversant with game theory and what it can and cannot do, and those who practice in the game theory field need to become aware of the potential of their profession to organizations concerned with occupational fraud. Brandenburger and Nalebuff put this situation as follows:

> Many businesspeople have heard of game theory and suspect that it's a poten-
> tially powerful tool. But all the mathematics can be baffling. . . . At the same time,
> game theorists are often unfamiliar with business practice. . . . Our experience
> in teaching, research, and consulting suggest that communication between the
> worlds of game theory and business practice is both possible and valuable.[54]

Game theory might be a sizable chunk for the average organization to bite off, although I suspect many of our organizational parents use it routinely in business operations. Collectively, however, it is certainly worthy of further exploration. We know (or at least we think we know) that fraud is probably an approximately $600 billion annual problem in the United States alone. Such numbers make even the largest auction in history look small. The scenario is perfect if we think of ourselves in the classic military/game model: I and an opponent are competing for the same prize; we both have strategies to achieve our objectives; we have some degree of knowledge of what the other strategy is; and we want to win. The applicability, I believe, is obvious.

Forensic Professionals as Organizational Pathologists

Goldstein's concept of the police, or in our case the forensic professional, as pathologist is also interesting. In many important ways, it is likely that the cop on the beat has a better understanding of what is going on in town than does the mayor. The cop, particularly in the community policing models discussed, has much more daily interaction with the citizens. Forensic professionals, likewise, may also possess important information and insights that are unavailable to the CEO. Even though hamstrung by poor information systems and inadequate staffing, these professionals probably have a better sense of the state of organizational disease and dysfunction. How can these data be made available and usable? How can they be generalized away from the anecdotal toward the abstract and, thus, be useful in informing and shaping organizational decisions and processes? How can they be presented to avoid the common filters that operate to prevent bad news from rising? In the interest of protecting the messenger, how can it be done without getting the messenger shot?

The terrain here may indeed be rugged. Donald Soeken, a clinical psychologist at Saint Elizabeth's Hospital in Washington, D.C., and his wife, a statistician at the University of Maryland, conducted a study of 233 whistleblowers in 1989. They found those likely to make such disclosures were family men in their forties, possessed of a strong conscience, and maintaining high moral values. Their experiences, however, were disheartening: 90 percent were fired or demoted, 26 percent had to seek physical or psychological care, 15 percent divorced, 10 percent attempted suicide, and 8 percent went bankrupt. Even so, 84 percent said they would do it again in the same circumstances.[55]

Such unfortunate consequences are not, it seems, unknown even in agencies whose primary mission is the detection and prosecution of misconduct. Martin Edward Andersen was a manager in the U.S. Department of Justice who complained in 1997 of what he called "' a cesspool of official misconduct,' including sexual favoritism in hiring, breaches of security and visa fraud in the department's overseas criminal training program." For these acts, he alleged, he was stripped of his security clearance and transferred to a meaningless job in a warehouse. After years of legal wrangling, he was finally awarded a cash settlement, and in 2001, after he voluntarily left the Department of Justice, he received a pubic service award from the Office of Special Counsel. Speaking of such situations, James E. Fisher, director of the Emerson Electric Center for Business Ethics at St. Louis University, commented: "The lone whistle-blower is often set up against a powerful corporate or government entity with more resources and power. . . . From the get-go, you have the likelihood of retaliation." Commenting on such situations, author Marci Alboher Nusbaum noted that while all but 15 states have some form of general whistleblower legislation, the protections afforded the employee are still a "patchwork."[56] Forensic practitioners are not in the identical position to whistleblowers since it is their job to discover bad news, yet even they may be censured for doing their jobs aggressively and well.

It will be unfortunate and unproductive if forensic professionals are viewed only as snitches or persons intent on playing a serious game of gotcha. Forensic professionals as pathologist have much to offer the organization beyond the immediate issues of who is doing something wrong. By training and the nature of their duties, they are one of the few entities in the organization that is interested in "looking under the hood," and not just seeing how fast someone can make the machine run. In this regard, they can be of immense immediate and long-term benefit to the organization well beyond the scope of their official duties.

Authors Argyris and Schon have written extensively of the issue of organizational learning and the peculiar strengths and weaknesses that organizations exhibit. Many of the issues they raise are pertinent to our consideration of the role of pathologist as an aid in the enterprise of organizational learning.

First, they note there are many way to conceive of the organization. These may include conceptualizations of it as an arena of social psychology and group dynamics; a structure of authority and information flow; an institution for the achievement of social objectives; a culture; or as a theater for the interplay of conflicts of interest.[57] To some degree, they contend, each of these perspectives has merit and, to the degree it is adopted as a frame of reference, has meaning for how the organization may be said to learn. Such learning, however, can occur only through the media of individuals—the persons who constitute the organization. Given this fact, there may be serious impediments for the achievement of learning by the organization, since information flow, particularly when the news is not good, may be severely constricted.

This may be the fault of the individuals themselves, who believe that rather than report bad news, with a little additional work on their part it can be turned into good news. Also, they instinctively understand that bad news is often not well received at the top. Were they so inclined to send bad news upward, they also understand that senior management usually adopts an orientation that requires that bad news be accompanied by proposed solutions in the same package— thus more disincentive to send the bad news upward.

Once middle management is in receipt of the bad news, they also have a tendency not to report it upward. Accordingly, it goes forward, if at all, in smaller, manageable pieces. Thus they contend, does upper management receive bad news in incremental bites, usually with firm assurances that those below have the situation under control and will have it resolved promptly. The net effect of these dynamics is that those at the bottom of the ladder, where the problem was first surfaced, remain ignorant and frustrated by the fact that bad news was reported and top management apparently is doing nothing about it.

Argyris and Schon see this as a classis example of problems in organizational learning and define the issue as follows:

> Organizational learning involves the detection and correction of error. When the error detected and corrected permits the organization to carry on its present policies or achieve its present objectives, then that error-detection-and-correction process is single-loop learning. Single-loop learning is like a thermostat. . . . Double-loop learning occurs when error is detected and corrected in ways that involve the modification of an organization's underlying norms, policies, and objectives.[58]

They go on to note that most organizations are fairly good at single-loop learning, but have great difficulties in double-loop learning. One can infer from their theory that rather than this being the problem half-solved, it is a compounding issue for most organizations. That this is so, they contend, is because most organizations have two theories of organizational behavior running at the same time. The espoused theory is that the organization is open and honest and welcomes the truth. The theory in use is that presenting news that suggests the organization made or is making a mistake is disloyal. Argyris and Schon see this as not unlike an individual who, when asked how he would behave in a given situation, replies with his espoused theory. In reality, however, he may well follow a different theory in use. Often, the person may not even realize that there are two theories in operation.[59] We may reflect back to our analysis of the reporting of occupational fraud. Many more respondents to surveys say they would report it than actually do.

With regard to decisions by top management Argyris and Schon summarize these dynamics thusly:

> Questioning the original decision violated a set of nested organizational norms. The first norm was that policies and objectives, especially those that top management was excited about, should not be confronted openly. The second norm was that bad news in memos to the top had to be offset by good news. These two interdependent norms require behavior that would be disloyal to the espoused theories of management and to the formal organizational policies. Hence, the fact that these two norms existed had to be camouflaged.[60]

They further note that the interplay of these dynamics produces a double bind. If they exposed organizational errors, they would call into question a set of organizational norms that were supposed to be kept covert. If they chose not to expose the errors, they hindered the ability of the organization to learn. Were this not bad enough, there are powerful organizational incentives, in Argyris and Schon's view, to even admit that the double bind exists in the first place. To suggest that such was the case meant that the organization's espoused theory was not the real theory in operation, implying a level of trickiness to top management. The result frequently was to remain silent.

One is reminded here of Delattre's comments on "noble cause" corruption. If I am damned if I do and damned if I don't, I might as well do what is easiest. Thus we can envision the production manager who knows he cannot meet quota with the equipment he has been given, and knows also that his complaints to upper management are not welcome and not acted on. So he fudges the production numbers on the theory that he has been put in an impossible position, and when it finally blows up it will be someone else's mess to deal with.

Building on these dynamics, Argyris and Schon contend that the result is that the organization always knows less, not more, than its members. Nor is it useful to think that the executive at the top does all the learning the organization needs. They note that executives come and go, while organizations remain, with their dynamics whirling away. Here, they see a paradox. Organizations are more than mere collections of individuals, but at the same time no organization can be said to exist without such a collection. At the same time, organizational learning is not merely individual learning, yet the organization can only learn through the experiences and actions of its members.[61]

The net effect of the interplay of these norms and theories is to instruct the members of the organization as to how they should behave. Several of the messages Argyris and Schon see are synopsized as follows:[62]

- Let buried failures lie
- Keep your views of sensitive issues private; enforce the taboo against their public discussion

- Do not surface and test differences in views of organizational problems
- Avoid seeing the whole picture; allow maps of the problem to remain scattered, vague, ambiguous
- Protect yourself unilaterally—by avoiding both direct interpersonal confrontation and public discussion of sensitive issues that might expose you to blame
- Protect others unilaterally—by avoiding the testing of assumptions where that testing might evoke negative feelings, and by keeping others from exposure to blame
- Control the situation and the task—by making up your own mind about the problem, and acting on your view, and by avoiding the public inquiry that might refute your view

There is, I suspect, much that experienced organizational hands will recognize here. I certainly do. We need only think of Steve McQueen in the scene from *The Sand Pebbles*. Everyone has an issue at stake, and the questioning of base-level assumptions is perhaps the surest way to produce anxiety and a negative response. The problem we face, simply, is how do we get better without doing exactly that?

To some small degree, this is what I have attempted in this book—to question the assumptions; to engage in double-loop learning. I realize that writing a book from the safety of a computer hundreds of miles away is safer and more fun than incurring the wrath of a snarling boss three doors down, but at some point it will have to be done, unless we choose to remain quiet and pretend the elephant is nowhere to be seen.

The issue of forensic professionals as organizational pathologists raises another interesting question. While we may learn much of value that can be shared as we delve into the innards of our organizational homes, we may also learn much from being examined ourselves. Bratton notes that the policing profession, once comfortable with the ideas of community policing and alternative strategies, became much more tolerant of outsiders probing within their ranks to increase understanding and improve performance. In this regard he specifically mentions the considerable assistance provided by the Police Executive Research Form (PERF) and the Executive Session on Policing at Harvard's John F. Kennedy School of Government.

A recounting of the series of Harvard executive sessions on policing may provide a flavor of how they operated and how they benefited the police. Lory Hough, writing about the many uses to which such sessions have been put in various fields, notes the observations of Mark Moore, professor of criminal justice and director of the Hauser Center for Non-Profit Organizations. Moore and Frank Hartmann had been involved in establishing the first set of sessions on policing.

Moore observed that the executive sessions on policing lasted almost seven years, much longer than sessions on other topics, due to the interest of the participants in continuing the dialogs. Ranking police executives from around the world were involved, as were Mayors and city officials. As these sessions rolled on, he notes, there was a subtle but profound shift in emphasis—from discussing the management of crime to considering the management of fear in the community. From this slight adjustment in perspective, much of what came to be known as community policing evolved.[63]

In approaching this basic issue—how do we do a better job—the law enforcement community came to realize that it had slowly been reduced to a predominantly reactive role of *case processors*, to use Kelling's term. Over time, six or seven years to be exact, they conducted a form of self-diagnosis with the assistance of outsiders and came to the conclusion they had been focusing on the wrong goal all along. While this realization was not quick, it appears to have been effective. *The Wall Street Journal* reported on April 11, 2002, that last year the U.S. inmate population grew at the lowest rate in three decades. Maybe that is a function of the fact that a lot of the bad guys are locked up—one in every 145 Americans, nearly two million, is incarcerated—but it is still an impressive number.[64]

Such openness to outside investigation and systematic analysis did not come easily to a profession typically as closed, rigid, and hide-bound as the police. Bratton observes:

> This was an interesting period in policing because the big-city chiefs opened up their doors to the research community. PERF and the Police Foundation let these social scientists, who ten years earlier they would have locked up for demonstrating outside the Chicago convention, into their station houses to interview prisoners and riffle their files. As a result, the field of policing included a generation of social scientists many of whom probably thought they would never get involved in this world. And, in an extremely conservative and intentionally isolated profession, the idea of the professionally informed and educated police chief began to emerge.[65]

There may, at this writing, be the beginning of a cultural appreciation of the forensic profession unseen for some time. *The Wall Street Journal* reports that several accountants involved with books detailing how to spot financial irregularities are now being invited to appear on talk shows. Several others interviewed for the article recount that their once-staid profession is now seen as exciting and even sexy, because of its element of danger. A few, however, note that this is probably the profession's 15 minutes of fame, and is likely to blow over once the public becomes bored with recent corporate revelations.[66]

Sexy or not, the forensic professional as organizational pathologist will continue to serve an important and continuing role in the organization's life, for the detection of disease is always vital. As we have seen on television, doctor shows come and go, lawyer shows come and go, but the continuing importance of their professional roles lives on. Perhaps we should enjoy our newfound sexiness while we can, but realize that while sex may come and go, the significance of our function endures.

As Yates noted so many years ago in his observations on the role of the internal audit function, it is tough to dance alone. Unless senior management is of the mindset that it is better to be aware of bad news and be able to act on it, the pathologist may find that while the patient is capable of being examined, he or she cannot hear. Thus is valuable, perhaps vital, information lost. Such concerns are far from academic. *The New York Times* reported in June 2002 of the experiences of analysts and auditors on Wall Street. They saw problems and reported them and got fired for their efforts. *The Times* notes of such actions:

> What if the people who want to do the right thing can get no support, especially from executives hired to make sure regulations are followed? What if people like these are in fact punished for speaking out?[67]

Perhaps it is necessary that the power of the federal government be the motivating factor to open the lines of communication. Perhaps wise executives and board members will come to this conclusion of their own accord. Perhaps neither will happen, but given the climate of the times, it appears unlikely. In that scenario, those who choose knowledge over risk, and action over inaction, will be the ultimate winners.

CHAPTER 12

PARTNERSHIPS FOR THE FUTURE

P artnership is a key element in most of the law enforcement models examined. What degree of partnership do we have already, and is it the proper amount with the pertinent partners, or must new alliances be forged? How, in times of resource constraints, do we ask more of other entities without being perceived as the organizational pest? From whom in the organizational hierarchy do we get permission to involve these resources?

We may be able to learn much from how at least one professional in a major company has approached this task. His concepts, while pertaining to the issue of partnerships, also speak significantly to areas such as leadership, advertising, and reconceptualization. George Campbell is the President of Fidelity Security Services, Inc., an arm of the massive Fidelity Investments financial services firm. In an address he gave to the National Food Service Security Council in July 2000, he touched on many of the lessons learned while building a highly successful corporate security function.[1] While occupational fraud, and not corporate security, is our immediate focus, there is much to be learned from his experience, as both professions share many of the same issues.

The first issue Campbell cites is that top management tends to have little understanding of the security function, perceives it as not being proactive, and does not see it as having much to contribute to business decisions. Campbell refers to these factors as being part of the Influence Quotient of a corporate security program. He then lists those program elements he believes are necessary if a corporate security program is to be successful. These he refers to as a Program Legitimacy Index:[2]

- Unhindered access to the top
- Influence the strategic direction of the business.

- Acknowledged stakeholder in the corporate risk management program
- Matters are escalated, no surprises.
- Senior management responds appropriately.
- Senior management exhibits support of the security policy.
- Sufficient resources to accomplish the protection mission
- Positive impact on the ethical hygiene of the firm
- Exclusive ownership of the firm's security program
- Customer base exhibits broad knowledge of the security program and risk awareness.

We may gaze on Campbell's list of successful program attributes in awe and wonder. We may say to ourselves, "Sure, who wouldn't want their occupational fraud program to be in that shape? If my program looked like that, my job would be a hundred times easier."

The point Campbell is making is that hardly anyone inherits a security, or occupational fraud, program in such solid shape. The points he goes on to make are concerned with how one begins to achieve such an organizational presence. The first key element he cites is a qualitative reporting and analysis program. It is simply impossible to be taken seriously in an organizational context when one cannot even articulate the dimensions of the problem(s) one is seeking to address or what is causing them.

This, unfortunately, is the common refrain throughout much of the forensic community when it seeks to address issues of occupational fraud. Our definitions are leaky, our statistics are weak, and causation has been little dealt with in almost 30 years, at least in any organized and available sense.

Campbell notes that the theme he used in developing his program within Fidelity was "Share the Responsibility," meaning that corporate security was not the sole purview of his department, but rather a partnership between the security function and every other element of the organization. In commenting on the rationale needed to make these partnerships work, he is pungent: "By and large, we've done a lousy job of linking ourselves to the value equation around risk management."[3] The reason, he counsels, is simple: "You cannot influence effectively without a qualitative reporting and analysis capability."[4]

This speaks directly to issues we have already discussed regarding the need for better definitions and reporting systems to begin to capture the true size and dimensions of occupational fraud. It is also a technique that J. Edgar Hoover used with brilliant result in building the FBI from a small, weak, and politicized agency. He was able to prove to various stakeholders, from bankers to insurance executives to Members of Congress, why the work of the FBI was potentially important to them and their interests.

Campbell is arguing that for the corporate security function to have meaning to various stakeholders in the organization, it must be capable of showing them, in their terms, why the function is important to them. Specifically, why it is important in reducing their risk exposure. I have mentioned previously that this is precisely the position I took in addressing the Academic-Practitioners Symposium of the American Society for Industrial Security. Until security, or the forensic profession, can anchor itself conceptually within the organization and within the academic community, it will forever drift in a state of weakness. Our anchor, I contend, is within the risk management function.

Campbell also addresses the taboo area of advertising. Many in our profession seem to believe that advertising is somehow beneath them; that it is unbecoming for a professional. I find this position curious, given that doctors, lawyers, universities, and hospitals routinely advertise, as do houses of worship. Have we set ourselves on too lofty a plain, or more likely, have we not adapted our self-perception and our message to changing times? We, like everyone else in the world, are competing for scarce resources, be they within or without the organization. We may feel better about ourselves in our purity by not seeking to compete in the commonness of the marketplace, but we pay a hefty price. The New York Yankees have won 26 World Championships and are acknowledged to be one of the classier operations in all of professional sports. They advertise all the time. Perhaps we need to rethink some of our assumptions.

In advertising, Campbell counsels that more than mere visibility is necessary. He advocates advertising to the entities with which we seek to partner. As he puts it, "We get results and advertise. Our messages are everywhere." He sets forth a matrix of how he goes about this task within Fidelity, and it is instructive. He advertises to employees within the company using 16 mechanisms, to include log-on scripts on computers to publicizing the ethics hotline. He further advertises through 15 channels to 15 specific groups in the company, from Recruiting—Human Resources to the cleaning staff. Finally, he utilizes 15 techniques to communicate with senior management, to include the Annual Report and frequent incident reports.[5]

Campbell's advice may well be based on either a studied or intuitive understanding of the advertising business. According to John Beck, director of research at the Accenture Institute for Strategic Change, and co-author Thomas Davenport, the competition for our attention is fierce. Accordingly, it is becoming more and more difficult to get and maintain the interest of customers or clients. By way of comparison, they note that the average Sunday edition of *The New York Times* carries more factual information than was available in all the written material in the known world in the 15th century. Not only information, but products also abound and clamber to be noticed; Beck and Davenport note that the average grocery store now stocks about 40,000 items, each striving to be one of the 150 or so products the average family buys each year.[6]

Again and again, Campbell counsels that, "Effective communication has to connect to the managers' frame of reference." That is, one size does fit all. The risk issues that may be important to one area are probably not the same for the next. Doing careful research and analysis allows Campbell to craft his message to his audiences, and *audiences* is the operative word here. There are many potential partners located throughout the organization, and each has its own issues and interests. By connecting in a manner that is important to them, Campbell is demonstrating the worth of his function and setting forth a rationale why partnering is in their best interest. In this regard he is much like Bratton, who was surprised to find that in New York City the cops and the citizens had radically differing views as to what was important for the police to deal with.[7]

Finally, Campbell posits what he calls Agreed upon Indicators of Success. We often, I believe, fall into the same conceptual trap as the cops did many years ago. We define success in terms that make sense to us, but that may not be shared by many of our clients. Please note the use of the word *clients*. This is the orientation that the police and Campbell took when rethinking their operations. Those we serve are, in fact, our clients, and we need their support and approval. That they may also be our partners, as in the sense the police involved the communities they were trying to serve in partnerships, makes them all the more important.[8]

Initially we may be tempted to dismiss a function such as corporate security as not being pertinent to what we are all about. Campbell's techniques and successes may be reason enough for us to rethink our assumptions. We, too, would like to inherit an operation with the prestige and resources of Campbell's, but we probably will not. He did not, either; he built it.

Dennis Drent, writing of the need for the internal audit function to maintain relevance to the organization it serves, cites several factors that can impede this process. His list of potential problems the internal audit director may face complement Campbell's thoughts well, and are a sort of a beware-of checklist for those seeking to improve the visibility and effectiveness of their function:[9]

- The director is not well-positioned in the corporate hierarchy. The audit director's supervisor will drive the audit process unless the director reports to a highly placed executive.

- The director does not have the confidence, communication skills, or presence to deal effectively with conflicts at the executive or board level.

- The organization or its audit committee members do not fully understand the concept of internal audit or the role of internal auditing.

- The internal audit staff is quick to seek credit for their work. This credit often comes at the client's expense. Therefore, auditors gain the reputation of watchdogs, and a consultative approach to auditing becomes problematic.

- The organization's auditors do not have the skill sets necessary to be effective as consultants.

- The auditors do not have the time to be effective consultants.

One may take from the comments of Campbell and Drent a sort of chicken and the egg feeling. Certainly, many if not most forensic professionals in organizations would like to be in the position where they had high-level executive access, were involved in important decisions, had sufficient resources, and found senior management responsive when they surfaced issues. The issue is not that this is not a highly desirable state of affairs. The task is how to move from a present position of relative weakness toward this state of increased visibility and enhanced effectiveness.

In this regard, Drent offers four suggestions:[10]

1. *Hire a professional services firm to evaluate and benchmark the function to industry best practices.* This can infuse new ideas into the function and also provide current industry comparisons for use in future discussions with executive management about resources and scope of responsibility.

2. *The function must have a conceptual framework from which to be able to articulate its role when holding discussions with key customers and partners.* In the audit field, the Institute of Internal Auditors Standards for the Professional Practice of Internal Auditing and the internal control framework developed and enunciated by the Committee of Sponsoring Organizations provide useful guidance and professional reference points.

3. *Never assume the internal audit function is doing a good job.* In this regard Drent is much like Campbell, who believes the need to remain relevant to the customers' needs and frames of reference is crucial to organizational success.

4. *Develop a few key performance measurements, but these must be relevant to customer needs and perceptions.* Again, like Campbell, Drent recognizes the need for a scorecard that makes sense to those whom the function serves.

It is important also to remember that the forensic function in a given organization may be isolated in a geographic sense, but may find substantial and continuing means of support from the greater forensic community and professional associations. As the field develops, there may well be a rising tide phenomenon that, through research, scholarship, visibility, and communication, will operate to assist individual entities in their efforts at growth and development. The International Federation of Accountants (IFAC) has already endorsed such a proposition, in *The Accountancy Profession and the Fight Against Corruption,* a paper released in 1999. In it, the IFAC suggests that the profession unite and team with other professions, the business community, governmental entities, legislative bodies, regulators, and other organizations to combat corruption. The IFAC also announced its plans to work with organizations such as the World Bank, International Monetary Fund, Organization for Economic Development, and the United Nations to pursue its agenda for anticorruption legislation.[11]

The idea of partnering may, even at its most basic level, be seen as a cost-effective way of improving the effectiveness of the forensic function within the organization. Carpenter and Mahoney have addressed this issue in an article on organizational fraud when they recount their understanding of the results of the Institute of Management and Administration/Institute of Internal Auditors 1999 Business Fraud Survey:

> [I]improvement in communications would tend to make organizations more proactive in their fraud detection efforts. This need to move toward a more proactive stance is consistent with the general observations of the respondents who cited a reactive mode of response to fraud detection. Sixty percent of the respondents characterize their departments' fraud risk analysis as being reactive in nature.[12]

Larry E. Rittenberg, the Ernst & Young Professor of Accounting at the University of Wisconsin—Madison and the President of the Institute of Internal Auditors Research Foundation, has also offered some guidelines for better partnerships between internal auditors and their most natural (if not always frequent) partner, the audit committee:[13]

- Lesson 1—Corporate governance is important.
- Lesson 2—Reporting structure does matter.
- Lesson 3—Accounting issues and controls are important.
- Lesson 4—Risk is the dominant framework for internal audit work.
- Lesson 5—The audit committee needs an effective information system.
- Lesson 6—Auditors Must Understand The Business. . . . What is the company's business? Answers to that question will significantly affect both revenue recognition and risks.
- Lesson 7—Auditors can assist in educating board and audit committee members.
- Lesson 8—Related party transactions and complex financial instruments present substantial risks.
- Lesson 9—Reporting is a process, not an event.
- Lesson 10—Commit to continuous improvement.

Were we to substitute the term *forensic professional* for *auditor* in the previous list, I believe we would see, as we did with Campbell, some suggestions for activities that are more likely to broaden our partnership opportunities and otherwise improve our organizational effectiveness.

Diane Sears Campbell, in discussing the new threats forms of cyberfraud represent to the organization, counsels the need for internal auditors to form partnership alliances with information technology professionals if truly effective controls are to be developed in these areas. To do this effectively, however, she warns that fears about compromise of audit independence will have to be set aside.[14] Partnerships, like marriages, carry an element of risk as well as reward. One can be judicious in limiting the amount of risk, but some element of it will always be present.

While they are separated by a fair amount of the alphabet, advertising and partnerships are, in many ways, quite close. Authors Brandenburger and Nalebuff provide a sense of this reciprocity when they discuss the merits of complements —finding firms or entities that are complementary to an organization's objectives or interests. Referring to the automobile industry at the beginning of the century, they observe:

> Having built a better mousetrap, the fledging auto industry didn't leave it to others. . . . While it couldn't pave all the roads itself, it got many started. In 1913 General Motors, Hudson, Packard, and Willys-Overland, together with Goodyear tires and Prest-O-Lite headlights, set up the Lincoln Highway Association. . . . The association built "seedling miles" along the proposed transcontinental route. People saw the feasibility and value of paved roads and lobbied the government to fill in the gaps. . . . by 1922 the first five transcontinental highways, including the Lincoln, had been completed.[15]

Likewise, they note, the Michelin company got into the tour guide and restaurant rating business, often pointing out the scenic beauty to be enjoyed on less-than-direct routes. In so doing, they sought to make the trip, and not just the destination, part of the fun. And, being in the tire business, longer trips meant people buying more tires.[16]

They also comment on the phenomenon of grouped stores. In New York City, for example, it is common to see many competing firms and companies operating literally side by side. West 47th Street has a mass of jewelry stores; West 48th Street has music stores; the lower east side contains many establishments selling lighting fixtures; and, perhaps most famous of all, Broadway is home to much of the theatrical industry. While each establishment competes vigorously with all the others in its line of endeavor, the fact of their grouping also helps create the market that sustains them all. Being close, potential buyers are drawn to the convenience of having multiple choices literally next door to each other. Suppliers likewise, find it easier, and therefore cheaper, to deliver when they can make several calls at one location.[17]

Partnership, we once noted, is an admission of weakness. Were things perfect, there would be no need to partner, absent altruistic motivations. The ideas discussed regarding partnership opportunities and issues are set forth as items to consider to create true synergies that will avoid the sort of zero-sum turf war mentality that is all too common in many organizations. Good partnerships, in the current management vernacular, can be win-win events where both parties come away enhanced, and not diminished. The old mass production mentality of organizational effectiveness decreed that for one to get better, they had to be bigger. This conceptualization of organizational dynamics is behind most of the turf wars we have all been through, in which my win is your loss, since we are locked into a zero-sum game. This was precisely the rationale that drove the police for many years—the insatiable and recurring need for more, since more was perceived as the only way to achieve better. Only when more and better were disconnected was significant progress made.

We should also allow for the operation in organizational environments of what is referred to as the Heisenberg principle in physics—you cannot interact with a system without changing it.[18] It is likely that by the act of attempting or exploring partnership opportunities, one will have some measure of impact on the system. The impact may be positive or negative, but either provides some value. A positive result is the potential beginning of a synergy not before recognized. A negative result, while disappointing, is more information than one possessed before the contact was made and, like the oil business, knowing where *not* to drill is also information that has value. One can direct one's efforts elsewhere. Partnerships, it appears, can offer a way out of more and movement toward better.

CHAPTER 13

ENVIRONMENTAL AND ORGANIZATIONAL INTELLIGENCE

Intelligence in an age of automation may be bountiful but out of reach. Certainly, most organizations rely heavily on computers, and they can produce a wealth of data useful to us in helping define the problems of our organizations. But we may have far less access to these systems than we need and, in my professional experience, most organizations have little skill in interrogating their own data systems. Are there ways to effectively leverage existing systems for the data we require, or must we build our own, and, if so, how and at what cost? If this is impossible or incomplete, how do we benchmark the effectiveness of what we attempt, much less use data (as in Compstat) as a design, management, and targeting input?

I am indebted to Carson Dunbar, the former Superintendent of the New Jersey State Police, for his thoughts on the issue of *discretionary law enforcement.* In using this term, he refers to the situation that most sworn law enforcement personnel find themselves in. They have more than they can handle and must develop some sort of mechanism, usually intuitive and experiential, as to how to prioritize what will receive their attention. Howard Cox, of the Office of the Inspector General in the U.S. Postal Service, has put this experience into a context most organizations face when he observes, "If you don't recognize that the threat is out there, you can't protect yourself against it."[1]

Unfortunately, one could well argue the proposition that most organizations do not have the luxury of being discretionary in their antifraud efforts. They probably have more than they can handle now, but without adequate organizational intelligence, they have no grounded, verifiable idea of what unseen threats they should be addressing. Thus, as Cox observes, they are in the unenviable position of being asked to defend against threats unknown and unseen.

An article in *The New York Times* reported on the success of a company called iJet Travel Intelligence. This Washington, D.C.–area organization is staffed with former intelligence officers and analysts, and provides, for a fee, travel intelligence for organization executives traveling abroad. This is possible, according to Chief Executive D. Bruce McIndoe, because of computers. He comments: "For a couple of thousands of dollars of technology, we're doing right now what would have cost the federal government from $2 million to $20 million only five to eight years ago, not to mention in the 1950s and 60s, when it wasn't even feasible to collect the same amount of data."[2] Among the types of data collected, analyzed, and made available to clients are transportation delays, issues, and advisories; political intelligence; health and epidemiology; environmental data; weather; and crime information.[3]

Organizational interest in such capabilities is interesting for three reasons:

1. It indicates that organizational executives are interested in both their personal safety and the efficiency of their travel schedules. To the degree that they have safety concerns, this is a form of risk management, just like their exposure to occupational fraud.

2. The power of computers, much like the Compstat program in New York City, is being harnessed to produce real-time information of value at competitive rates.

3. It may unfortunately indicate that many executives are more concerned about risk when away than while at home. The latter is disturbing, since home is where they spend most of their time and home is where a significant portion, if not most, of the organizational resources in their custody are located.

Have they been lulled into a false sense of security by the familiarity of their home surroundings? Perhaps, and if so this is unfortunate, because we have seen how the routineness and sameness of faces and names can mask a plethora of occupational fraud. Away is strange, and therefore to be feared. Home is familiar and, therefore, assumed to be safe. Those interested in committing fraud in the workplace count on this protective coloration to protect them. The executives, rightfully concerned about so many risks of which they have awareness, blissfully ignore those they have never bothered to expose, even though these unseen threats may do them and their organizations substantially more damage than foreign travel.

In thinking about home and how little most of us really know about it, Henry's history of the Compstat program may offer some useful insights. As noted, the program was a vast improvement over the push pin system of the past, and it was also inexpensive to implement, requiring just some off-the-shelf software and a couple of personal computers. Its reports were intentionally structured to be simple and easy to digest. Police commanders are busy people and, at least at the time Compstat was introduced, not usually familiar with the more esoteric forms of statistical analysis. After a bit of experience with the program, the

NYPD learned that Compstat could provide deeper insights as well. Injuries and sick time, analyzed by precinct, could provide indications of the morale in that location and have implications for the efficacy of crime reduction efforts. The old push pin system might show that one shooting, two drug arrests, and three robberies took place near one corner in a 36-hour period. Compstat could provide additional information that might be able to link these incidents through analysis of common participants, types of weapons used, gangs involved, or other data. Finally, Compstat helped flush out a problem created innocently by a vagary of the NYPD's measurement systems.

At the time, an incident could be cleared by an arrest. The operative word here is *an*. Under the old system of analysis, a robbery, for example, was one pin on the map and could represent one perpetrator or a half a dozen; however, under the system used at the time, as soon as one arrest was made in a given matter it was considered cleared. The pin was removed from the map, although there were five more bad guys out there. Some commanders in some busy precincts saw the effort to nail remaining offenders after the first arrest as wasting resources, creating even more dreaded paperwork, and consuming precious overtime that could be used on fresh offenses.[4] That this worked to defeat the department's objective of reducing crime was overshadowed by the fact that it maximized the score in a game the department had unintentionally created.

On a national basis, the experience of the FBI in the development and evolution of its Uniform Crime Reporting Program (UCRP) may be both instructive and, perhaps, a bit discouraging in this endeavor. The UCRP collects data from cities with more than 10,000 inhabitants, suburban and rural counties, colleges and universities. Some 17,000 agencies contribute data to the system, which results in the annual *Crime in the United States* report. A handbook is distributed to reporting agencies to try to ensure that data are uniformly collected and characterized.[5] By 1968 this reporting covered 97 percent of people living in major cities, 75 percent of people living in rural areas, and 92 percent of the overall U.S. population.[6]

Begun in 1930, the UCRP began to undergo a significant revamping and updating in the late 1970s to better capture crime and related data, and is now in its third incarnation, the National Incident-Based Reporting System (NIBRS).[7] The objectives of the NIBRS are described as follows:

An indispensable tool in the war against crime is the ability to identify with precision when and where crime takes place, what form it takes, and the characteristics of its victims and perpetrators. Armed with such information, law enforcement can better make its case to acquire the resources it needs to fight crime and, after obtaining those resources, use them in the most efficient and effective manner. NIBRS provides law enforcement with that tool because it is capable of producing more detailed, accurate, and meaningful data than those produced by the traditional UCR Program.[8]

Such a comprehensive system, designed to capture data about hundreds if not thousands of types of crimes and the circumstances under which they take place is no small undertaking, even after 70 years of development and evolution. Chilton, Major, and Propheter, in a paper presented at the 1998 annual meeting of the American Society of Criminologists in Washington, D.C., attempt to address this complexity when they note this is an effort "to fill an information gap produced by the conversion from the UCR summary statistics system to an incident-based UCR system. . . . We examine some of the difficulties related to the conversion to the new approach, including counting rules, table titles, and the possibilities for confusion among recipients of the information."[9]

They go on to recount some of the factors that make the seemingly straightforward task of collecting crime data a larger task than one might imagine:

An incident in the National Incident-Based Reporting System (NIBRS) is defined as one or more offenses committed by the same offender or group of offenders acting in concert, at the same time and place. However, counting offenses in the new system is more complicated than it is in the summary statistics program because NIBRS collects information about incidents, offenses, victims, offenders, the property involved, and arrests. Counting is further complicated by the possibility of multiple offenses, multiple victims, multiple offenders, and multiple arrests within an incident.[10]

Such complexity is suggested by the fact that the National Incident-Based Reporting System, *Volume 1: Collection Guidelines*, is 128 pages in length. Even in the era of NIBRS, a system built on decades of organizational experience in capturing crime data, there are still problems. Kramer and Fiedler note that even in an NIBRS environment there may still be important issues left open:

Law enforcement is data-driven. Departments collect lots of numbers and are calculating and aggregating numerous police activities. These data are used to make operational decisions. Often decisions are made on anecdotal information, leaving open the possibility for subjective rather than objective information. Even the numbers that are collected may not reflect the reality of the situation. Why?

To put it simply, there is a problem in the policing profession with traditional measurements. The problem begins with the data we capture, how we capture it, and what we do with it.

Traditional measurements, such as the Uniform Crime Report Rate, the NIBRS report, arrests, and tickets, tabulate only events. They do not measure whether the activities were completed efficiently and effectively, and they don't describe what impact the activities had on the community.[11]

The authors go on to argue that the only realistic answer to addressing continuing issues around data collection is to create and implement a learning organization that is continually in the process of self-examination and self-improvement.

As poorly equipped as the forensic profession, and its practitioners, may be to effectively measure the volume and nature of the problems they are being asked to face, there may even be a glint of good news in this relative vacuum. It may be that the only thing worse than having no system at all is having an existing system, in this case the Uniform Crime Reports, and trying to manage the changeover to a new environment, namely the NIBRS. *The Law Enforcement News*, one of the leading police newsletters in the nation, recently ran an article about the experiences of one department, Memphis, Tennessee, in making the transition. Command officers involved in the process reported the effort was a "nightmare," requiring the installation of a new reporting system; finding and paying for a vendor to install the new system; training police officers how to use the new system, which had more than five times the number of data entry possibilities for the recording of incidents; doubling the number of data-entry support personnel; and having to run parallel systems for the 18-month changeover period.[12] The good news was that, once implemented, much valuable and useful data was being captured.

Is the FBI experience good news or bad news for the forensic profession as it attempts to better define the size and nature of the occupational fraud problem in the United States? I would argue it is a bit of both. Certainly 70 years of development is a long time, and surely the effort consumed a huge amount of resources along the way, but we must remember the law enforcement task is vastly greater than ours, in simple terms of the sheer number of offenses they are trying to track. Complexity has been added with time. The basic UCRP sought to record arrests and reports to police of crimes committed. The NIBRS is much more comprehensive, in an attempt to better capture the state of crime in the United States, including incidents known to the police, rather than just formal police reports and arrests. It also attempts to capture much more data pertaining to the personal characteristics and circumstances of both the victim(s) and offender(s).

We can learn from the UCRP and its successes and failures along the way. We can also adopt a much more narrow range of offenses we wish to track. Since we are dealing with occupational fraud, we have an inherent advantage, in that we already have substantial amounts of personal data (e.g., age, sex, education, length of service) available to us, since the perpetrators here are, by definition, our own employees. We will have to deal with the issue of standard reporting formats, but this again is a much easier task than that faced by the UCRP, with 17,000 reporting agencies. We will have to make some tough and sometimes subtle decisions with regard to issues of compromise of intellectual property and computer crimes, but this must be done, as both become issues of greater and greater import to us and our profession on a daily basis. We need a central rule-making body to set definitions, collect data, perform analysis, and issue reports.

Henry, in his history of the Compstat program, has commented on its utility for the field of corporate and private security and has set forth his thoughts on the demands of such a system if it is to be of maximum value to the organization. While he notes such systems must be capable of answering the classic, "who, what, why, when, where" array of questions for significant effectiveness, a typology of offenses or conditions must be developed and appropriate training provided in the proper use of the system.[13]

One effort in this direction, albeit much broader in scope, was made in 1995 by the National Fraud Investigation Center. In 1995, with input from law enforcement agencies and professional groups, it attempted to create a system of Fraud Identification Codes to better capture fraud data. By its conclusion, the project had identified over 600 types of fraud and concluded that some system of this type was vital to gaining an understanding of the true extent of these problems.[14]

These observations are well taken. The FIC concept is interesting but obviously designed to capture a broad range of economic offenses well beyond occupational fraud. These include banking, credit cards, health care, insurance, securities, telecommunications, intellectual property and computer crime, and identity theft.[15] Further, as the National Fraud Center indicates, there are still significant issues to be dealt with in regard to reporting mandates and incentives. We should note also that in the list of areas the FIC seeks to address, occupational fraud is not among them. This is not a fault of the FIC or its sponsors; they were simply looking at a huge problem—economic crime—from a different angle.

We might also be well served by looking closely at the work being done by the Ethics Officer Association (EOA) in its effort to develop an ISO-type standard for ethics and compliance programs that will be usable across industry and national boundaries. In writing about this project, Essrig has raised several issues of definition and the potential relevance of related fields that are highly similar to what we encounter when we begin to think systematically about occupational fraud. Perhaps the EOA and its affiliated organizations and institutions can provide us with some valuable guidance from their experiences in this regard. Other organizations of potential value in such efforts include, at a minimum:[16]

- The Ethics Resource Center
- The Institute For Global Ethics
- International Business Ethics Institute
- European Institute For Business Ethics
- Lockheed Martin Corporation, Corporate Ethics Online Information
- KPMG Business Ethics
- The Institute for Applied and Professional Ethics
- Illinois Institute of Technology, Center for the Study of Ethics in the Professions, Codes of Ethics Online Project

It may be that our greatest challenge will be the reluctance of victim organizations to make reports. In this regard they seem to behave much like individual victims. The National Public Survey on White Collar Crime conducted by the National White Collar Crime Center reported that less than one in ten fraud incidents were reported to a law enforcement agency, and the Ernst & Young LLP—Canada fraud survey found there was a 50 percent drop from those who said they would report a fraud in the workplace and those who actually did file such reports. Likewise, at least with regard to computer incidents, both public and private organizations appear to be similarly silent. Reporting on an FBI survey of public and private organizations, *The New York Times* reported:

> The survey found that about 90 percent of respondents detected computer security attacks in the last year but that only 34 percent reported those attacks to authorities. Many respondents cited the fear of bad publicity about computer security.[17]

The *2002 Report to the Nation* also seems to bear this tendency out. We have seen that larger losses are more likely to be reported to law enforcement authorities than are smaller losses, and that fear of bad publicity, reaching private settlements, and the victim organization's desire for closure are the most cited reasons for taking no legal action.[18]

Shover and Wright, writing about corporate crime, also advance several rationales for this state of affairs. Although their focus is corporate crime, I suspect many of these motivations apply to occupational fraud as well. They include the fact that the offense may look routine in its initial appearance; victims may be unfamiliar with regard to where to report the offense; and they may have embarrassment, shame, or a sense of feeling "I should have been more careful."[19] Probably compounding this behavior is the fact, as noted by Moore and Mills, that for many decades victims of street crime were also ignored by researchers interested in criminal justice matters.[20]

If researchers, the courts, and the police could ignore victims of often-violent street crime—victims who had faces and voices and names and injuries—for so many years, is it any wonder that impersonal organizations garnered even less attention? As a consequence of that, could it be that many organizations simply gave up, adding yet another motivation to their already stout list of reasons for underreporting? Moore and Mills, again speaking of corporate fraud, recount several studies that tended to demonstrate that many victims found the official responses to their complaints less than encouraging, to the point where they finally gave up.[21] Perhaps not surprising, but again these were people with legitimate complaints of having been swindled. If they encountered resistance and indifference, how does the faceless organization fare? At what point does it, too, give up?

Organizational America also appears reluctant to report other problems as well. The Bureau of Justice Statistics reports that only 44.2 percent of violent victimizations that occur in the workplace are ever reported to the police. Without such reporting not only is the size of the problem masked, but the police are unable to work with companies to craft more effective deterrence strategies. Stephen Doherty, writing of his experiences in working with companies in Wakefield, Massachusetts to reduce such violence, puts the consequences of this posture as follows:

> This failure of businesses to report lower-level incidents and the reluctance of police to aggressively tackle the issue only empowers the perpetrators and diminishes the victims. Ultimately, these unreported smaller incidents are precursors to larger acts of violence. If you don't deal with the simple assault, you may eventually have to deal with homicide.[22]

That organizations choose not to report is perhaps not surprising, since organizations are nothing more than collections of people, and they also tend not to report. Richard Titus has observed that while the FBI's UCRP is arguably the best-known and most-used source of crime data, surveys indicate that fewer than half of all criminal incidents ever get reported to a law enforcement agency.[23] Because of such issues, note Jenkins and Braithwaite, they and other researchers into corporate offending rates tend to rely on case studies, absent the availability of better statistics.[24]

Even schools, which are highly sensitive to issues of personal safety after the events at Columbine and other locations, have imperfect records when it comes to reporting issues and incidents. The National Association of School Resource Officers, representing those police officers who are routinely assigned to schools, is the largest such organization of its kind. In a survey it conducted of 689 members, it found that 99 percent of officers believed their presence made a difference in school safety and 86 percent believed it improved school reporting of incidents. Eighty-four percent, however, believed that in general crimes on school properties are still underreported to the police.[25]

Issues of organizational reporting will represent a major hurdle for the forensic profession to overcome if it is to move toward greater congruence in defining the size and nature of the problems that confront it. At the same time, the profession is not totally at the mercy of the discretion and motivation of others. David Banks, for example, has written of the promise shown by marrying the concepts of Benford's Law—a statistical analysis technique developed in the 1930s to attempt to determine if a given distribution of numbers was the product of chance or indicated some sort of human intervention—with the modern powers of computers and automated spreadsheets. At this stage, Banks notes, in the hands of a skilled and experienced forensic investigator, such analytical capabilities may be useful in an increasing number of circumstances to make early assessments as to the possibility of fraudulent activities having taken place.[26]

It is, admittedly, one thing to be able to look at the activities in one account or series of invoices and make informed judgments as to the likelihood of fraud or human manipulation being present; it is quite another to be able to look at the financial and quantitative representations of an entire organization and make similar judgments. The developments around the use of Benford's law in an age of automation may offer promise for those in the field to continue to explore approaches to organizational diagnosis based on experience, statistical analysis, and the increasing power of computers.

CHAPTER 14

RECONCEPTUALIZATION

In thinking about issues of reconceptualization, there is perhaps no set of examples as large and immediate as the high-tech/dotcom companies. Although their rise was rapid and the demise of many was just as swift, they perhaps forever changed how at least a portion of the business psyche operates. Hype and overblown projections aside, they forced a fundamental rethinking of many previously held business axioms and assumptions: revenue and cash flow were vital to attract financing and achieve success; customers had to be able to "see, feel, and smell" a company before they would trust it; intellectual works such as records, books, and movies were the clear property of their creators and owners; ordinary people would not consummate sizable financial transactions or invest over the anonymous and impersonal Internet; no one in their right mind would give away a revolutionary piece of software like Linux; someone in Maine could only buy a rocking chair from someone in Arizona if they happened to be there on vacation; serious issues of technological development were the stuff of corporate laboratories and PhDs in white smocks, not students, dropouts, or teenagers; people would not bid on items that had a set price, like airline seats, nor would companies permit this; and the Saturday afternoon visit to the car dealership to kick the tires and talk to the guy in the plaid sports coat was how automotive purchasing decisions were made.

These and many other assumptions about business decisions were forever altered by the presence of technology that permitted a fundamental rethinking of business models that had been in existence for centuries. It may be instructive to sample some of this "new age" thinking and speculate as to how it may be applied to the forensic profession.

Fast Company is a magazine devoted to doing business in the high-tech/dotcom environment. In its February 2002 issue, it featured a series of articles about how

even these young and changing companies needed to adjust in a period of economic softness and uncertainty. The underlying tone of much of the advice was
established by author Fara Warner, quoting Dennis Pawley, a former Chrysler
executive charged with bringing Chrysler into a more competitive position vis-à-
vis its rivals: "We had all the tools. But what I failed to recognize was that the
way people think is more important than the tools they use."[1]

To more fully appreciate the importance of thinking, or perhaps more accurately, rethinking, about a business in need of change, we can turn to another
article in the same issue, "Nine Ways to Fix a Broken Brand," by Scott Bedbury.[2]
Bedbury helped build both Nike and Starbucks into national brands before starting his own branding company. While Bedbury is speaking to issues of product
branding, his observations are equally applicable to service branding. And, I
would argue, the forensic profession is fully capable of being thought of as a
service industry, much like law or medicine.

Bedbury offers nine factors to be analyzed when brands begin to die:

1. *A brand is broken.*

Bedbury notes that the common reaction to signs of trouble is to do something—quick. This may lead to crash meetings of the brass, counsel to spend
more, advice to spend less, impulses to fire the marketing director or outside ad
agency, and so on. The good news is that everyone has an opinion; the bad news
is that that is all they are—opinions. Bedbury counsels careful research to determine what went wrong, when, and why before launching into a premature fix.

How many times have we in the forensic profession been in the same boat?
Our superiors and clients decide one day, for whatever reason(s), that we are not
getting it done, or we are too expensive, or there has been yet another horror
show in some department. In short, our brand is broken. What do we normally
do? We respond—everyone has an idea (or opinion). We tighten up, we become
more aggressive and visible, we write blistering memos, we nail a couple of high-
profile violators. Our crackdowns on fraud, or travel and expense excesses, or
personal telephone use, or accepting gifts from vendors are just that—crackdowns. They are not responses to the problem because we really do not know
exactly what the problem is, but we display our intent, energy, and, hopefully,
worth, by getting busy.

2. *A brand is disjointed or without direction.*

Bedbury suggests following the advice of Plato: focus on essence. What is the
core essence of your product or service, and how has that essence been portrayed? If incremental adjustments have weakened or changed the message
around essence, then confusion is the probable result. To a large degree this issue
lies at the heart of reconceptualization: How do we view ourselves? Are we part

of the audit function, corporate finance, risk management, or some other function? Have our daily activities branded us within the organization as something we did not wish to become?

There is a story told about five monkeys in a research cage. A banana is suspended in the cage above a set of steps. When one monkey climbs the steps to reach the banana, the others are sprayed with cold water. Soon, any monkey that attempts to climb the steps is attacked by the others, since they do not want to be sprayed. Then, one by one, the monkeys are replaced and the cold water is eliminated. Each new monkey learns to attack any other monkey who tries to climb the steps because that is what it sees the other monkeys doing. Soon, the entire population of monkeys is new, none having ever been sprayed with cold water. They still follow the pattern of punishing any monkey who tries for the banana, since that is what they have learned.

James Lardner and Thomas Repetto have commented on this phenomenon in police departments in their book *NYPD: A City and Its Police*. Lardner was a member of the Washington, D.C. police department before embarking on a successful career as a journalist and senior writer for *U.S. News & World Report*. Repetto, the head of the New York Citizens Crime Commission, is a former police commander with a doctorate from Harvard. Regarding the power of institutional memory, they note:

> [T]he NYPD has demonstrated time and again—that its appointed leaders are no match for what more prescient observers called its "inner life." In chronicling the affairs of this remarkable institution, we mean to zero in on that inner life—on the traditions, the fears, the lore, and all the lessons, official and unofficial, spoken and silent, that cops pass along from generation to generation, beginning with that fateful first night on patrol, when the veteran tells the rookie: "Forget everything you learned in the academy, kid."[3]

3. *A brand is old hat and boring.*

Bedbury here notes the significant contributions of Abraham Maslow and his now famous hierarchical need theory. Basically, Maslow contends that basic survival needs are at the bottom of the pyramid, with higher needs becoming more and more psychological in nature. He postulates that as basic needs are satisfied humans tend to seek satisfaction at higher and higher levels. If we accept Maslow's proposition, how does it relate to what we do?

Bedbury notes that the highly successful Starbucks chain became so because it realized that while coffee was a commodity, much like any other commodity with dozens of choices available, one could sell the coffee experience. To depart from Bedbury for a moment, let us think of a meal. Let us assume it was possible to take a pill that would provide all of the nutritional benefit of a four-course dinner in a fine restaurant. Let us envision the restaurant—soft music, crisp linen, gleaming silverware, flowers, attentive waiters, and candles. Now let us envision the pill—small, round, pink. Are we buying the nutrition or the dining experience?

Think, if you will, about Listerine. The product has been around, largely unchanged, since 1879. That's 14 years after the end of the Civil War! Owned by Pfizer, it recently underwent a spectacular rebirth, as recounted in an article by Kevin Markey about Pfizer executive Maurice Renshaw:

> America's ceaseless war on bad breath gained a mighty weapon last fall— Listerine PocketPaks. In place of a rinse, the thumbnail-size carrying cases from Pfizer Inc. contain green ultra-thin, celluloid-like strips, which melt on the tongue and pack a familiar Listerine wallop. The new product promises to rein- vent oral hygiene by making mouthwash edible, highly portable, and arguably, tasty. It has already had a topsy-turvy effect on domestic breath freshener sales; after a mere four weeks in stores, germ-killing Listerine PowerPaks strips stormed to the top spot. . . . Pfizer took a venerable brand with great name recognition, applied new technology—dissolvable film—and spun off a thor- oughly contemporary product.[4]

But, we may respond, we are not in the selling business. We are necessary pro- fessionals, highly trained, our existence even mandated by law, custom, or policy. That may well be true, but even that which is mandated can be boring. One of the more frequent complaints I hear from forensic and security professionals is that they are viewed by their organizations as a necessary evil that does not add to the bottom line. Perhaps selling is more important than we think.

4. *A brand is lifeless.*

Even good ideas can run their course and become stale, says Bedbury. Banana Republic started out as a chain with a cute gimmick, a safari atmosphere, and was successful for a while. But, time caught up with it and it was only when the Gap acquired it that it could be reinvented and rejuvenated as a different type of clothing retailer.

In our experience, we have all seen people who seemed to languish in one depart- ment or function, then take off in another. So, too, can departments and functions also become reborn by a change in organizational scenery. I have cautioned against change for the sake of change, and I believe the observation is valid; however, some- times movement can result in a better fit and an increase in productivity and vitality.

Perhaps we, too, need to change—without moving or being acquired. There is perhaps a point where concepts like brand, culture, and community begin to merge. Dana Beth Ardi, a human capital partner at JPMorgan Partners, has commented on this phenomenon in a recent issue of *Forbes ASAP* magazine. She noted that the new economy represented by the "dot.com" revolution was really a reconceptualization of the very definition of "work." The knowledge workers of the new economy wanted to join communities, not companies. They rallied to the concept of "brand" and "culture" as ways of identifying with these communities, and saw the building of a brand as a sort of process of creating their own identities as they went. Aided by flat forms of organization, she notes, the "...seeds of the Human Capital Movement were planted and cultivated. This has forever changed the way Americans work."[5]

Perhaps we as a profession can more profitably think of ourselves not only as employees of organization A or B, but also as members of a community defined by professional skills and interests. In being members of that community—of forensic professionals—we may find more value to ourselves and bring more value to our organization, whether it be A or B.

5. *A brand represents only its past.*

Bedbury here notes that success can be a double-edged sword: It can build and sustain growth—to a point, but if the base product or message is too narrow, there will eventually come a time when the flower outgrows the pot. He notes that Nike had this problem. They were highly successful with competitive male athletes and had adopted a "wimps need not apply" tone to their corporate message. The problem was that there was a natural limit to the size of this market. Nike needed to expand its market to women, casual athletes, older people, and those who would purchase the brand for simple mall walks, but they needed to do this without losing their solid male/serious athlete base. Bedbury notes the "Just Do It" campaign was the answer they found after one or two false starts. It had a much broader appeal without losing contact with the base of support.

We are not in the shoe business, but we do have an audience—customers, if you will. Who are they? Is this base too narrow and, if so, how can we expand it without losing touch with the primary core? If we are part of the organization's audit function, does this mean we have no value to corporate finance, legal, human resources, public relations, or risk management? We may perhaps benefit greatly if we start thinking about our profession as a sales organization with customers. How do we get more customers?

6. *A brand lacks width.*

Bedbury suggests five steps to increase brandwidth. The first is *co-branding*; partnering with another entity that brings value to your core business because they have resources or capabilities that you do not. We saw earlier that this was one of the more common strategies adopted by many law enforcement organizations as they began to rethink the business they were in. Bedbury notes that when Starbucks aligned with United Airlines, each partner got a benefit: United was able to serve its customers a premium coffee during their flight and Starbucks got exposed to people who had perhaps never tried their product.

Second, try to achieve *brand extension*. Bedbury recounts the experience of *Time* magazine, which for years had a popular section in each edition about interesting people. *Time* saw the potential in expanding on this interest, and *People* magazine was born. So successful was *People* that it, in turn, spun off another publication, *Teen People*.

Starbucks also sought *new distribution channels*, Bedbury notes third. In addition to their effort with United Airlines, Starbucks also put whole bean and ground coffee products into 30,000 grocery stores to create a complementary channel for their product. Now the folks coming off those United flights had even more opportunities to find the product to which they had been exposed.

The fourth step cited by Bedbury is *new product categories*. Ralph Lauren now has a line of home paints. Martha Stewart moved from culinary interests into an entire line of clothing and other products. Starbucks, in the coffee business, launched a brand of coffee ice cream that in six months became the best-selling coffee ice cream in the country.

Finally, per Bedbury, consider creating a *subbrand*. Nike is a successful brand, but Air Jordan is an even more successful subbrand. Toyota has long been a force in the automotive business, but its Lexus subbrand is even better known, and many buyers are only vaguely aware that it is a Toyota product.

The possibilities of these concepts in the forensic profession are intriguing. Partnerships seem to be a natural avenue to explore, and perhaps many forensic professionals operate in that mode today. Other possibilities are surely present, if not evident. We need to think clearly about what we produce. Is it investigations, service, analysis of data, responsiveness, or some mixture? Whatever it is, it is capable of being thought of as a product and, thereby, may well obey the laws of marketing and branding. We may wish to ponder the benefits of so doing.

7. The brand is too new and is yet to be accepted.

Bedbury here notes that raising a brand is much like raising children. It takes commitment, consistent values, and a long time. The payoff is that it can be done, can be done well, and the brand can outlive the parents. This may not be possible if one is subject to excessive turnover and shuffled responsibilities. In this regard Bedbury is much like Kelling and Barsky, who have both commented on the need for consistency of leadership to achieve significant social change.

The possibilities for change we are discussing within the forensic profession may be, in some instances, profound. Can we realistically expect these changes to take place if there is significant movement at the top? Within a given organization that is probably a reasonable assessment. There are few long-tenured coaches in Division I-A college athletics, since immediate performance or rapid dismissal seems to be the common model; however, those coaches that have remained in place for decades are almost always associated with notable programs, both athletically and academically.

We may find such tenure and security in some organizations, but it will probably not be the common case. One remedy we may have at hand is professional associations. These are natural catch basins for the collected wisdom and experiences of their members, and they often have more stable leadership to assist in the guidance of change. In short, it may not be necessary to be about the task of reinventing the wheel simultaneously in hundreds of organizations. If that happens, fine. I believe the profession will be stronger for it, but should that not occur, there may still be significant advances to be made from a professional, associational level.

8. *A brand is seen as a commodity.*

Anything that is left to sit long enough runs the risk of becoming a commodity. Bedbury notes that there were great coffee sellers long before Starbucks, but these companies saw themselves as being in the business of keeping grocery chains—their distribution channel—happy. Eventually, their goods were stacked next to each other—rows and rows of red and green cans, each trying to catch the eye of a potential purchaser. From time to time a promotion could raise one can an inch higher than the others, a significant advantage when all the cans look essentially the same and are filled with about the same stuff. But, promotions are just that—short-lived events that eventually end and restore the rows to their previous uniformity. The idea of a continuous promotion really made no sense, since a continuous promotion—a contradiction in terms, really—is a price reduction. In a war of price reductions, no one wins in the long run, as American automobile manufacturers have learned several times over.

We, too, risk becoming a commodity. One of the more common complaints heard from audit partners in the Big Four professional services firms is that auditing has become a commodity. Once the province of long-term relationships, the industry seems over the past several decades to have become a commodity, with buyers seeing one pound of auditing being pretty much like the next. As a result, there has been price pressure to attract or retain business and this, in turn, has caused firms to seek greater and greater efficiencies in the conduct of audits as they become more competitive and less profitable.

However one views the impact on the accounting profession, this is not an ideal stance into which to be thrust. There are only so many efficiencies that can be drained out of a system before quality begins to suffer or the business is simply unworkable at the profit margins involved. Some in the profession see audits as loss leaders to establish and maintain a client relationship, hoping to make up lost profits on the provision of other, higher margin services. But these too are being impacted by regulatory and financial market concerns about independence, particularly in the aftermath of the Enron situation.

The forensic profession runs the same risks. If it is thought of as a commodity, the rules of the marketplace apply. Those rules say over time people will buy a like product at the lowest possible price. For a while one can strive to be more efficient, and this will buy time, but ultimately price pressures will prevail upon any commoditized service offering.

Some, perhaps many, of the thoughts set forth in thinking about the message of Bedbury's piece may seem novel, even goofy. Fine. If they are, it is a clear attempt to recast the construct of our profession and what we do. To do less is to risk being just another can in a long row of cans.

Bedbury offers the following ideas to counter the momentum toward becoming a commodity:

- *Set your sights high.* Do not be content to be in the field—be a leader in the field.

- *Elevate your product.* Can you argue persuasively that who you are or what you do or how you do it is in some way unique? If not, why not? Bedbury notes that Krispy Kreme is not just a doughnut and that protects them and makes them highly profitable. The country singer Loretta Lynn is reported to have offered the following advice some years back to those interested in making a name for themselves in that field: "Be first, best, or different." It is not bad advice.

- *Offer more than the minimum.* Think, if you will, of Starbucks or the dinner in the fine restaurant. Are we offering a plain vanilla product, or is it somehow more complete, useful, or interesting than the thousands of other reports that get shoved up the line in every organization every day? How can we stand out from the crowd?

Perhaps there is an even more pressing problem: How can we move beyond our pasts? For better or worse, external audits, internal audits, and even forensic investigations are now decades, if not many decades, old. We have track records trailing us, and in many important respects they are at odds with who we are now and, especially, with who we desire to become in the future. Our problem may not be so much with who we are ourselves, but who our peers and superiors see when they look at us. Many senior executives and board members had their primary learning experiences in organizations two, three, or even four decades ago. They were exposed to a much different controls and investigations environment than exists at present, yet many still retain images of our prior selves and modes of operation. A sizable amount of education needs to be done, and I suspect it will fall to the practitioners reading these words to begin to address it. It can be done; Henry has commented on the success of the corporate security field to move in this direction.[6] We need to begin to take similar steps.

- *Remember that the company is the brand.* Customers often look past the product to the core values of the organization that produces it. In a crowded field, reputation can be a differentiator, and truly it can be the little things that count. Consistency can be viewed as plodding repetitiveness and more of the same, or it can be portrayed as "Never missed a deadline!" I suspect many in our field are proud of their reputations and methodologies, and those are built on sound foundations of professional competency, devotion to duty, adherence to details, and thorough documentation. We could, with but a little tinkering, apply these same attributes to a robot on an assembly line, Or, we can put them before our customers as statements of value brought to the table: "Never missed a deadline," "Certified professional," "If it's there, we'll find it," and "We can back up what we say." This is, after all, advertising.

9. *The brand doesn't appeal to the young.*

Bedbury cautions against the pursuit of cool, whatever that is, since it is defined necessarily by others and is a volatile and changing thing. An enduring attempt to always be cutting edge can leave one without roots and having expended a significant amount of energy. Instead, Bedbury advises to stick with the core of the business and concentrate on being respectful of employees, customers, and the environment, while remaining honest and principled.

There is little to add to Bedbury's prescription, other than to again counsel against change for the sake of change or trying to always be the flavor of the month. Fashion in management is as changeable as it is in clothes and cars, as any perusal of a bookstore's Management section will reveal. Few titles survive more than a couple of months, only to be replaced by the newest proscriptive. Endless tinkering with our professional persona and message will probably do us more harm than good. One is reminded of Bedbury's injunctive in his first prescription for brand revival: Analyze and think before taking action.

An example from the heartland of America will perhaps convey the manner in which such thoughtful, measured, yet significant change can be achieved. The Northeast Ohio Technology Coalition, or NorTech, makes annual awards to companies in that area. As writer Ann Quigley recounts:

The awards program, now in its eighth year, rewards creators of novel products or services that increase company value. Companies inspired to innovate would do well to look to their strengths, judging by the strategy of seven-time NorTech Award winner Keithley Instruments, Inc., based in Cleveland, which develops product testing methods for the electronics industry. To develop its winning product, a test for fiber optic networks, Keithley avoided copying the competition, Silicon Valley industry giant Agilent Technologies. Instead, to create a climate of innovation, it drew on the assets of northeastern Ohio, a long-time manufacturing seat that still espouses small-town values like loyalty and a solid work ethic. Keithley encouraged employee input and employee-customer partnerships, trusting that its employees weren't solely motivated by stock options, bonuses and raises.

Developing its winning product... involved a large amount of customer interaction. About 40 percent of Keithley's development engineers—the folks usually holed up in labs—visit customers, according to Linda Rae, a general manager at Keithley. "It's very important for the design guy to actually hear the customer's voice in a manufacturing environment," she says.[7]

Reconceptualization of ourselves and our function will move us within the organizational structure. This need not be a move of up or down, with attendant issues of status, pay, and reporting. Even a move sideways may be seen as threatening to other organizational elements. How do we deal with the political and organizational dynamics of these efforts? Washington, D.C. Mayor Tony Williams, speaking in 2002 about his efforts to reshape and revitalize that city's police department, termed these effects *wake turbulence*. He observed that as a boat passes through water, it creates a wake. So too, he noted, does changing a municipal department. Not everyone will be happy with the changes. He counseled that the only way to avoid creating a wake is for the boat not to move or, in organizational terms, to do nothing.[8]

Should we decide to proceed on this journey, there will not only be wake to contend with, but also some element of professional risk. In the post-Enron environment, this perhaps seems obvious and a somewhat simplistic statement, but it has older roots. In 1977, Erroll Yates, writing in *Internal Auditor* magazine, called for auditors to assume expanded consultative and managerial roles in the organization, but offered the following words of caution:

> There is the danger that in his consultant role an internal auditor might lose some—if not all—of the independence needed for control reviews. The enthusiastic internal auditor with ability and ambition might well take over where the manager fears to tread. But I believe this is a risk which, if recognized and watched, is well worth taking considering the benefits that can be achieved for both the internal auditor and the organization.[9]

Written almost three decades ago, such cautions may seem today to be mild. When Yates wrote those words was he thinking of—could he even envision—the collapse of a multibillion-dollar international company? Do his cautions and hopes still have meaning, or are they hopelessly outmoded by recent events? I think we need not worry, at least from the perspective of the forensic profession. Granted, we have discussed at some length the issue of whether the forensic profession would benefit from reconceptualizing itself, and in this regard we resemble that scenario about which Yates wrote, but there is a profound difference. Yates saw reinvention as bringing the internal auditor more substantially into the mainstream of daily operations and organizational management. In this regard he is highly consistent with those who worry about audit independence, given the scope of nonaudit services routinely offered in today's environment. But ours is a different focus: We seek to consider reconceptualization of the forensic profession not simply to expand its breadth, but also to increase its effectiveness. Our process of reinvention will not operate to dilute controls, but rather enhance their effectiveness.

Caution is prudent when embarking on any process of change, but I do not believe our level of caution need be an impediment if we maintain our focus. Such possibilities are suggested by Norman Marks, writing in *Internal Auditor* magazine. Speaking about the rate of change endemic to the New Economy, Marks postulates that:

> Internal auditors can thrive in the midst of this confusion and, in fact, are needed more than ever before. As our organizations sail to the new world of e-business, auditors can be at their side. We can provide necessary advice and counsel as our clients embark on new explorations. In fact, the recently updated definition of our profession emphasizes the auditor's role as consultant and risk manager. In this capacity, we can help identify and assess new business risks so that management can make wiser decisions. If necessary, we can shout a warning when we see icebergs ahead.[10]

In thinking about how this reorientation of the audit function will be played out, Marks foresees a much different audit landscape in the future:

> Instead of focusing on a list of audits from an audit schedule, we will be concerned primarily with assurance: providing peace of mind to our clients that business risk is being managed effectively—even, or especially, in turbulent times. Most importantly, however, we will need to start looking further ahead and rethinking our traditional approach to audits.
>
> When continuous change and transformation occurs, continuous risk assessment is needed. As auditors, we will need to make sure our eyes remain on the areas of greatest risk. The days of an annual audit plan, where projects are set in stone, will disappear. Risks can change rapidly and with little warning, as Cisco found when its sales plummeted and forced the company to write off $2.5 billion in inventory. Auditors will need to change their schedules constantly to ensure that present and future risks are being addressed—not the risks of the past. . . . Our audits will be future-looking projects, rather than audits of history, and our mantra will be "assurance through prevention.[11]

While recognizing there are differences between the forensic profession and the audit function, Marks' vision is worth consideration. We shall discuss in the final chapter the need for forensic professionals to look both up and down within the organization. We have examined the benefits to be gained from looking for ideas and assistance both within and outside the profession. It may be that we are moving toward a 360-degree model, in which we will look to the past and the future to identify areas of potential fraud risk.

Such concepts may, at first, seem revolutionary, but they are no more extreme than many things being tried in U.S. manufacturing at this writing. Confronted with new demands and the need for new answers, companies are beginning to experiment with cross-training employees to be able to respond where needed and when needed, rather than be caught in a job description and skill set whose utility may experience highs and lows. Other companies rely on floating reserves of workers ready to be called up as needed, while others share temporarily idle employees with other companies who have needs at the moment.[12] The need to be mobile and capable of responding to shifts in the economy or production requirements was sensed, and met, by these companies by rethinking their assumptions about how their people could be utilized. We may have to be just as flexible and nimble as we consider the challenges we face.

Even as this book is written, there are significant corporate reconceptualizations underway. Consider, if you will, one of our close organizational cousins— corporate security. For many years, decades even, corporate security was the province of locks, alarms, and guards. Usually staffed with a former law enforcement officer, the mission was normally to protect people, product, and premises, sometimes with a bit of executive protection and stockholder meeting security thrown in. While the events of September 11th have changed much of the focus on and attention to the corporate security function, significant rethinking of the function and its role was underway well before that. Steve Lohr, writing in *The New York Times*, has documented the rise of a new player on the organizational horizon—the Chief Security Officer. The imperative, he believes, is for the new security professional to possess analytic skills, business acumen, and leadership ability. As he puts it, "roughly equals parts top cop, business manager and computer geek." He reports that executive search firms now advise that qualified individuals can command in excess of $400,000 per year in such positions, and that a new magazine, *CSO*, is due out in September.[13]

Such thinking is perhaps sweeping the private sector, as Lohr reports that a survey by Christian & Timbers, a search firm, found that of 300 companies surveyed, 95 percent said they needed to hire a chief security officer. One practitioner already in the field, working for a major technology company, is a former policeofficer with an MBA. He notes that security in his firm is a business process, that requires setting strategy and priorities, establishing procedures and programs to achieve goals, and measuring effectiveness.

Lohr notes that about 15 years ago the Chief Information Officer (CIO) concept was greeted with derision and misunderstanding when it first appeared on the organizational playing field, but with time has grown to be viewed as more than a narrow specialty. CIOs, he contends, are now routinely accepted as important contributors to overall business and organizational success.

Some of this change, Lohr contends, is directly the result of the increasing use of automation in organizations. While it allows them to move faster and adapt more quickly, it also presents new levels and forms of risk. While in the past there were two separate tracks in the organization's security environment— physical security and data security—many are beginning to see the benefits to be gained from bringing them together. Certainly people can compromise systems, and this brings into play issues as varied as preemployment background checks and access controls. At the same time, systems can be a door so open to intruders that all of the physical access controls in the world become useless. It seems that many organizations have come to the realization that these elements must be coordinated to be truly effective.

Such concerns may be well founded. A recent article highlighted very well the necessary but fragile interface between people and machines:

> Posing as computer help-desk employees, U.S. Treasury inspectors telephoned 100 Internal Revenue Service workers at random, asking them to change their password to one the callers specified. . . . an astounding 71% complied, meaning total strangers could gain access to the supposedly secure IRS computer system.[14]

The largest professional organization in the field, the American Society for Industrial Security, Lohr reports, is already developing a set of criteria and qualifications for this new position.[15]

Others report revived interest in an old concept, the organizational ombudsperson. These positions, with Scandinavian antecedents, were popular in the 1970s when I was in the government. They function as sort of an employee advocate, where aggrieved employees can bypass their boss and normal reporting channels if they think their concerns are not being addressed. Following some of the larger corporate financial implosions in 2002, Monte Burke reports that some organizations are now investigating this concept as providing a safe haven for whistleblowers who have concerns about corporate activities. He notes also that the mere existence of such a mechanism may bode well for the organization caught up in a federal prosecution, even if the conduit was not the source of the information leading to an inquiry. The theory is that having a viable function such as this is proof of some level of intent to self-police one's organization.[16]

Has the time come for the forensic function in the organization to undergo a similar rethinking? I believe the immediate answer is "yes," and that is the easy answer. I hope I have established the need to engage in this process. The more vexing question is who should do the rethinking? Is it executive management or the board, or must it come from the profession itself? I suspect events will show that a little of both is required, but forensic professionals should be prepared to do one of two things. First, if the door swings open on such issues, they must be ready and armed with thoughts, theories, ideas, and proposals to advance the process. This will require time and research, but the sooner these items are addressed the better for the forensic professionals and for the organizations they serve. Second, if the door remains closed in a given organization, precisely the same materials will be necessary if any attempt to open it is to meet with success.

CHAPTER 15

LEADERSHIP

That leadership is a crucial element of any significant endeavor in an organizational setting approaches being a tautology. Yet, we often fall into the trap of thinking of issues of leadership in a hide-bound and highly personalistic fashion. We challenge ourselves, if we are so inclined, to be a leader: to have vision, energy, and courage to seize the situation and make something happen, much like the athlete on the playing field. This is a common and frequently accepted definition of the term, yet it is often incomplete in either its conceptualization or acknowledgments. Few of us have the organizational stature or personal charisma to make significant events occur in a vacuum. Certainly we can, within reason, lead our subordinates with little outside assistance, but how about our peers or, more important, our superiors? How do we lead our bosses, who may be crucial to the achievement of our objectives?

Thinking of instances of success in our organizational pasts, how often were we able to consummate those achievements without support either laterally or from above? The common leadership speech after victory is to acknowledge the team and praise the loyal and selfless subordinates who were crucial to success. That is well and good, appropriate to many situations, and often the sign of an enlightened leader, but how often do we neglect those to the side of us or those above us?

Erroll Yates observed almost 30 years ago that the growth of the internal audit function from technical expertise to management legitimacy could come only with support from "the highest level."[1] Charles M. Elson, director of the University of Delaware's Center for Corporate Governance, has noted with regard to codes for corporate behavior that they also need substantial topside support if they are to be effective.[2] If we are truly to begin to reconceptualize the foundations of our professional existence, can this be done without leadership, both laterally and vertically? Or, to redefine ourselves, must we also redefine our conceptualization of leadership? I think the answer is "yes."

It appears the Institute of Internal Auditors (IIA) may already be heading in this direction. In the April 2002 edition of *Internal Auditor* magazine, Christy Chapman notes that in December 2000 the IIA approved the new Standards for the Professional Practice of Internal Auditing (Standards), seeking to "better reflect current practice and the new definition of internal auditing."[3] Chapman goes on to note the impact these Standards will have on the profession:

> "The old Standards were narrowly constructed around internal control assurance and compliance," says Tony Ridley, former IIA chairman of the board and chairman of the Guidance Task Force responsible for recommending changes to the Standards. "The revision depicts a much broader focus incorporating consulting, risk, and governance, three areas that have not been addressed before at the standards level." For example, the new Standards prescribe a more proactive role for internal auditors in risk management and governance processes.... The nature of internal audit work itself is described in terms of evaluating and contributing to the improvement of risk management, control and governance systems. The revised Standards even address what chief audit executives (CAEs) should do when they believe senior management has accepted an inappropriate level of risk—take their concerns to the board.[4]

We have long dealt up in our organizational lives, but usually these were occasions of asking permission: requests for resources, adjustments to reporting relationships, and the like. We are now approaching a new and largely uncharted part of the forest, which will require new thinking and new approaches. We have seen the innovative and challenging rethinking of assumptions taking place in the advertising business with the advent of neuroscience research.[5] Likewise, we have examined the almost-inconceivable changes in the manner in which some law enforcement agencies go about their work. Advertisements are but a mechanism to influence human choice. Is that not what we are about when we deal with our subordinates, peers, and superiors?

In thinking of such activities, we should be mindful of the issues at the top— in the boardroom and executive suite. Risk management has for many years sought to protect the organization and its assets through several mechanisms and activities, with various forms of insurance being high among them. Recent developments in the industry, following the dotcom collapse, September 11th, and Enron, may have forever altered the landscape. Insurance may now not be the automatic panacea to placate concerns about various forms of risk; it is simply becoming prohibitively expensive. A recent article in *Risk Management* magazine put this issue as follows: "A few risk managers report that underwriters have not been interested in negotiation or in risk and claims mitigation issues— only in rate hikes. As a result, not much could be done in the short term to avoid significant price increases for significantly less coverage."[6]

Such a position by the insurance industry, if growing, could significantly alter the risk landscape for many years to come. It suggests three alternatives—none of them good, but at least two of them manageable. The first is to accept the status quo, pay increased rates for reduced coverage, and learn to live with it. The net effect will likely be increased product and service prices to pass this cost along to customers; lower profits to absorb the increased costs; or dropping of higher-risk (and probably higher-profit) services lines or products to reduce risk. The second alternative is to focus on risk mitigation to such an extent and in such a manner that insurers will relent on price increases and coverage reductions. But even were an organization successful in this endeavor, it is still a mutual situation— the other side, the insurers, can still say "no."

The third alternative is identical to the second with a shift in focus. It consists of maintaining a level of risk mitigation insurance that appears reasonable at prevailing prices, but attempting to move toward a posture of being self-insured, at least for those risks over which the organization has sufficient control and influence. In this scenario, the organization is spending resources formally designated for insurance coverage on active risk mitigation. As an organizational strategy, this may pay ancillary dividends. Risk mitigation surveys, whether they are for occupational fraud, physical security, or some other purpose, usually produce volumes of important and useful organization data that go far beyond pure risk mitigation. In one sense, it is a two-for-one activity, with increased operational efficiencies gained from vastly improved knowledge about organizational processes and capabilities.

This alternative may be seen as a significant gamble, largely because it has not been widely used before. This is true, and it may fall to the forensic professionals within organizations to become the advocates for consideration of such proposals, but this will not occur in a vacuum. Environmental drivers, like the changing dynamics of the insurance industry, may not only make such concepts and proposals more likely to be well-received, but may even mandate them in terms of economic logic.

If the levels of board and executive concern, in the post-Enron environment, approach those that appear to have manifested themselves in the post-September 11th time frame, the issue may be far from academic. Carol Hymowitz, writing in the *Wall Street Journal* about "Business's New Agenda," makes the following observations:

> Until six months ago, corporate security was a back-burner issue.
> Then, came Sept. 11th, . . . A few weeks later, the threat of anthrax-tainted mail stirred panic in offices throughout the nation.
> Today security is a main concern from corporate boardrooms to mailrooms everywhere.[7]

In this article, Hymowitz goes on to cite a study conducted by Booz Allen Hamilton in November and December 2001, which found that 75 percent of chief executives at large companies had an increased concern about security issues. Specifically, she advises, the study reflected the following areas of focus among those interviewed:[8]

Mail processing	86%
Travel	85%
Protection of employees	79%
Protection of infrastructure	75%
Risk assessment	71%
Protection of offices and physical plants	69%
Employee morale	69%
Supply-chain distribution	51%

Certainly, the horrible events of September 11th are in a different league than issues of occupational fraud, but we must now be more alert to the possibility that the financial actions of one or at most a few can also seriously injure an organization. For many years we assumed that organizational size alone would protect us and operate as a de facto form of self-insurance. The events at Enron, and other companies that fell or faltered because of financial issues, may be a warning. Size alone, as the tragedy at the World Trade Center demonstrated, may not be enough.

Is it then appropriate that we begin to consider utilizing neuroscience or other developments in the art of advertising in crafting a campaign to facilitate our goal(s) of organizational redefinition? That is perhaps too literal an application of the concept, but it is intriguing to begin to think in neuroscience terms about how our product (us) is perceived in the marketplace (them—bosses, peers, subordinates, other employees). It may be that our current forms of advertisement—periodic and annual reports as to how much we produce, how responsive we are, how much money we save the organization, even how we dress and comport ourselves in day-to-day activities—are much less effective than we think.

Reconceptualizing our message will almost surely produce moments of discomfort for those around, below, and above us, and also for ourselves. The major changes in life—birth, puberty, aging, death—are always painful, yet necessary. We would be less than realistic were we to assume that profound changes in the context of organizational life will be any less stressful. We can and should work to minimize and mitigate these consequences, but it is not realistic to believe they will not occur. Or, as Mayor Tony Williams noted, there will be wake turbulence. But, as he also noted, the only alternative is to lie still in the water. That is an option we as a profession may not have. The sheer size of the fraud problem is turbulent, in and of itself. Add the Enron situation and others like it, and the waters become agitated. Should we choose to lie still, we will still be buffeted.

Continuity of leadership was cited by one theorist as important, if change is to be effected. How do we attempt to promote continuity or, in its absence, maintain the momentum necessary to effect productive changes? Writing a book review of *Times Square Roulette*, a work about the revitalization of Times Square, Neil Barsky noted the groundwork for this successful endeavor required many years and a good deal of continuity at both the political and project levels, and could have been derailed at many points:

> But under the surprisingly consistent leadership of Gov. Mario Cuomo and Mayors Ed Koch and David Dinkins, the city's public development forces chalked up impressive accomplishments. . . . The real heroes . . . are the unheralded public officials who stood behind the governor and the mayor during their press conferences. . . . [9]

Is it useful and appropriate to think of ourselves, the forensic professionals, as a professional class of organizational servants, holding true to our mission and beliefs as top leadership comes and goes? Can we function as institutional memory so our message is not lost or unheard? That may be a good and worthy conceptualization of both our function and ourselves, yet it may well be a double-edged sword. Certainly, continuity in the face of change is valuable, if for no other reason than one does not endlessly reinvent the wheel. But, do we run the risk of becoming the organizational furniture, accepted but unseen in a cognitive sense, much like Montague's "buildings that don't move?"[10] That is a threat and one that perhaps all too many practitioners are all too familiar with. Yet, at the same time, we can ill afford to constantly be at the front of the organizational stage, lest our performance become wearisome. Susan Blakeslee and the researchers on whom she reported seem convinced that thrill, excitement, and the unexpected are important components to both human learning and human psychic satisfaction, but any circuit can become overloaded. Like the carnival funhouse, where we are intrigued when our sense of up and down is momentarily challenged, continual excitement of that sort can quickly become draining and an irritant.

We as human beings appear to need a certain level of normalcy and a certain amount of excitement to both survive and grow. So, too, does the organization. Rock-solid consistency has its uses, but it can lead to economic extinction. Marks, for example, has noted that "only one of the 12 largest U.S. industrial organizations from 1990, General Electric Co., still exists today."[11] Probably many factors were responsible for this result, but certainly inability to change and grow was one of them. Conversely, within the past decade we have seen the explosion of dotcom companies, with few rules, little structure, murky objectives, and changing participants. Some still survive and prosper, but most are gone and forgotten, their dreams and founders scattered, as if they never existed.

Even with committed, informed, courageous,and persistent leadership we may still have significant hurdles to overcome. Terry Cooper has commented on the leader's problems with role conflict or ambiguity of authority when attempting to effect change.[12] We may find there is a need to develop clear channels of support from the top, as Yates has counseled and Campbell has demonstrated. Greanias and Windsor note this may extend to the organization itself, since it has various constituencies with differing expectations,[13] and Andrews observes this phenomenon may apply as well to corporate boards of governors.[14]

There will probably be considerable inertia to overcome. Bhide and Stevenson have reported on their analysis of the operation of ethical codes in the marketplace, and find that victims may often not identify themselves as such, due to personal, financial, or psychological reasons. For this reason, they contend, much impropriety goes unreported and unpunished.[15] So, too, with many organizations, in my experience.

Leaders and organizations also have a tendency, it appears, to pay attention to the extremes of the spectrum and avoid dealing with the all-important middle. John Rohr has described this issue thusly: "We tend to focus on narrow, rather legalistic questions. . . or we aspire to articulate vast schemes of general ethics."[16] Thus it is the case that many organizations have lofty statements of organizational codes of behavior and can also probably tell you how many people got caught fudging their travel expenses in the last year, but tend to have incomplete information as to what is going on in the middle.

Still other executives, organizations, and professions tend to sit. Organizational consultant Frank J. Navran has commented on this tendency of companies and organizations in the area of corporate values.[17] Researchers and theorists Lloyd Nigro and William Richardson have also studied this phenomenon. Following a call by Moneypenny in a 1953 edition of *Public Administration Review* for public agencies to move from a stance of "pious declaration" to actual implementation of ethical codes, they tracked progress in the pages of that same journal. As of 1990, they declared they had found none in the intervening 37 years.[18]

Still others opt, consciously or unconsciously, for a path of suboptimization. Since they have difficultly measuring the effects of their efforts on the major objectives they seek to attain, they begin to move down the food chain until they find matters capable of measurement and then hope that these will suffice as surrogates for the intended goal measurements. Terry Cooper has commented on this tactic as follows: ". . . The fact that ultimate goals often do not lend themselves to quantification usually leads to an attempt to work down the hierarchy of subordinate goals until one or more are found to which numbers can be assigned."[19]

Randall and Gibson have also commented on measurement issues. They conducted a review of more than 700 articles published with regard to business ethics and found that only 94 offered any parameters for measuring the effectiveness of business ethics programs. Further, they found that even among the 94 articles there were substantial open questions as to how well research design and sampling issues had been dealt with.[20]

Still others see dangers in attempting to resolve significant organizational issues through incremental steps that will never achieve the desired objective. Henry Mintzberg has noted his considerable research into operations of organizations and has commented on their tendency to operate in an ad hoc, discontinuous mode in a number of areas. He argues that absent a systematic or coordinated plan for implementation, it is unlikely one will appear from such idiosyncratic initiatives.[21]

There is a danger also that the mere declaration of intent can become a surrogate for effective implementation and meaningful progress. While the figures are somewhat dated, it is interesting to speculate on the meaning of four studies conducted between 1964 and 1987 that showed that corporations were adopting codes of conduct at an increasing rate. By 1987, 85 percent of reporting corporations advised they had such a code. What is perhaps telling from the studies is that in a 1980 study, 91 percent of respondents said they were satisfied with the performance of their firms' codes.[22] So high a rate of satisfaction may be indicative of a comprehensive and well-functioning ethical system within those organizations, or one could speculate that the mere adoption of a code was being perceived as having solved any existing problems.

Having delineated some of the obstacles likely to be faced when attempting to develop a comprehensive and effective conduct and compliance program, what positive guidance may we look toward? Peters and Austin suggest, as with any effort at achieving excellence in organizations, that it will require "a million little things done with obsession, consistency and care."[23] Kirk Hanson advises that corporate compliance and conduct codes are capable of being effectively implemented, but this will require multiple implementation measures and mandatory reporting systems.[24]

Four researcher/theorists offer their thoughts on the necessary elements for effective compliance and conduct systems and also for their effective implementation:

1. John Fleming recommends:[25]

   - Recognition of the objective by top management
   - A Chief Executive Officer with a high degree of integrity to set an example
   - Information flow to key personnel about ethical issues
   - Formal policies for ethical enforcement
   - Attention to ethical dimensions in recruitment and selection
   - Frequent pronouncements on ethical issues by key executives
   - A written ethical code
   - Formal training for all employees

- Alternate channels of upward communication
- Development of operational definitions of ethics and corporate social responsibility

2. Mark Frankel suggests that compliance and conduct programs, once developed, can serve as:[26]

- Enabling documents
- Sources of public evaluation
- Vehicles for professional socialization
- Enhancers of professional reputation and public trust
- Preservers of professional biases
- Deterrents to unethical behavior
- Support systems
- Frameworks for adjudication

3. L. J. Brooks cites the following areas as being important for compliance codes to cover if they are to be effective:[27]

- Confidentiality guidelines
- Hearing processes
- Employee protection
- Employee rights
- Compliance motivation
- Conflicts of interest
- Coordination of code requirements

4. Gatewood and Carroll articulate the following suggestions if measurements are to be effective within the context of a given organization's history and culture:[28]

- Measurement should be linked to the culture and goals of the organization
- Measurement should be at all levels
- Multiple measures should be used
- Different measurement systems should be used for different organizational units
- Measurement should be of an individual or a group
- Measurement should address both short- and long-term performance;

- Both behaviors and results should be measured
- Whatever is measured should be under the control of the individual being evaluated

Interested or concerned forensic professionals may wish to conduct a type of self-assessment of their home organizations against these or other criteria. The difference between the theoretical ideal and present reality may provide some general indication as to the size and nature of the leadership that will be required to close the gap. In many instances, it is likely that leadership will have to come, at least in part, from the forensic professional.

CHAPTER 16

THE NEXT FIVE YEARS

Funding

As with most things in life, money sooner or later raises its ugly head. It is well and good to look across the organizational landscape and marvel at the many things, great and small, that the law enforcement profession has accomplished in the past 30 years. Likewise, it is intriguing to imagine what contributions, known or unsuspected, other fields of endeavor, from game theory to neuroscience, may bring to our profession. Certainly, many of the accomplishments realized in the law enforcement arena were achieved with little monetary cost. Others, however, were more expensive, and then there is still the issue of environmental intelligence—how big is the problem and what does it look like?—and also basic deterrence research. All of these things will cost money. The question is, where does it come from?

I am reminded of a story, allegedly true, I heard during one of my tours at FBI Headquarters. As the story goes, a young Supervisory Special Agent in the FBI's Legal Counsel Division was busy at work one day when a Bureau executive burst into his office in a state of near-panic. The executive explained that there was an incredibly important project that had to be done perfectly in two or three days and he was assigning him to do it. The executive also informed the young agent that he could expect no help, as everyone else was tied up on other important matters. The young fellow pondered the task at hand and the deadline for several seconds and is reported to have replied: "You can have it good, quick, and cheap. Pick two."

I wish, many times in my career, I had thought of those words, much less had the courage to say them. If we are honest with ourselves and others, we all acknowledge that there is no free lunch. If something is good and quick, it is not cheap; if it is cheap and quick, it is not good; and if it is cheap and good, it is not quick. Thus do most forensic professionals in organizations face their daily tasks: they are asked to perform important tasks in a timely fashion with limited resources. So, too, the profession. If we, in fact, have a $600 billion annual problem on our hands, we are going to require something a good bit more rigorous and substantive than we have now. The question, again, is where does it come from?

Organizations may also have a sort of mental disconnect when it comes to spending money in areas with which they are not familiar. The firm of Booz Allen Hamilton conducted a survey of 72 CEOs of companies with more than a billion dollars in annual revenue after the terrorist attacks of September 11th. Among other things they found that while 80 percent of them believed that corporate security was more important than before, fully one-third did not anticipate substantial increases in spending for their corporate security functions. They further found that 72 percent of these executives did not believe that the quality of their companies' security function was more important to customers after the attacks than it was before. Booz Allen officials were reported to have been surprised by these findings with one, Vice President Mark Gerencser, noting: "Corporate security is now a strategic issue that can no longer be delegated."[1]

In terms of how organizations perceive workplace fraud and their resource response to it, the Institute of Management and Administration/Institute of Internal Auditors *1999 Business Fraud Survey* may be unfortunately instructive. Carpenter and Mahoney commented on these findings as follows:

> Because increasing attention has been devoted to fraud prevention and detection, one might expect to observe increased funding for internal audit departments and, more specifically, to their fraud-related training. However, only 39 percent of the respondents indicated that their internal audit department's budget had increased. More surprisingly, the respondents indicated that only a small fraction of that amount was allocated to fraud-specific training. In fact, the study found that the average percentage of an internal audit department's budget devoted to fraud-specific training was a mere 3 percent, and the median amount was an extremely small 0.1 percent.[2]

If the results of this survey can be reasonably assumed to reflect the attitudes of a majority of organizational America, securing adequate funding for more substantial and expansive research may well be a significant challenge.

The government is often the first place many people look to for funding, and it is tempting to consider this, but obstacles may lie ahead. The government, in the form of the FBI's UCRP and NIBRS, is a valuable source of intelligence, but its focus is on many matters other than occupational fraud. Fraud is not even a priority category for which it collects information. Adding to this limitation are the events of recent months after September 11th that find Congress and high administration officials actively discussing moving the focus of the FBI and other elements of the Department of Justice (DOJ) away from other areas of criminal and intelligence activities and toward terrorism. This is certainly understandable, but it does not bode well for increased assistance from federal sources in the near future.

The Securities and Exchange Commission (SEC) is already voicing concerns about the adequacy of its funding and resources in a post-Enron environment.[3] At least one influential U.S. Senator, Banking Committee Chairman Paul Sarbanes of Maryland, has written to President Bush to renew his request that the agency receive an emergency appropriation.[4] If a federal agency has difficulty getting resources from the government of which it is an important part, we may suspect that any new request or tasking will face stiff competition. Such concerns are hardly new in the information age. The SEC reported in 1998 that it was receiving 120 complaints per day over the Internet from online investors alone.[5]

There are also the consequences of the terrorist attacks of September 11th to deal with. In April 2002 the federal government announced a sweeping revision of its antimoney laundering regulations. Some reporting requirements have been expanded and others amended, and the range of financial services industries and institutions has been broadened.[6] While the burden of complying with these mandates will fall most immediately on the private sector, there will be consequences for the public sector as well. As more and more information is required to be reported to the government, there will be a concomitant requirement that this information be received, recorded, analyzed, and disseminated. Each of these activities will require people and resources, thus exacerbating already tight agency budgets. As agencies turn to Congress for additional funding, the net effect will be to push other worthy objectives to lower priority levels.

Likewise, a search of the DOJ website is not terribly encouraging. There are grant and funding programs listed for a number of categories: Bureau of Justice Assistance, Corrections, Support Programs, Drug Court Programs, Weed and Seed Programs (narcotics), Violence Against Women, Victims of Crime, Juvenile Justice and Delinquency Prevention, and National Institute of Justice. Nothing appears to be pertinent to occupational fraud. Again from the DOJ website, we can see what types of programs have been funded in the immediate past. The programs supported in Fiscal Year 2001 included Empowering Communities, Breaking the Cycle of Drug Abuse and Crime, Combating Family Violence, Addressing Youth Crime, Managing Offenders, Protecting and Supporting Victims of Crime, Using Technology in Addressing Crime, Enhancing Law Enforcement Initiatives, Countering Terrorism and Ensuring Domestic Preparedness, Crime and Justice for American Indians and Alaskan Natives, and Enhancing Criminal Justice Administration through Research and Evaluation. Still other programs supported through the Bureau of Justice Assistance include Church Arson Prevention Grant Program, Emergency Federal Law Enforcement Assistance Program, Public Safety Officers' Benefits Program, Public Safety

Officers' Benefits Educational Assistance Program, Denial of Federal Benefits Program, National Auto Theft Prevention Program, and the Defense Procurement Fraud Debarment Program.

Such is the nature of governmental agencies: they are large, complex places full of programs for just about everything, and the aforementioned search was hardly exhaustive. There may be help available from the federal government, but when it comes to occupational fraud, absent a truly effective (and expensive) lobbying campaign, immediate assistance does not seem to be at hand.

Actually, there may be benefits to be gained from not attempting to rely on governmental sources for the primary, or even significant, levels of funding. Ted Gest, a veteran reporter on law enforcement matters and the politics of Washington, has written of the often erratic and turbulent history of efforts to inject the federal government, and its dollars, into matters of local law enforcement. Tracing this perspective of local crime as a federal issue to the Johnson administration, he recounts how each succeeding administration has brought its own views, priorities, and politics to the issue, often with unintended or disruptive consequences. It may be that in the quest for better solutions to the issues of occupational fraud, this area is just as well left undisturbed.[7]

Some academic institutions appear to be taking a heightened interest in occupational fraud and some are adding courses on the subject to their academic programs. As has been noted, the arena of occupational fraud may be a particularly rich one academically, since it spans areas such as accounting, law enforcement, social science, mathematics, psychology, sociology, and bioscience. Such actions are welcome, but the history of institutions of higher education is that they are normally looking for sources of funding rather than providing them.

Associations are another potential source of funding, but this may prove inadequate to the substantial needs at hand. While organizations such as the American Association of Retired Persons, the Better Business Bureau, the National Consumers League, and others all have an interest in fraud, it is usually fraud committed by persons against other persons, not occupational fraud. Also, the vast majority of their mission is public awareness and education, rather than research, recordkeeping, and analysis.

The ACFE is by far the largest organization in the world devoted exclusively to fraud, and its mandate easily encompasses the conceptual arena of occupational fraud. The founder and chairperson of the ACFE, Joe Wells, has written a highly successful book of the same name (*Occupational Fraud and Abuse*, see Chapter 3, note 3). The ACFE also has an extensive research library and about 24,000 knowledgeable and motivated members. In many ways it is a logical place to begin to think about creating the research and data collection capability necessary to advance the profession and its capabilities, but money is still an issue.

Although the ACFE is now firmly established and highly successful, it is doubtful that it has the resources necessary to make any more meaningful contribution to this area than it has already, and the existing contribution has indeed been impressive.

Assuming that the ACFE has 24,000 dues-paying members and that its dues are $125 per year, that gives it a rough cash flow of about $3 million per year. Set against this are the need to support its membership, publish materials, produce and ship a monthly magazine, and maintain its headquarters and staff. There is not much left for either data collection and analysis or research, and when we compare it with the $5 billion Pfizer alone spends annually on research it is indeed puny.

This brings us to organizations that, after all, are the locus of all occupational fraud in the United States. Is it in their interest to consider funding some sort of coordinated data collection and analysis program? I think the answer is yes. They and their forensic professionals have benefited greatly from the work of the ACFE and those few other organizations and academics that evidence an interest in this field, but their vulnerabilities are still vast. If we accept the ACFE figure that occupational fraud may be a $600 billion annual problem in the United States, that means that U.S. organizations, mainly companies and corporations, lost an average of $1.64 billion each day this year, including weekends and holidays. To try to apprehend the magnitude of so staggering a sum, please assume that it will take you about one minute to read this page. At the estimated rate of $1.64 billion per day, U.S. organizations lost $1.14 million to occupational fraud during that minute. At this astonishing rate, one hour's worth of losses—slightly more than $68 million—would pay for all the fraud data collection and fraud research that has probably ever been done in the United States.

While funding for research, data refinement and collection, and clarification of definitional issues is desperately needed, we should not forget the mainstay of almost all existing fraud deterrence programs—internal audit and forensic investigations. These requirements, too, must be reexamined. We cannot stand still while the forensic field addresses its profound developmental needs, and the mainstream audit and investigations activities have been shown time and again to have a positive impact in reducing occupational fraud or, at least, lessening its impact. In some regards, I am sure there are those who would say this is taking both sides of the argument—questioning our traditional activities while calling for the development of more effective tools and processes. I would disagree. When the first car was produced, all the horses in the United States were not turned loose. There will be a period of overlap, when traditional activities, effective activities, continue as new concepts are developed and tested. The end result will likely be an amalgamation of the old and the new, hopefully in a new and more highly effective paradigm.

Even were our monumental research and related needs properly funded, we would still be faced with the significant task of organizing a professional body of knowledge. Even the police, after the better part of three decades of research, experimentation, and innovation, are still concerned that they lack an organized body of available knowledge similar to that found in law and medicine. Scott and Sampson, writing in *Subject to Debate*, the newsletter of the Police Executive Research Forum, one of the most prominent law enforcement think tanks in the world, bemoan both the relative lack of research and the availability of that research. They point to the Office of Community-Oriented Policing Services (COPS), funded by the DOJ, as an important first step in this process. COPS, they report, will with the assistance of university professors begin to produce a series of guides for police on how to address law enforcement and community issues from the perspective of community policing precepts.[8] That this is taking place after several decades of productive experience in law enforcement may give some flavor of how large and daunting a task this may be, notwithstanding its necessity.

We have seen from ACFE data that traditional activities are effective, just as we saw that during their time of greatest experimentation law enforcement budgets were also rising. Prudent public policy is often not to put all of one's eggs into one basket, and this will hold true for organizations as well. It may well be in their best interests to make a renewed investment in tried-and-true programs and procedures even as new methodologies are being developed to make them more effective, replace them if warranted, or produce an amalgamation of the old and new. If occupational fraud has increased 50 percent in the United States in seven years, there may indeed be a high price to be paid for standing still.

Some will respond: Isn't that what we pay the cops for? Yes, we do pay the cops, probably not enough in many instances, but self-protection is perhaps more common than we think. There are cops in every jurisdiction and neighborhood in the land, but most organizations have security guards, fences, access badges, lighting, video cameras, and alarm systems. These items, and many more, are elements of self-protection. The cops will be happy to show up—after the crime has occurred. They cannot realistically patrol the corridors of organizational America to deter occupational fraud. Even if they could, would we want them to?

Even the cops are not finished learning, no matter how impressive many find their records. There are still respected researchers and scholars who believe that the crime reductions we have discussed, no matter how impressive, are really the result of many factors—drug issues, gun issues, and incarceration rates. In questioning the efficacy of the law enforcement initiatives often cited as the primary reason for crime reduction, these persons raise interesting and useful questions, for crime, like all of human behavior, is a terribly complex business. In making these criticisms, they cite the paucity of research, even in an area as apparently front burner as crime.[9] If this is so, what must surely lie ahead for us in an area buried for so long as occupational fraud? But it is a process we must go through if we are to gain important knowledge, and it will be a process that will be measured in decades, not years.

People have an interest in protecting what is close to them—their family, their property, their neighborhood, even their piece of the Internet. Jennifer Lee has commented on the unpaid, self-appointed vigilantes who patrol the Internet to identify and shut down auction fraud artists. They do this sometimes out of anger at having once been a victim themselves, but others do it to protect what they rightfully conceive of as a piece of their turf, the Web sites they enjoy visiting to browse or purchase.[10] Organizational America may likewise have to decide if it needs to do a better job of protecting its neighborhood, the organization itself.

During speeches I have given to organizational executives, especially those in the private sector, I like to pose a hypothetical question. I ask them if they bought a luxury vehicle, say for $50,000, if they would spend $500 for an alarm system for the car. Invariably, the answer is "yes." I inform them that the cost of the alarm system is 1 percent of the vehicle's value. I then ask them if they spend 1 percent of their company's net revenue on corporate security and financial controls. Usually, I get looked at as if I had just grown another head. The comments are typically, "Are you kidding? That would be crazy!" I then ask them to explain to me why they protect their car better than they protect their company. I normally do not get too many insightful answers, usually just puzzled or irritated looks.

While this story is anecdotal, it finds a remarkable degree of support in real-world statistics. The 2002 Pinkerton survey of corporate security directors found that only 9 percent had a budget that was greater than 1 percent of annual corporate revenue, while 26 percent had budgets that were less than .001 percent of annual revenue. Given that fully 44 percent of respondents did not know how large a percentage their budgets were compared to annual corporate revenue, we may presume that many of these are quite small percentages, as well.[11]

With occupational fraud accounting for such staggering losses, even the most incremental of reductions would represent a phenomenal rate of return on investment. As we have seen from the experience of law enforcement in reducing crime rates, there is good reason to hope that the reductions will be more than incremental. Given this scenario, it seems the issue is not so much whether to make such an investment, but how best to do it. This consideration should be given careful attention not only by the forensic professionals but also by boards of directors, corporate officers, shareholders, and the investment community. This is not a question of good or evil, or "nice to have, but." It is a simple and basic question of safeguarding precious corporate assets, protecting shareholder value, and ensuring the financial futures of millions of working Americans.

It may also be useful, particularly from a corporate perspective, to consider the monster that has been lurking in many corporate closets for many, many years— OSHA. The dreaded Occupational Safety and Health Administration has long been pilloried in corporate America for writing needlessly demanding, costly, and strict regulations and enforcing same in a draconian manner to promote worker safety. In November 2000, OSHA "issued the most far-reaching set of work-related rules ever, provoking an immediate barrage of criticism that the new ergonomics regulations are too broad, overly vague, and scientifically unsound," reports *CFO Magazine*. The article goes on to note, "In response, more than 60 companies have signed on to overturn the new rules, which take effect January 16 but give businesses until October to comply."[12]

OSHA estimates it will only cost businesses $4.5 billion to comply with the new regulations. Business groups counter that the cost will more likely be $18 billion to $126 billion.[13] The lower figure is 3 percent of the estimated occupational fraud loss, and the higher one is 21 percent. Unlike OSHA's one-time compliance cost, occupational fraud losses continue year after year.

Visibility

Let's face it, we in the forensic profession labor in an obscure corner of the vineyard. We are the carefully selected, trusted, highly trained guardians of one of the last great secrets remaining on the face of the earth—the $600 billion, more or less, annual problem nobody knows about.

In New York mob circles there is a saying about "making your bones." It refers to a long-standing La Cosa Nostra (Mafia, for those not familiar with such matters) rule about becoming a made guy (full member). After passing all the apprenticeship tests, the final chore before becoming made is to kill someone. This is usually not a random killing, but more likely a piece of mob business—knocking off a suspected informer, dealing with a reluctant deadbeat, and so on. In management terms we would refer to these, respectively, as protecting intellectual property and receivables management, but that is another story. Obviously, when one dies the body begins to decompose, finally arriving at the skeleton. Thus the term "making your bones."

Perhaps we need someone out there, somewhere, to "make their bones" on occupational fraud. You will, I suspect, see more coverage in the next month on child car seats, college athletes' graduation rates, and tongue piercing than you will see on occupational fraud in a year. In the news business this is called underreporting a story. It is important, but nobody seems to care. Conversely, we are all too familiar with the normal tendency of the press—the pack mentality—when they discover something, they beat it to death.

Michael Kramer has written of the debilitating effect fraud and corruption have on foreign aid provided to third world nations. Some estimates indicate that as much as 40 percent of such aid is siphoned off in the form of bribes, kickbacks, substandard supplies and workmanship, and the like. Such losses are systemic and long term and have the effect of keeping the citizens of those countries in a perpetual state of poverty and of weakening the resolve of contributing nations, who believe their best efforts are being thwarted by the dishonest actions of a few.[14]

Occupational fraud in the United States is, thankfully, nowhere near the 40 percent level, but if we accept the 6 percent bottom-line figure advanced by the ACFE, it is not insignificant either. How can $600 billion per year disappear from our economy and not have an impact? How many investment opportunities were stunted or lost because of workplace fraud? Until we begin to think about such issues, I fear far too many people inside and outside of organizations will continue to accept occupational fraud as the cost of doing business.

Perhaps occupational fraud is the media's dirty little secret. It is, however, a secret with profound public policy implications. Donald Schon wrote many years ago of a concept of "ideas in good currency."[15] In using this term, Schon was speaking to the fact that the public, the government, or an organization can only focus its time and attention on so many things at once. Those items that are on the plate at a given period are "ideas in good currency": ideas that will receive time, discussion, attention, and resources. With time, some of these ideas will evolve, resolve, or dissolve, to be replaced by others. But without their turn at bat, a truly serious issue like occupational fraud will never receive the truly serious attention it deserves.

Schon's formulation has antecedent roots in an intelligence concept called "news content analysis." During World War II, British intelligence services placed a high premium on getting their hands on every newspaper they could find from enemy and axis countries. They studied these newspapers avidly to make predictions about what was happening in those economies and societies. Their theory was brilliant in its simplicity. They understood that editors were not only in the business of correcting style and spelling, but also functioned as filters. In this role they literally decided what was news and what was not. For every story printed there are dozens that are discarded. Thus does the editor make informed judgments about what is important in that town, region, or country. While their individual judgments may be flawed or skewed, cumulatively dozens or hundreds of editors produce an accurate portrayal of a society and its issues. Thus is the power of the press. One may like it or dislike it, but it is true, and the insightful advocate of any issue is well advised to be aware of it.

Even press exposure may not be a permanent panacea. Columnist Jonathan Alter recently wrote of the events of 9/11, six months later:

> Some days, the country seems to have changed little. After a brief surge, recruitment figures for the armed forces and community service are up only slightly.... Getting hassled at the airport, once a gladly fulfilled patriotic duty, is growing tiresome.... Buying habits,... changed almost not at all.[16]

Joseph S. Nye, Jr., Dean and Don K. Price Professor of Public Policy at the John F. Kennedy School of Government at Harvard, Former U.S. Assistant Secretary of Defense for International Security Affairs, and Former Chairman of the National Intelligence Council, spoke to these issues at a conference sponsored by that university in May 2002. He commented on the vicissitudes of public opinion and of the need for senior politicians and policymakers to seek to craft a sustaining level of public support for a counterterrorism effort that might last years, if not decades. Although he did not mention Edelman or his formulations, he was counseling against the sort of crisis mentality that sets inherent time limits for action and, thereby, success. The thrust of his comments was that crafting this level of public support over the long haul was going to be a significant challenge.[17]

Earlier research also commented on the tendency for pressing issues to remain unaddressed over long periods. James Bowman, in 1989, conducted a survey of 750 public administrators who were members of the American Society for Public Administration and found that most were hopeful that interest in public-sector ethics was more than a transitory issue. While they saw the need for the public sector to improve its ethical standards, many felt there was insufficient, sustained energy in the body politic to maintain needed momentum. Adding to this sense of frustration was the fact that over half these administrators believed that supervisors were from time to time under pressure to compromise standards, usually by their superiors, and well over half thought that organizations had no consistent approach to encouraging ethical behavior and discouraging unethical acts.[18] Such findings remind us again of Schon's ideas about "ideas in good currency." Employees are attuned in many ways to what is going on about them, and the organization that does not tend to its ethical dimensions, and certainly tolerance for occupational fraud is among them, may do so at some degree of peril.

Such inertia has consequences. The U.S. Merit Systems Protection Board conducted a study of 2,800 employees who left the federal government in Spring 1989. Of the 10 most common reasons for leaving, five—job stress, inconsistent policies/procedures, poor manager–employee relations, unfair promotion practices, and low morale—could be considered relevant to the status of the ethical environment in the workplace.[19]

This may represent our greatest challenge. If the horrific events of 9/11 can begin to fade, at least in their ability to affect human awareness and choice, how will our little fraud problem ever gain enough attention to be dealt with properly? Perhaps this is both a curse and a blessing. Fraud certainly has some emotional component; no one likes being cheated, but if we seek to ground our future efforts on a base of vengeance or moral indignation, we may also fade fairly quickly. Perhaps we are better served, in the long run, to view this as a purely business decision. We have the opportunity to improve financial performance in a cost-effective manner. That may lack sex appeal, but it may be more enduring. As the Pennsylvania Dutch in the section of Pennsylvania where I was raised were fond of saying, "Kissing don't last. Cooking do."

The development, adoption, and implementation of more consistent codes of conduct and controls may be more welcome than some might think. As far back as 1961 a special *Harvard Business Review* study of business practices indicated that most executives favored the establishment of codes of conduct in their areas of endeavor, and 71 percent said doing this would raise the standards of conduct in their fields. Perhaps most surprising, 88 percent said they would welcome such developments, since they believed they would be better equipped to resist unwarranted pressures to commit wrongful acts.[20]

Even earlier, in 1955, the *Annals of the American Academy of Political and Social Science* examined the state of ethical standards and professional conduct in several occupations and professions and found a continuing need to improve, update, strengthen, and coordinate mechanisms designed to promote ethical behavior. Fields surveyed and found in need of improvement included public accounting, architecture, medicine, engineering, public education, public service, and business.[21]

We may face a long and draining process if we are to seriously rethink our assumptions and approaches to occupational fraud, as the aforementioned material suggests. It will be a lengthy effort and will require unending attention. We must remember that for all their apparent successes, the law enforcement profession did not begin to make a significant impact on crime rates for the better part of 20 years into their new era of thinking and acting.

We must have the resolute support of those at the top if this effort is to succeed. Yates, writing more than 20 years ago, spoke to the need for topside support if the internal auditing profession was going to achieve anything close to its full potential. Observers of the political scene in New York City have likewise commented tellingly that the renovation of Times Square could not have happened were it not for the consistency of support throughout three mayoral administrations. Flowers are easy to plant, but they require continuing care to grow. Will such support be available, as we embark on what will certainly be a long and difficult process? It almost assuredly will, at least in spots, for there are certainly many farsighted and committed executives who will see the economic, if not moral, imperative to address issues so massive and persistent. Yet, we must temper our enthusiasm with the realization that not all will join our parade, at least not at first. *USA Today* published a poll in June 2002 that perhaps indicated a bit of the strange psychology that seems to appear from time to time. While the focus of this book has not been on executive misdeeds, I believe the following numbers speak for themselves as we consider the issue of upper-level support for a more effective response to occupational fraud. The poll, conducted by Starwoods Hotels, interviewed 401 top executives who golf.[22] The results?

Consider themselves to be honest in business	99%
Played with someone who cheated at golf	87%
Cheated themselves at golf	82%
Hated others who cheated at golf	82%
Believe that business and golf behavior parallel	72%

As they say in New York City—go figure.

Where We Go from Here

In 2001, Dave Richards, the chief audit executive at FirstEnergy Corporation and the then newly appointed chairperson of the Institute of Internal Auditors, spoke of the need for the profession to have a vision for the future if it was to progress and meet increasingly demanding challenges:

> Possessing a personal vision affords several benefits. A vision can empower us to take the actions necessary to drive our careers and lives in the direction we desire. A vision will help us attach the necessary importance to initiatives such as education and training, for example. It will also exact from us a level of commitment that enables us to stick with a project when we want to quit.
>
> Vision helps us remain focused when confronted with alternatives that are not in line with our vision, and it drives us to perform at levels never thought possible. Believing in a particular outcome awakens within us the ability to perform difficult tasks that are necessary to achieve the goal. In addition, people with vision are happier because they know where they are going and they have a plan for getting there.[23]

Richards then suggests six distinct steps that the profession and its members must take if they are to achieve their vision:

1. Take stock of where I am.
2. Decide what is important.
3. Determine where I want to be in the future.
4. Visualize what that target state would look like.
5. Condense the vision into a concise, memorable statement.
6. Link this statement to performance objectives and measures.

I believe we can take to heart Richards' vision and his view of how to get there. Our first task in thinking about the future of the fight against fraud in the workplace will be to decide what our vision shall be, then begin to work on the measures necessary to get there.

I would suggest the following as the beginning tasks of a vision toward which we can proceed:

- Develop uniform definitions and measures of what constitutes occupational fraud.
- Develop methods to share information on effective or innovative deterrence programs.
- Develop methods to encourage self-reporting of occupational fraud losses.

- Develop improved awareness of occupational fraud as a serious societal problem.
- Organize and promote research on methods to deter, detect, and investigate occupational fraud.
- Develop a more comprehensive and useful theory of occupational fraud causation.
- Secure the funding necessary to advance these activities.

If we accept these initial thoughts toward a vision for the future, how do we begin to form the learning community necessary to share to achieve these goals? The ACFE may be a logical place to consider, but even there we may need to self-define the mission of the entity. Certainly, there is much sharing and exploration that already takes place, but most of it is in the context of our more traditional activities. The National Fraud Center report describes several things as future needs in the effort to better address the broader arena of economic crime. Among these are laws, regulations, and better reporting systems; uniformity in reporting systems; public–private partnerships, and balancing privacy interests.[24] Following the issuance of their *1998 Fraud Survey*, the firm of KPMG is reported to have advanced the following as areas for additional focus in the future: reviewing and improving internal controls; improving the focus of senior management on fraud issues; improved training; better corporate codes of conduct; background checks on employees; and improved ethics training.[25] We may wish to consider whether these somewhat different goals should be part of the preliminary vision I have suggested.

Perhaps there are other professional groups or even academic institutions willing to assume a leadership role, but they must be willing to step forward and assume a formidable task and a variety of roles: fundraiser, research coordinator, arbitrator of definitions, liaison to other interested groups, and promoter of visibility of the issue. How do we begin, as individuals, a group, or a professional community, to break out of our normal frames of reference and explore other fields for promising theories and answers? How do we make contact with other professional associations, in say the fields of law enforcement, organizational behavior, social science, criminology, and psychology, to name but a few, to explore areas of common interest?

Bratton has noted his view that the policing profession benefited greatly from two complementary forces operating together—the infusion of outside social scientists into the inner sanctum of police departments and the continuing leadership and continuity provided by entities such as PERF and the Police Foundation. He also mentions an ancillary benefit that should be afforded serious consideration—the interest of an entire generation of social scientists in law enforcement matters. This is a two-way street or, in today's parlance a win-win situation. There is much research that needs to be done, and our profession can benefit mightily from it. At the same time, what we do for a living is inherently interesting. What causes an apparently loyal and competent employee to violate that trust, and how can they be dissuaded from doing it? Also, attempting to answer such questions is the stuff of which doctoral dissertations and research grants are made—a true win-win scenario.

Here, we enter into an area of duality that can, unlike a dance, move forward productively no matter which partner leads. We have examined several theories of white-collar crime and, in the case of the general theory, a construct that claims to explain all crime, white-collar crime included. Robert F. Meier, a professor and chair of the Department of Criminal Justice at the University of Nebraska—Omaha, has written of the history and sometimes-maddening complexity of theories of white-collar crime, noting: "If there is one persistent issue in the field of white-collar crime, it is its definition. More scholars have weighed in on this topic than perhaps any other, and there is relatively little to show for this fervent attention."[26] Meier goes on to quote Dr. Gilbert Geis, a professor, author, and authority on the subject, as observing: "The task of defining white-collar crime...is in many ways wearisome, perhaps best left to those with a predilection for medieval theological debates."[27]

These are specifically the sorts of debates I hope we as a profession can avoid, or at least limit, as we seek to move forward. In the face of a $600 billion (and probably growing) national problem, these debates can be interesting, but distracting and unproductive. It is a bit like pondering the chemical properties of aluminum while someone is stealing your hubcaps. Most of the issues Meier deals with in his examination are around what I have referred to as corporate crime. The issues that learned and articulate researchers and writers have devoted much of their time to have to do with whether the executive who sins to benefit the corporation is doing so as an individual or as the corporation. These are serious and consequential issues, and I do not wish to minimize them, but as both Meier and Geis have noted, much time has already been spent on these topics with little discernible result. This is not to say this debate should not go on. It should, for such matters are worthy of professional and public attention because they have significant consequences.

At the same time, we are still in need of theories and research—in my mind the two are reciprocal—as to why Susie in accounting or Bob in purchasing decides one day to start looting his or her employer or organization. In focusing on the boulders, we tend to ignore the sand. While the boulders are easier to see, in the aggregate there is an infinitely larger amount of sand.

Geis, Meier notes, seems to capture the essence of this perspective:

Geis has maintained that white-collar crime is a distinctive form of criminality, that the white-collar offenders are qualitatively different from conventional criminals, and that, as a result, different theoretical approaches may be required. It is also possible that efforts to control white-collar crime may be quite different from those used in restraining conventional criminality, although Geis consistently has advocated the use of the criminal sanction in the control of white-collar criminals.[28]

I find myself close to Geis' camp, issues of corporate crime notwithstanding. Through research, introspection, and the promulgation and testing of theories, we must become better and more effective in understanding this creature called occupational fraud. In taking this position, I am ever mindful of Putnam's telling observation that "the last refuge of a social-scientific scoundrel is to call for more research."[29] I hope I have, to at least some small degree, avoided hiding behind that rather large and convenient rock. I have attempted to offer thoughts, suggestions, and insights as to the specific needs for research and how that effort can best be organized and funded. With all due deference to Mr. Putnam, I note the next sentence he used after his pithy observation: "Nevertheless, I cannot forbear from suggesting some further lines of inquiry."[30]

If we are indeed ignorant in important areas where we should by this time have some degree of insight it is, I would argue, better to admit our ignorance and begin the necessary process of education rather than remain mired in the mud. Ideally, I hope we achieve a sense of *praxis*, a term I first encountered at the Washington Public Affairs Center of the University of Southern California in the late 1970s. It was *praxis*, a blending of theory and practice, which sought to enrich both the practitioner and academic sides of the field.[31]

The occupational fraud community, I believe, is well positioned to achieve precisely such a blending, to the benefit of all participants. There is substantial academic and research interest in the broader area of white-collar crime and, surely, some of that can be directed to occupational fraud. At the same time, there are scores of thousands of forensic professionals with an interest in these issues. The challenge is to bring them together in the most productive forum to advance the needs of the profession and, more important, those it serves.

Thinking of this agenda, as Greenfield notes, it is, literally, in our hands. Now will we do it? As Bess Myerson, a former Miss America and one-time New York City Commissioner of Consumer Affairs has noted: "The accomplice to the crime of corruption is frequently our own indifference."[32] (Myerson, it is noted, was charged with shoplifting later in her life. Perhaps a testimonial to the power of dopamine.) Our focus is not the public corruption the public appears to tolerate; it is theft by insiders that organizations and, even more important, their stakeholders appear to tolerate.

There are many drivers, in the current management vernacular, to begin this process. Certainly, management and shareholder expectations are high among them. When one reads of national delivery service companies such as Federal Express training its drivers which finger of which hand to carry their vehicle keys on, to save a few seconds on each delivery, or of production or assembly-line studies focusing on how to save a second here and there in manufacturing processes, it seems clear that organizations are already striving to achieve peak efficiency. Such things, in the aggregate, are important since they directly affect production costs, margins, and financial performance. If this is true, as it clearly appears to be, how can occupational fraud and its attendant losses continue to be considered the cost of doing business?

The professional pride and integrity of forensic practitioners is another powerful incentive, since any professional worthy of the name should have an innate curiosity and responsibility to improve their craft and calling. Finally, there are the employees themselves. While they may grumble about the company cops or the audit weenies, they also look to these same professionals to be the guardians of the organization's financial health and integrity. Perhaps recent corporate events were not all bad, if a healthy skepticism now abounds in the workplace. As one former vice president of a stricken company noted, "Whatever company I work for in the future, I'll never again trust at face value what top executives say."[33] This may indeed be a sad commentary, but it is also the perceived, if unstated, reality for many employees at various levels whose income, health and life insurance, and retirement may be put in jeopardy by the actions of but a few persons who will almost certainly not suffer like consequences.

At least on an international level, the utility and worth of the forensic profession seems to be gaining in acceptance and recognition. The Ernst & Young study of more than 10,000 international organizations and their exposure to fraud, released in 2000, is reported to have found that of those respondents who used forensic professionals to address issues in their organizations, 80 percent were pleased with the results.[34] While this obviously implies that 20 percent either were not pleased or did not respond to the question, it appears to compare favorably with many of the comments often heard about client satisfaction with outside professional service providers.

Even for the conscientious and energetic board member or executive officer, the task may be becoming increasingly difficult. Some executives are already expressing their frustrations at trying to manage the flow of data concerning business operations scattered widely throughout the globe. The increasing use of computers that can instantaneously amass and transmit reams of data may only exacerbate this information deluge.[35]

Because of technology and public sentiment, the number of potential allegations against once-sacrosanct corporate seniors may be growing. Shortly after the Enron scandal broke, one member of Congress who was interested in the matter had his staff create an Enron Tip Line Web page. A number of leads came into this site, including one of the first allegations that Enron's auditors may have been destroying documents. The FBI, the National White Collar Crime Center, and the Software Business Alliance also operate tip line Web sites, as do several groups interested in other forms of criminal activity.[36] The director of enforcement for the SEC, Stephen Cutler, noted recently that since the Enron controversy the online complaint center of that agency received an average of 525 e-mails per day, up 45 percent from last year's average volume. He also noted that on February 5, 2002, the agency received 763 e-mail alerts to possible fraudulent activity—a record.[37]

As mentioned previously, the forensic professional may increasingly be in the difficult position of the Roman god Janus, who had two faces, one looking forward and one looking back. We can do little about how senior executives are chosen, but we may be called on in the future to monitor more closely how they act. At this writing, the pressures pushing in this direction are clear and growing. Unions, whose huge pension funds are heavily invested in corporate America, have both a clear financial interest in the well-being of these investments and, by the rationale of their existence, a long-standing distrust of corporate management. After a recent meeting about such issues, *The Wall Street Journal* made the following observation:

> Investors, including public funds, "let down their guard" during boom years, says Richard Trumka, AFL-CIO secretary-treasurer. But no longer, he says. About 30 public-fund trustees over the weekend heard from AFL-CIO officials about executive compensation, Wall Street research and corporate conflicts of interest.[38]

The possibility, indeed likelihood, of the need for increased scrutiny is also coming from other sources as well. *The Wall Street Journal* also reported on high-level deliberations within the Bush Administration in the wake of the Enron situation, noting that the Administration was seeking alternatives to increase officer and director responsibiltity when shareholders were mislead, even if this was the result of carelessness rather than actual malfeasance. The story further reported Treasury Secretary Paul O'Neill cautioning corporate executives that they would now be held to a standard of negligence that is more encompassing than in the past. Essentially, the standard goes beyond the commission of a wrongdoing and would now include the failure to become aware of a wrong-doing.[39]

Such sentiments may also be shared by the public at large. A *Wall Street Journal*/NBC poll has shown that 57 percent of respondents said that corporate leaders' standards and values have dropped in the past 20 years, as opposed to 38 percent who said they either rose or stayed the same. This represents a sharp departure from views expressed just four years ago, when 53 percent of respondents rated corporate leaders' standards as being the same or higher than in the past. Perhaps even more telling, fully 60 percent of professionals and managers— persons familiar with the business landscape—said business standards today are lower. Such sentiments may also have political consequences. Forty-nine percent of persons polled in the survey favored increased government regulation of business practices, as opposed to 39 percent who did not.[40]

Corporate and organizational boards are not deaf to such concerns, at least for the time being. *The Wall Street Journal* reports that many boards and board members are actively seeking outside professional assistance to help educate and guide them in the pursuit of their duties. Some boards are even setting up dedicated Web sites for this purpose, to increase their awareness of company activities, to improve their access to management, and to be able to ask questions in a more rapid and efficient manner.[41]

While some may attribute such attitudes to the propensity of the news media to produce saturation coverage of events of interest, other data suggest that these opinions may have more of a solid footing in fact. The U.S. Sentencing Commission has reported that in 2000 there were 133 companies prosecuted for fraud, tax, or antitrust actions. These organizations were ordered to pay an average of $2,282,646 in fines.[42] Such volume and frequency, an average of about 2.5 incidents per week, may help explain why the media appears to be relentlessly pounding organizational America. It may not be the prejudice of the so-called antibusiness media; it may just be that they are reporting the news. If the cases were not there, they could not report them.

The concept of the government looking to the private sector for self-policing activities that benefit governmental programs and objectives is hardly new. The development and evolution of anti–money laundering policies in the United States has always relied heavily on policing, compliance, and reporting by affected institutions. Starting with banks more than 20 years ago, these requirements have spread over time to casinos, stock brokerage houses, and other groups that routinely deal in high volumes of liquid assets. So too, in a post-Enron environment, I suspect we will see a broadening of reporting and recordkeeping requirements with much, if not most, of the burden being pushed downward to the private sector by the federal government. The SEC is already complaining about a lack of resources and a strained budget as it confronts a burgeoning workload in the post-Enron weeks and months, and it appears that these issues will more likely worsen than abate.[43]

Such pressures may be motivated by positive, as well as negative, consequences. A current survey of opinion leaders—1,155 shareholder groups in the United States, institutional investors, CEOs, financial analysts, and the like—announced that 48 percent believe that a CEO's reputation has an impact on the valuation of that stock. Of those holding this belief, 95 percent advised such an opinion would influence their decision as to whether to buy that stock, 93 percent stated it would influence their decision to partner or merge with that company, and 92 percent advised that their opinion of the CEO would affect their confidence in that stock during a market slump.[44]

A growing number of law enforcement agencies, which have pioneered so much in their efforts to become more effective, have already accepted this rationale. Through the efforts of organizations such as the Commission on Accreditation for Law Enforcement Agencies (CALEA), they pay for outside bodies to come in and survey and benchmark their activities and operations. The benefits CALEA attaches to meeting their standards are as follows:[45]

- Reduce exposure to liability.
- Have a comprehensive, thought-out written directive system.
- Implement modern management practices.
- Increase public and governmental support.
- Be recognized for excellence

Such benefits seem to make sense to the many law enforcement bodies that go through CALEA examination and certification. They also, upon reflection, make sense for just about any organization interested in its occupational fraud risk profile.

In this regard, we may be looking up in the organization more than we have done in the past. At the same time, we will spend most of our time looking down, at the broad, sprawling, and twisted mass of occupational fraud that has confounded us so to date. Our task, it seems, is never simple and appears to be growing more complex and demanding. For these reasons and more, we must begin to explore alternative methods of doing our work. If we stay with our old models, Chief Bratton's paradigm of "rapid response, rapid patrols, and reactive investigation," we will be forever doomed to return to the same noisy street corner again and again, without discernible effect.

Steve Huggins is the Senior Vice President for Strategic Resources and Information Technology at the Goodrich Corporation. As such, he is part of the team that helped change the tire and plastics manufacturer into a $4 billion global aerospace company. In discussing this transformation process, he offered the following observation about the best quality a person can have when confronting the business of change: "Curiosity. To go where no one has gone before. To seek out new worlds and new civilizations. A fine sense of wonder and a hunger to learn make every day a quest. The alternative is incremental, linear thinking, which never creates the breakthroughs necessary for business—or personal—growth."[46]

Brandenburger and Nalebuff, in their book about new business strategies based on the capabilities of game theory, put it this way:

> An old Chinese proverb explains: if you continue on the course you're headed, that's where you'll end up. Sometimes that's good, sometimes not.... That's because you're playing the wrong game: you need to change it.... Real success comes from actively shaping the game you play—from making the game you want, not taking the game you find.[47]

I believe it is appropriate for a forensic practitioner writing for an audience of other forensic practitioners to first and foremost, be honest. The opening line of this work said it would be long on questions and short on answers. I did not lie to you. Throughout this work I have questioned some of what organizational

America and the forensic profession does. I have spent, with considerable pride, my entire adult life in large organizations, most of it in one form or another of forensic investigations. To some, I may appear disloyal. If that is the case, so be it, but it is not my intent. I am aware of the old story, recounted by author Chris Offut, of the axe being carried into the woods. When the trees saw it, they gazed at it and said, "Look, the handle is one of us." I have tried to be the loyal watchman, shouting "Fire!" because I believe we can do better. I hear the river running. The next tidal wave will happen someday—it always does. But we are foolish, as it recedes and we survey the damage, if we do not listen for the river.

ENDNOTES

Introduction

1. Michael S. Sitrick, with Allan Mayer, *Spin* (Washington, DC:Regnery Publishing, 1998), 123–124.

2. Ward made these comments at a Northeast Regional Breakfast Meeting of the FBI National Academy Associates in New York City in the late 1980s. The author was present.

3. Erroll J. Yates, "Internal Audit: A Managerial Control," *Internal Auditor* (1977), reprinted and recounted in Jeffrey Ridley, "Worth Repeating," *Internal Auditor* (December 2001), 37–39.

4. The Association of Certified Fraud Examiners, *2002 Report to the Nation: Occupational Fraud and Abuse* (Austin, TX: 2002), 17.

5. When Frank Gruttadauria, a fugitive stockbroker suspected of absconding with as much as $125 million of client money over a 15-year period, turned himself in to the FBI in Cleveland, Ohio, on February 9, 2002 he is reported to have said: "I was surprised I got away with it for so long" (CBS Evening News, February 10, 2002). Likewise, when convicted spy Robert Hanssen, a career FBI agent assigned to highly sensitive counterintelligence investigations, was arrested in Northern Virginia on February 18, 2001 for selling secrets to the Russians over a period of many years, he is reported to have said: "What took you so long?" We normally do not think of espionage as a form of fraud, but it is. Issues of classifications and national security damage aside, it is merely the selling of trade secrets or intellectual property to a competitor for money. For a recounting of Hanssen, his career, and likely motivations see: David A. Vise, *The Bureau and the Mole* (New York: Atlantic Monthly Press, 2002). As to the frequency of "What took you so long?" comments, we may wish to ponder, especially from a game theory perspective, whether our opponents (the fraud perpetrators) view us as being more effective than we view ourselves. If such is the case, it is still useful information when crafting a strategy in a game theory environment.

Chapter 1

1. Laura A. Hauth, "The History of New York's Finest," in *Selected Readings in Criminal Justice*, ed. Philip L. Reichel (San Diego, CA: Greenhaven Press, 1998), 74–76.

2. *Crime in America: Causes and Cures* (Books by *U.S. News & World Report*, 1972), 13–15.

3. Randall R. Rader and Patrick B. McGuigan, "Criminal Justice Reform: A Blueprint," from the book *Criminal Justice Reform: A Blueprint* by Randall R. Rader and Patrick B. McGuigan, 1. Copyright 1983 by Henry Regnery Publishing. All rights reserved. Reprinted by special permission of Regnery Publishing, Inc. Washington, D.C.

4. Ramsey Clark, *Crime in America: Observations on Its Nature, Causes, Prevention and Control* (New York: Simon & Schuster, 1970).

5. James Lardner and Thomas Repetto, *NYPD: A City And Its Police* (New York: Henry Holt and Company, 2000), 256, 271, 278.

6. Milton Meltzer, *Crime in America* (New York: Morrow Junior Books, 1990), 19.

7. *Id.*

8. *Id.*, 18–19.

9. The American Bar Association Criminal Justice Section and the Center for Continuing Legal Education, *White Collar Crime 2002* (Chicago: ABA, 2002). Proceedings of meetings held at Miami Beach, Florida, February 27 to March 1, 2002.

10. The Hastings Center, *The Teaching of Ethics in American Higher Education* (Hastings-On-Hudson, NY: The Hastings Center, 1980), 2–3.

11. James H. Auten, "Productivity: A Challenge for the 80's," Police Training Institute, University of Illinois, in *Selected Readings in Law Enforcement Management* (Washington, DC: FBI Academy, U.S. Department of Justice, undated), II-47–52.

12. Special Agent William L. Tafoya, Editorial Note to "Futuristics: New Tools for Criminal Justice Executives," presented March 25, 1983, at the 1983 Annual Meeting of the Academy of Criminal Justice Sciences, March 22–26, 1983, San Antonio, Texas. Reprinted in *Selected Readings In Law Enforcement Management.*

13. *Id.*, II-57, citing Jack L. Kuykendall and Peter C. Onsinger, *Community Police Administration* (Chicago: Nelson-Hall, 1975), 13; and Thomas A. Reppetto, *The Blue Parade* (New York: The Free Press, 1978), 11.

14. *See* note 4, 33.

15. Malcolm W. Klein, *The American Street Gang: Its Nature, Prevalence, and Control* (New York: Oxford University Press, 1995), 90–91.

16. *Id.*, 34.

17. *Id.*, 114.

18. *Id.*, 120.

19. *Id.*, 199.

20. *See* note 8, 40.

21. *Id.*, 39–46.

22. U.S. Department of Justice, Federal Bureau of Prisons, National Institute of Corrections, *www.fbi.gov.* Accessed on January 12. 2002.

23. Morgan Reynolds, "Q: Will Building More U.S. Prisons Take a Bite out of Crime?," *Insight* (June 7, 1999), available online at *www.findarticles.com.*

24. "Private Prisons Benefit Local Economies," *PR Newswire,* (October 25, 2001), available online at *www.findarticles.com.*

25. Nicholas Kulish and Joseph T. Hallinan, "States' Tight Budgets Compel Easing of Prison-Sentence Policies," *The Wall Street Journal* (February 7, 2002), B-7.

26. Janine Latus Musick, "Keeping Would Be Thieves at Bay," *Nation's Business* (October 1998), available online at *www.findarticles.com.*

27. William Bratton, with Peter Knobler, *Turnaround: How America's Top Cop Reversed the Crime Epidemic* (New York: Random House, 1998), 8.

28. *Id.*, 98.

29. *Id.*, 93.

30. *Id.*, 213.

31. *Id.*, 94.

32. Peter K. Manning, *Police Work: The Social Organization of Policing* (Cambridge, MA: MIT Press, 1979), 103.

33. *Id.*, 111–116.

34. *Id.*, 117.

35. *Id.*, 127.

36. *Id.*, 129–132.

37. *See* note 29, 142–143.

38. *Id.*, 151.

39. *Id.*, 209.

40. *Id.*, 215–216.

41. *Id.*

42. Graham T. Allison, *Essence of Decision* (New York: Little Brown & Co., 1971).

43. Albert A. Seedman and Peter Hellman, *Chief* (New York: Arthur Fields Books Inc., 1974), 434–435.

44. Irwin Garfinkel, "Foreword," in Murray Edelman, *Political Language: Words That Succeed and Policies That Fail* (New York: Academic Press, 1977), xiii.

45. Michael Lipsky, "Introduction," in Murray Edelman, *Political Language: Words That Succeed and Policies That Fail* (New York: Academic Press, 1977), xiii.

46. *Id.*, 3.

47. *Id.*, 4.

48. *Id.*, 43–44.

49. *See* note 29, 242.

50. Edwin J. Delattre, *Character and Cops: Ethics in Policing* (Washington, DC: American Enterprise Institute for Public Policy Research, 1989), 211–212.

51. The public still, however, puts a heavy emphasis on crime and issues related to it. In a Gallup poll conducted between August 29 and September 5, 2000, 60 percent of respondents rated crime as an extremely or very serious issue. Poll Topics & Trends—Crime, The Gallup Organization, *www.gallup.org*. Accessed January 12, 2002.

52. *See* note 6, 107.

53. Fox Butterfield, "Study Finds Steady Increase at All Levels of Government in Cost of Criminal Justice," *The New York Times* (February 11. 2002), A-14.

54. In 2001, *Forbes* magazine conducted a special survey to attempt to determine how the changing demographic and social makeup of the United States would affect the nation's business. It consisted of "original research from 4,000 interviews on the attitudes, behaviors, and perspectives on life in the U.S." The research commenced in August 2001 (p. 3). On the issue of crime and policing, four groups (White, Non-Hispanic; Hispanic; African American; and Asian) were asked "How Much Do You Trust" various institutions: the police, the legal system, the current government, news on TV, and the daily newspaper. The police were trusted most by White/Non-Hispanic; were trusted second most, by one percentage point under the legal system, by Hispanics; were tied with the legal system as most trusted by African Americans; and were trusted third-most by Asians, following news on TV, and the legal system (p. 31). "Portrait Of The New America: A Multicultural Marketplace," special supplement to *Forbes*, (January 21, 2002). Generally speaking, from these figures is does not appear that trust in the police is a primary problem in effecting crime control. The somewhat good showing the police made versus other institutions may be a result of their current crime control efforts.

Chapter 2

1. As of the publication date of their review of crime in the United States, *U.S. News & World Report* listed improving the police, improving the courts, and improving corrections. Community involvement is mentioned in regard to these initiatives, but in no focused or systematic fashion. *Crime in America: Causes and Cures* (Books by *U.S. News & World Report*, 1972), 172–179

2. Clark, *Crime in America*, 133–137.

3. All references to Goldstein and his work are from "Professor Herman Goldstein, the 'father' of problem-oriented policing," interview by Marie Simonetti Rosen, *Law Enforcement News* 23, no. 461, (February 14, 1997), 8–11. Reprinted with permission of *Law Enforcement News* (John Jay College of Criminal Justice, New York: 1997).

4. It is often the reaction of the general public that police discretion is an oxymoron since cops, by definition, enforce the law, and the law is what it is. Any deviation from this strict standard is often assumed to be the result of police corruption or favoritism. To most police officers and knowledgeable observers of the police function, this view is simply incorrect. There are, of course, elements of corruption and favoritism in law enforcement, just as there are in any profession or calling, but confusing discretion with corruption is a serious mistake most of the time. The interesting thing is we all know this instinctively, since almost none of us drives at 55 (or 65) on any U.S. interstate highway so marked. We understand police tolerance for some degree of speeding and adjust our behavior accordingly in a sort of informal and undocumented pact with the officers who patrol those roads.

5. 221 F.3d 329 (2d Cir. 2000), cert denied, 122 S.Ct.44 (2001), cited in Elliot B. Spector, "Stopping Suspects Based On Racial And Ethnic Descriptions," *The Police Chief* (January 2002), p.10. *The Police Chief* is published by The International Association of Chiefs of Police, Inc.

6. *See* note 3, 8.

7. *Id.*

8. *Id.*

9. *Id.*

10. *Id.*, 9.

11. Conversations with Carson Dunbar, April 9–10, 2002.

12. *See* note 3, 10.

13. *Id.*

14. *Id.*

15. *Id.*, 8.

16. "Prof. George Kelling, co-author of 'Fixing Broken Windows'," interview by Marie Simonetti Rosen, *Law Enforcement News* 25, no. 511, 512, (May 15 and 31, 1999), 8. Reprinted with permission of *Law Enforcement News* (John Jay College of Criminal Justice, New York: 1999).

17. *Id.*

18. Lardner and Repetto, *NYPD: A City and Its Police*, 295.

19. *See* note 16. For a critique of the effectiveness of "broken windows" theories and applications, see "The Broken-Windows Myth," by Bernard E. Harcourt, *The New York Times* (September 11, 2001), A-23. Harcourt notes, among other observations, that increased levels of enforcement in New York City have produced a 66 percent jump in misdemeanor arrests and "sharp increases in stop-and-frisks that allow more searches for guns, more checks

for outstanding warrants, and more fingerprint collection." He observes, however: "This enhanced surveillance has come with a big price tag: a 37 percent increase in complaints of police misconduct from 1993 to 1999, significant racial disparities in enforcement, illegal strip searches, and many traumatic encounters"

20. *See* note 16.

21. Id. The "root causes" philosophy is not found solely in law enforcement. Writing about the U.S. and international military response to the events of September 11, 2001, author Victor David Hanson has noted that many tend to believe war itself emanates from concrete injustices, ignorance, or insanity, rather than mere evil. *See* Victor Davis Hanson, "The Longest War," *American Heritage* (February/March 2002), 45.

22. *See* note 2.

23. Malcolm Gladwell, "Why Some People Turn into Violent Criminals," in Reichel, *Selected Readings in Criminal Justice*, 33–46.

24. Sarah Glazer, "Does Better Policing Reduce Crime?," in Reichel, *Selected Readings in Criminal Justice*, 94–96.

25. Philip Terzian, "Idle, Addicted, Violent . . . and Self-Pitying" (review of *Life at the Bottom*, by Theodore Dalrymple), *The Wall Street Journal* (February 21, 2002) A-16.

26. Russell Kirk, "Criminal Character and Mercy," from the book *Criminal Justice Reform: A Blueprint* by Randall R. Rader and Patrick B. McGuigan, 219. Copyright 1983 by Henry Regnery Publishing. All rights reserved. Reprinted by special permission of Regnery Publishing, Inc. Washington, D.C.

27. William A. Stanmeyer, "Making Criminal Justice Work," from the book *Criminal Justice Reform: A Blueprint* by Randall R. Rader and Patrick B. McGuigan, 239. Copyright 1983 by Henry Regnery Publishing. All rights reserved. Reprinted by special permission of Regnery Publishing, Inc. Washington, D.C.

28. Robert J. Kelly, "Crime Causation from the Inmates' Standpoint," in Reichel, *Selected Readings in Criminal Justice*, 47–52.

29. *See* note 16.

30. A classic, and oft-cited, example of this secondary effect of enforcement of public-order crimes affecting the rate of more serious crimes was seen in the New York City subways. When fare-beaters were targeted the number of concealed weapons arrests rose sharply, thus lowering the rate of more serious crimes on the subway, a chronic problem for many years. *See* note 16, 10.

31. Neil Barsky, "From Triple-X to Just Extraordinary" (book review of *Times Square Roulette*, by Lynne B. Sagalyn), *The Wall Street Journal*, (February 20, 2002) A-20.

32. *See* note 16.

33. *See* note 16, 6. Again, with regard to the painful issue of making hard social choices, such as incarcerating people for relatively minor offenses, Hanson (*see* note 21, 46), is instructive. He notes, with regard to the military actions against bin Laden and other terrorists: "Real morality does not permit hesitating out of fear of injuring the innocent or suffering casualties. . . . Lincoln called such sacrifices 'the terrible arithmetic' . . . (and) which Thucydides called the 'harsh schoolmaster'."

34. *See* note 16, 10.

35. Peter C. Dodenhoff, "LEN Salutes Its 1996 People of the Year, the NYPD and Its Compstat Process," *Law Enforcement News* 22, no. 458, 1, 4. Reprinted with permission of *Law Enforcement News* (John Jay College of Criminal Justice, New York: 1996).

36. *Id.*, 4.

37. *Id.*

38. William K. Rashbaum, "Crime-Fighting by Computer: Scope Widens," *The New York Times* (March 24, 2002), 43.

39. Andy Newman, "Crime Shows Biggest Drop in Five Years," *The New York Times* (January 1, 2002), B-1.

40. Vincent E. Henry, *The COMPSTAT Paradigm: Management Accountability in Policing, Business and the Public Sector* (Flushing, NY: Looseleaf Law Publications, Inc., 2002), 245–248.

41. National Institute of Justice, Office of Justice Programs, U.S. Department of Justice, *Excellence in Problem-Oriented Policing: The 2000 Herman Goldstein Award Winners*, (November 2001), 1.

42. *Id.*, 4–47.

43. Police Executive Research Forum, *Excellence in Problem-Oriented Policing: The 2001 Herman Goldstein Award Winners* (December 2001), 3–62.

44. Butterfield, "Study Finds Steady Increase," A-14.

45. Marc Mauer, "The Social Cost of America's Race to Incarcerate," Reprinted from *Phi Kappa Phi Forum* 82, no. 1 (Winter 2002), 30. Copyright by Marc Mauer, reprinted by permission of the publishers.

46. Bratton, *Turnaround*, 290.

47. John D. Bessler, "America's Death Penalty: Just Another Form of Violence," Reprinted from *Phi Kappa Phi Forum* 82, no. 1 (Winter 2002), 17. Copyright by John D. Bessler, reprinted by permission of the publishers.

48. "If You Love Police Stats," *Community Links* (Magazine of the Community Policing Consortium), (March 2002), 19.

49. "For Some Cities, Crime Continues to Drop," *Law Enforcement News* 28, no. 575 (April 15, 2002), 7. Reprinted with permission of *Law Enforcement News* (John Jay College of Criminal Justice, New York: 2002).

50. *Id.*

Chapter 3

1. Jack Bologna, *Handbook on Corporate Fraud* (Boston: Butterworth-Heinemann, 1993), 4. Also see William C. Cunningham, John J. Strauchs, and Clifford W. Van Meter, *The Hallcrest Report II* (Stoneham, MA: Butterworth-Heinemann, 1990), 31.

2. Bologna, 5. Also see Henry S. Ruth, *The Nature, Impact, and Prosecution of White Collar Crime* (Washington, DC: U.S. Government Printing Office, 1970), "Foreword."

3. Joseph T. Wells, CFE, CPA, *Occupational Fraud and Abuse* (Austin, TX: Obsidian, 1997), 35.

4. "Fraud Statistics," The Association of Certified Fraud Examiners, *www.acfc.org.* Accessed March 28, 2002..

5. ACFE, 2002 *Report to the Nation,* ii.

6. Davita Silfen Glasberg, "The Dialectics of White Collar Crime: The Anatomy of the Savings and Loan Crisis and the Case of Silverado Banking, Savings, and Loan," *The American Journal of Economics and Sociology* (October 1998), available online at *www.findarticles.com.*

7. U.S. Department of Justice, *Fiscal Year 2000 Performance Report* and *Fiscal Year 2002 Performance Plan.*

8. Matthew Weinstock, "Erroneous Payments Cost Government $20 Billion in 2001," *www.govexec.com.* Accessed May 31, 2002.

9. Meltzer, *Crime in America*, 50.

10. *Id.*, 49.

11. Training and Research Institute, National White Collar Crime Center, *The National Public Survey on White Collar Crime* (Morgantown, WV: NWCCC, 2000), 2, citing President's Commission on Law Enforcement and Administration of Justice, "Challenge of Crime in a Free Society (Washington, DC: Government Printing Office, 1968).

12. *Id.*, 2.

13. *Id.*, 6.

14. Telephone interview with John Kane, National White Collar Crime Center, March 14, 2002.

15. *See* note 11.

16. Brian W. Carpenter and Daniel P. Mahoney, "Analyzing Organizational Fraud," *Internal Auditor*, (April 2001) 34–35.

17. *Id.*

18. *Id.*

19. Pinkerton, "Top Security Threats and Management Issues Facing Corporate America: 2002 Survey of Fortune 1000 Companies," 2–10.

20. "Obese Nation," 60 Minutes (February 10, 2002).

21. Alex Rodriguez interview, "Mike and the Mad Dog," radio program, WFAN-AM, New York City (March 5, 2002).

22. John R. Wilke, "Visa, MasterCard Face Huge Potential Damages in Suit," *The Wall Street Journal* (June 6, 2002), B-1.

23. Michael Brzezinski, "Re-engineering the Drug Business," *The New York Times Magazine* (June 23, 2002), 26.

24. *Fiscal Year 2001 Federal Financial Management Report*, Office of Management and Budget, 16.

25. Richard M. Sheridan, "Working the Data Mines," *Security Management* (April 2002), 72.

26. *See* note 14.

27. *FraudInfo Newsletter* 2, no. 11, (March 17, 2000), published electronically by the Association of Certified Fraud Examiners.

28. Jerry Adler, "The 'Thrill' of Theft," *Newsweek* (February 25, 2002), 52–53.

29. *White Collar Crime Study*, FBI National Press Office (March 6, 2002).

30. *See* note 3, 513.

31. Carol Hymowitz, "Managers Must Respond to Employee Concerns about Honest Business," *The Wall Street Journal* (February 19, 2002), B-1.

32. Michael R. Young, "The Origin of Financial Fraud," in *Accounting Irregularities and Financial Fraud*, ed. Michael R. Young (New York: Harcourt Professional Publishing, 2000), 1.

33. Holman W. Jenkins, Jr., "The New Business Casual: Prison Stripes," *The Wall Street Journal* (March 13, 2002), A-19.

34. L. J. Brooks, "Corporate Ethical Performance: Trends, Forecasts and Outlooks," *Journal of Business Ethics*, no.8 (January 1989), 31–32.

35. Kenneth Labich, "The New Crisis in Business Ethics," *Fortune* (April 20, 1992), 167–176.

36. "Employee Fraud Prevalent in the Workplace: Ernst & Young Study," press release by Ernst & Young LLP—Canada, (Toronto: Ernst & Young, 2001). Poll conducted by Ipsos-Reid between October 4–15, 2001.

37. For example, a recent survey of taxpayers and their attitudes toward cheating found that 76 percent said they should not cheat on their taxes, indicating that almost one-quarter of respondents felt otherwise. Eleven percent said it was all right to cheat a little, and 5 percent said it was all right to cheat as much as possible. A similar survey conducted in 1999 found those who said they should not cheat to be 87 percent of respondents. It appears, then, that those disinclined to cheat to some degree declined by 11 percent. "As Audits Decline, Fewer Taxpayers Balk at a Bit of Cheating," *The New York Times* (January 19, 2002), A-11.

38. *FraudInfo Newsletter* 4, no. 15 (April 10, 2002), published electronically by the Association of Certified Fraud Examiners, Austin, Texas.

39. Diane Sears Campbell, "Focus on Cyber-Fraud," *Internal Auditor* (February 2002), 33.

40. *See* note 16, 36.

41. *The Small Business Fraud Prevention Manual*, (Austin, TX: The Association of Certified Fraud Examiners), quoted in *FraudInfo Newsletter* 4, no. 13 (March 27, 2002), published by The Association of Certified Fraud Examiners, Austin, Texas.

42. *FraudInfo Newsletter* 4, no. 18 (May 1, 2002), published electronically by The Association of Certified Fraud Examiners, Austin, Texas.

43. Jennifer S. Lee, "Making Losers out of Auction Winners," *The New York Times* (March 7, 2002), G-7.

44. Brian Krebs, "Internet Auction Fraud Is Top Consumer Complaint—FBI" (April 10, 2002), *www.Newsbytes.com*.

45. *See* note 39, 30.

46. "Cyber Crime Bleeds U.S. Corporations, Survey Shows; Financial Losses from Attacks Climb for Third Year in a Row," news release, Computer Security Institute, San Francisco, California (April 7, 2002), in conference proceedings, *Undermining Terrorism: New Concepts and Policies for an Interdependent World*, John F. Kennedy School of Government, Harvard University (May 3–4, 2002).

47. *FraudInfo Newsletter* 2, no. 3, (March 7, 2002), published electronically by the Association of Certified Fraud Examiners.

48. Douglas M. Watson, "Whom Do You Trust?" *The White Paper* (March/April 2002), 28.

49. Al Cameron, "How to Stop Internet Credit Card Thieves," in *Working Together to Reduce the Impact of Economic Crime*, conference proceedings of the Economic Crime Summit, Crystal City, Virginia (May 6–8, 2002), 20.

50. *See* note 43, G-1.

51. Adam Clymer, "Arrests Made in a Sweep Against Thefts of Identities," *The New York Times* (May 3, 2002), A-16.

52. *Id.*

53. John F. Ellingson and Christopher S. Williams, "Facing the Identity Crisis," in *Working Together to Reduce the Impact of Economic Crime*, conference proceedings of the Economic Crime Summit, Crystal City, Virginia (May 6–8, 2002), 22.

54. David Pace, "Investigators Cannot Estimate Extent of Government Credit Card Abuse," Associated Press Newspapers (May 1, 2002).

Chapter 4

1. Wells, *Occupational Fraud and Abuse*, 8–10.

2. *Id.*, 10–11.

3. *Id.*, 12–14.

4. *Id.*, 22.

5. *Id.*, 22–23.

6. *Id.*, 25–26.

7. *Id.*, 25.

8. *Id.*

9. This observation is remarkably consistent with a comment made by former NYPD Detective Bob Leuci during a seminar in the early 1990s at the FBI Academy in Quantico, Virginia. Leuci had been the subject of a major police corruption probe by the NYPD, had evidence developed against him, began to work with the authorities conducting the probe, and wore a wire (a concealed tape recorder) against many of his former associates. Many were dismissed as a result of the probe, some went to jail, and one or two committed suicide. The tale of Leuci's exploits was turned into a book and a movie, both titled "Prince of the City." On occasion he would be hired by the FBI as a guest lecturer on the dangers of corruption in law enforcement in general, and in undercover operations in particular. During one of these sessions, with about 30 FBI undercover agents in attendance, he made the following observation. Leuci noted words to the effect that, "In every organization, 5 percent of the people are dirty. No matter what you do, they are going to be dirty. And in every organization, 5 percent of the people are clean. You can't tempt them to do anything wrong. The rest are waiting to see what happens."

   To the writer, who was in attendance, Leuci was speaking to issues of organizational culture and organizational socialization processes. I understood Leuci to be saying that if the culture of the organization, at the working level, is that certain things are okay, regardless of what the rulebook says, most people will be influenced to follow this guidance.

10. All references to Hollinger-Clark are found in Wells, 25–26. *See* also note 9.

11. *White Collar Crime Study*, FBI National Press Office (March 6, 2002).

12. *See* note 1, 29–30.

13. *Id.*, 31–32.

14. *Id.*, 32. *See* also note 9.

15. James S. Bowman, "Ethics in Government: A National Survey of Public Administrators," *Public Administration Review*, 50, May-June 1990, 350.

16. *See* note 1, 33.

17. Bologna, *Handbook on Corporate Fraud*, 21–22.

18. *Id.*, 30–31.

19. George Van Nostrand and Anthony J. Luizzo, "The Hidden Cost of Downsizing: Where Loyalty Dies, Fraud Grows," *The White Paper* (Association of Certified Fraud Examiners) 10, no. 5 (September/October 1996), 23–25.

20. *Id.*, 24.

21. Carpenter and Mahoney, "Analyzing Organizational Fraud," 36.

22. Michael R. Gottfredson and Travis Hirschi, *A General Theory of Crime* (Stanford, CA: Stanford University Press, 1990).

23. *Id.*, 255–256.

24. *Id.*, 256.

25. *Id.*

26. *Id.*

27. *Id.*, 89–90.

28. *Id.*, 182.

29. *Id.*, 183–184.

30. *Id.*, 185–186.

31. *Id.*, 186–188.

32. *Id.*, 188–190.

33. *Id.*, 190.

34. *Id.*, 191–192.

35. *Id.*, 192–196.

36. *Id.*, 196–201.

37. Darrell Steffensmeier, "On the Causes of 'White-Collar' Crime: An Assessment of Hirschi and Gottfredson's Claims," *Criminology* 27, no. 2 (1989), 346.

38. *Id.*, 347.

39. *Id.*, 349.

40. *Id.*, 352–354.

41. Gary E. Reed and Peter Cleary Yeager, "Organizational Offending and Neoclassical Criminology: Challenging the Reach of a General Theory of Crime," *Criminology* 34, no. 3, (1996), 357.

42. *Id.*, 363–365.

43. *Id.*, 364–367.

44. *Id.*, 376–377.

45. ACFE, *2002 Report to the Nation*, 9.

46. *Id.*

47. *Id.*, 8.

48. *Id.*, 10.

49. Grace-Marie Turner, "Healthy Start," *Forbes* (May 27, 2002), 32.

50. *See* note 45, 5.

51. *Id.*, 12.

52. *Id.*, 15.

53. *Id.*, 16.

54. *Id.*

Chapter 5

1. Quoted in Dean Randolph W. Westerfield, "Vital Statistics," *Marshall Magazine*, The Magazine of The Marshall School of Business at the University of Southern California (Spring 2002), 4.

2. John A. Rohr, "Ethics in Public Administration: A State-of-the-Discipline Report," in *Public Administration: The State of the Discipline*, eds. Naomi B. Lynn and Aaron Wildavsky (Chatham, NJ: Chatham House Publishers, 1990), 97.

3. Wells, *Occupational Fraud and Abuse*, 3, citing The Association of Certified Fraud Examiners, *The Report to the Nation on Occupational Fraud and Abuse* (Austin: ACFE, 1996), 4.

4. William G. Mister, Diana M. Rose, Beverly J. Rowe, and Sally K. Widener, "The Contingent Workforce," *Internal Auditor* (April 2001), 40–41.

5. See, for example: "The Old Rules No Longer Apply," by Baruch Lev; "Major Boo-Boo," by Rich Willis; "SEC Loves IC," interview with Commissioner Steven Wallman; "New Metrics For A New Age," by Michael S. Malone; "You're a Fool if You Buy into This," by John Rutledge; and "We're Microsoft, We Don't Need IC," by Mike Brown; all articles appearing in *Forbes.ASAP* (April 7, 1997).

6. Geanne Rosenberg, "An Idea Not Yet Born, but a Custody Fight," *The New York Times* (September 8, 1997), D-3.

7. Eric W. Pfeiffer, "Mine Games," *Forbes.ASAP* (June 24, 2002), 62.

8. Emily Heller, "Building a Case," *The National Law Journal* (November 5, 2001), 1.

9. Lenita Powers, "Companies Escalate Fight against Espionage," *USA Today* (December 18, 1996), B-1.

10. "Runway Robbery," *TIME* (March 18, 1996), 34.

11. Robyn Meredith, "VW Agrees to Pay G.M. $100 Million in Espionage Suit," *The New York Times* (January 10, 1997), 1.

12. Owens Hughes, "Video CD Crackdown Planned," *BILLBOARD* (April 10, 1999), 47.

13. Daniel Eisenberg, "Eyeing the Competition," *TIME* (March 22, 1999), 58.

14. *Id.*

15. *Id.*

16. *Id.*

17. Emily Nelson and Raju Narisetti, "Kodak Alleges Theft of Data by Ex-Staffers," *The Wall Street Journal* (November 8, 1996), A-3.

18. Anne Reifenberg, "How Secret Formula for Coveted Slick 50 Fell into Bad Hands," *The Wall Street Journal* (October 25, 1995), A-1.

19. "Economic Espionage Explosion," *SECURITY* (May 1998), 14.

20. "Cops Versus Robbers in Cyberspace," *Forbes* (September 9, 1996), 134.

21. Glenn R. Simpson, "A '90's Espionage Tale Stars Software Rivals, E-Mail Spy," *The Wall Street Journal* (October 25, 1995), B-1.

22. William M. Carley, "Secrets Suit: What Did He Know?," *The Wall Street Journal* (January 9, 1998), B-1.

23. *Id.*

24. *Id.*

25. "Oil Business Gushes Patents," *National Law Journal* (February 16, 1998), 1.

26. Bologna, *Handbook on Corporate Fraud*, 13.

27. *White Collar Crime Study*, FBI National Press Office, March 6, 2002.

28. Meltzer, *Crime in America*, 49.

29. Lal Balkaran, "Curbing Corruption," *Internal Auditor* (February 2002), 41–42.

30. *Id.*

31. "The Growing Global Threat of Economic and Cyber Crime," The National Fraud Center, Inc., in conjunction with The Economic Crime Investigation Institute, Utica College, (LEXIS-NEXIS), December 2000, 14.

32. The Office of the National Counterintelligence Executive, Annual Report to Congress on Foreign Economic Collection and Industrial Espionage 2001, NCIX Web site (*www.nacic.gov*), 3. Accessed March 28, 2002.

33. Campbell, "Focus on Cyber-Fraud," *Internal Auditor*, 30.

34. See note 32, 16–19.

35. "The Threat to U.S. National Security from Loss of U.S. Intellectual Property to Foreign Interests: Crime and National Security in the Information Age," (speech) by John Harley, Deputy Assistant Director, National Security Division, FBI, to the National Seminar, American Society for Industrial Security, Atlanta, Georgia, September 12, 1996.

36. Dan T. Swartwood and Richard J. Heffernan, "Trends in Intellectual Property Loss, Special Report," sponsored by the American Society for Industrial Security International, March 1998.

37. *See* note 33, 2.

Chapter 6

1. Wells, *Occupational Fraud and Abuse*, 8.

2. National Fraud Center, "The Growing Global Threat," 14.

3. Neal Shover and John Paul Wright (Eds.), *Crimes of Privilege: Readings in White Collar Crime*, (New York: Oxford University Press, 2001), 1.

4. The significant initiatives, programs, and policies that have been developed to deal with sexual harassment, racial intolerance, and other forms of bigotry in the workplace seem to be a direct refutation of at least the concept of "root cause" causality. If they were not, they would be ineffective and wasteful. For many years the "root cause" rationale for some of these behaviors, "boys will be boys," seems to have been accepted as an adequate, if uncomfortable, basis for causation.

5. Donald A. Schon, *Beyond the Stable State* (New York: W.W. Norton & Company Inc., 1971), 17.

6. ACFE, *2002 Report to the Nation*, 21.

7. Lal Balkaran, "Management Fails Fraud Test," *Internal Auditor* (August 2000), 11.

8. Beryl Radin "Nevertheless, the Mail Arrives," (review of *Bureaucracy: What Government Agencies Do and Why They Do It*, by James Q. Wilson), *New York Times Book Review* (February 11, 1990), 22.

9. Thomas L. Peters and Nancy H. Austin, *A Passion for Excellence: The Leadership Difference*, (New York: Random House, 1985), xviii; Robert H. Hayes and William J. Abernathy, "Managing Our Way to Economic Decline," *Harvard Business Review* (July-August, 1980), 67–77.

10. William G. Scott and David K. Hart, "Administrative Crisis: the Neglect of Metaphysical Speculation," *Public Administration Review*, 33 (September-October, 1973), 416–417.

11. "Diane Vaughan, Transaction Systems and Unlawful Organizational Behavior," in Shover and Wright, *Crimes of Privilege*, 136.

12. *See* note 3, 174.

13. Andy Hochstetler and Heith Copes, "Organizational Culture and Organizational Crime," in Shover and Wright, 213–216.

14. James William Coleman, "Competition and Motivation to White Collar Crime," in Shover and Wright, 342–346.

15. *Id.*, 353.

16. Courtney Thompson (ed.), "Just Stopping the Fraud," *Internal Auditor* (August 1997), 70.

17. *See* note 5, 31–60.

18. *Id.*, 31–32. Morison's book was published by M.I.T. Press.

19. Lipsky, in Edelman, xix.

20. *Id.*, xix.

21. *Id.*, 13.

22. *Id.*, 36–37.

23. Yuval Levin, "Bookshelf: A Political Idea and Its Empty Promises" (book review of *Heaven on Earth*, by Joshua Muravchik), *The Wall Street Journal* (April 1, 2002), A-10.

24. For example, to its credit, the top-ranked graduate accounting program in the country for the last eight years, offered by the University of Texas at Austin, recently added fraud examination to its curriculum. "Top U.S. Accounting School Adds Fraud Examination to Curriculum," *FraudInfo Newsletter* 4, no. 3 (January 16, 2002), published electronically by the Association of Certified Fraud Examiners.

25. "Weird Science," interview by Amy Barrett, *The New York Times Magazine* (February 3, 2002), 9.

26. Bureau of Justice Statistics, U.S. Department of Justice, "Violence in the Workplace, 1993–1999," quoted in "A Dangerous Place to Work," *Law Enforcement News* (January 15–31, 2002), 1.

27. Mike Freeman, "Theft by Teammates Is a Troubling Issue," *The New York Times* (March 17, 2002), SP-9.

28. "Senator Cites Misuse of Government Credit Cards," *The New York Times* (March 14, 2002), A-29.

29. "Pentagon Moves to Stop Credit Card Abuse," *The New York Times* (March 28, 2002), A-20.

Chapter 7

1. Chris Argyris and David Schon, *Organizational Learning: A Theory of Action Perspective*, Reprinted with permission of Pearson Education, Inc., Upper Saddle River, NJ. © 1978, 13.

2. Roger Harrison, "Understanding Your Organization's Character," in *The 1975 Handbook for Group Facilitators* (La Jolla, CA:University Associates Publishers, 1975), 200.

3. Adapted from "Paradigms, Metaphors, and Puzzle Solving in Organizational Theory" by Gareth Morgan. Published in *Administrative Science Quarterly* 2, no. 27-46, 611–612, by permission of *Administrative Science Quarterly*.

4. *Id.*, 605. See also Karl Mannheim, *Ideology and Utopia* (New York: Harcourt, Brace and World, 1936).

5. *Id.*, 608—609.

6. As a member of the American Society for Industrial Security (ASIS), the author was invited to speak at several symposia held between officers and members of ASIS and academic practitioners. These annual meetings are an attempt on the part of ASIS to help the academic community develop courses pertinent to corporate security, which is the primary interest and focus of the association. These concerns developed as ASIS and some of its

members came to appreciate the fact that security had no conceptual home in academic institutions. It was usually a stepchild of some law enforcement curriculum and, even there, was poorly served. The author argued, in his presentations, that security should most properly be part of the business school and be conceived of as an element of the risk management function of the firm/organization.

As an aside, the author has also been on the advisory board of the Program for Continuing Criminal Justice Education at Pennsylvania State University. From participating in many board meetings, I now appreciate that even the law enforcement programs sometimes have trouble finding a firm and comfortable footing in the university's academic environment. If they are in this shape, then their stepchildren must, indeed, be wearing hand-me-downs.

7. There is an old joke in law enforcement circles about agency budgets. If crime is going up, the Chief asks for more money, since the problem is getting worse. If crime is going down, the Chief asks for more money, since he can now prove that what he and his department have been doing works.

8. An amusing story is told about the legendary U.S. Marine Corps General, "Chesty" Puller. Purportedly a Colonel during the Korean War, so the story goes, Chesty got word that a forward position was under attack by Chinese troops. Phoning the front, Chesty got a Republic of Korea Colonel on the line and asked how many Chinese were attacking. "Many Chinese; many, many Chinese," replied the Korean Colonel. Chesty exploded into a stream of obscenities and demanded that the Marine liaison officer, a Captain, be put on the line. Chesty then asked him the same question, to which the Marine Captain replied, "Sir, there's a whole s---pot full of them," to which Chesty replied, "Well, thank God some-body up there can count!"

Unfortunately, our intelligence on the size of the problem(s) we are facing seems to be in about the same shape. We can say, with great confidence, that we are somewhere between "many, many" fraud problems and a whole "s---pot full."

9. Kevin Markey, "A Breath of Fresh Growth," *Continental Airlines* magazine (March 2002), 35–36.

10. Andrew Pollack, "Despite Billions for Discoveries, Pipeline for Drugs Is Far from Full," *The New York Times* (April 19, 2002), C-1.

11. Jeffrey L. Seglin, "An Ethics Code Can't Replace a Backbone," *The New York Times* (April 21, 2002), BU-4.

12. *FraudInfo Newsletter* 4, no. 6, February 6, 2002, published electronically by the Association of Certified Fraud Examiners.

13. T. Barr Greenfield, "Organizations as Social Inventions: Rethinking Assumptions about Change," *The Journal of Applied Behavioral Science* 9, no. 5 (1973), 551.

14. Leonard P. Murray, "An Approach That Works," *Internal Auditor* (December 2000), 52.

Chapter 8

1. Carpenter and Mahoney, "Analyzing Organizational Fraud," 34.

2. *Fraud Examiners Manual*, ed. 3, vol. 1, (Austin, TX: ACFE, 1998), 1.302.

3. Barry Lipton, "Where's the Architect?" letter to *Internal Auditor* (April 2002), 8.

4. W. Steve Albrecht, "Employee Fraud," *Internal Auditor* (October 1996), 28.

5. *See* note 1, 34–35.

6. Alessandra Galloini, Benjamin Pedley, and Michael R. Sesit, "Lax Controls May Explain Trading Loss at Irish Bank," *The Wall Street Journal* (March 8, 2002), C-1.

7. Charles Gasparino and Susanne Craig, "Lehman Broker in Alleged Big Swindle also Supervised the Compliance Officer," *The Wall Street Journal* (February 20, 2002), C-1.

8. "Watching Employees," USA Today Snapshots, *USA Today* (February 25, 2002), 1-B.

9. *See* note 1, 35.

10. Thomas H. Oxner and Jimie Kusel, "Job Market Outlook," *Internal Auditor* (June 2002), 28–35.

11. Pinkerton, *Top Security Threats*, 6, 12.

12. Courtenay Thompson (ed.), "Responsibilities Defined," *Internal Auditor* (June 2002), 63–65.

13. Michael J. Corcoran, letter to *Internal Auditor* (April 2002), 8.

14. Marilyn Stieneke, "Mastering the Manual," CALEA Update, Commission on Accreditation for Law Enforcement Agencies, no. 78, (February 2002), 4.

15. Delattre, *Character and Cops*, 81.

16. Mike White, "The Problem with Gratuities," *FBI Law Enforcement Bulletin* (July 2002), 20–21.

17. Marie Simonetti Rosen, "A LEN Interview with Prof. Edwin J. Delattre of Boston University, Author of 'Character and Cops'," *Law Enforcement News* 23, no. 467 (May 15, 1997), 12. Reprinted with permission of *Law Enforcement News* (John Jay College of Criminal Justice, New York: 1997).

18. David Wessel, "Why the Bad Guys of the Boardroom Emerged in Masse," *The Wall Street Journal* (June 20, 2002), A-6.

19. Harold Koontz and Cyril O'Donnell, *Principles of Management: An Analysis of Managerial Functions* (New York: McGraw Hill, 1972), 85.

20. Robyn Robertson and Herb Simpson, "DWI Enforcement: Solutions to Nine Common Problems," *The Police Chief* (July 2002), 51–52.

21. *FraudInfo Newsletter* 3, no. 35, (September 6, 2001), published electronically by The Association of Certified Fraud Examiners.

22. ACFE, *2002 Report to the Nation*, 11.

23. *Id.*, 12.

24. *Id.*, 19.

25. Dale L. Flesher, "Attitudes toward Whistle-Blowing Hotlines," *Phi Kappa Phi Journal* (Spring 1999), 5.

26. *See* note 22, 19.

27. *Id.*, 20.

28. L. Miller, "Wanted: Ethical Environments," *Internal Auditor* (September 1999), 13.

29. William C. Boni, "Keeping the Digital Jewels in the Vault," *Security Management* magazine (May 2002), 96.

30. Craig Fink and Richard Miller, "Pulling the Plug on Employee Fraud," *The White Paper* (Association of Certified Fraud Examiners), 14, no. 2 (March/April 2000), 51–53.

31. Ashton B. Carter, "The Architecture of Government in the Face of Terrorism," *International Security* 26, no. 3, 19, presented in "Undermining Terrorism: New Concepts and Policies for an Interdependent World," conference proceedings, John F. Kennedy School of Government, Harvard University, May 3–4, 2002.

Chapter 9

1. Cyrus C. Perry, "A Code of Ethics for Public School Teachers," *Annals of the American Academy of Political and Social Science*, no. 297, (1955), 76–82.

2. Raymond Baumhart, *Ethics in Business*, (New York: Holt, Rinehart & Winston, 1968), 153–157.

3. Karen J. Stensgaard, "Have You Audited Your Compliance Department Lately?" *Internal Auditor* (April 2002), 47.

4. *Id.*, 49.

5. Balkaran, "Curbing Corruption," 42.

6. Jerry G. Kreuze, Zahida Luqmani, and Mushtaq Luqmani, "Shades of Gray," *Internal Auditor* (April 2001), 50.

7. Stephen J. Burns, "Combating Corruption," *Internal Auditor* (June 1997), 56,

8. The Ethics Officers Association, *www.eoa.org*. Accessed March 4, 2002.

9. C. Lee Essrig, "An International Management System Standard for Business Conduct," *ethikos* (November/December 2001). Obtained from: The Ethics Officers Association, *www.eoa.org*. Accessed March 4, 2002.

10. Paul E. Fiorelli and Cynthia J. Rooney, "COSO and the Federal Sentencing Guidelines," *Internal Auditor* (April 1997), 57–58.

11. *Id.*, 60.

12. Carpenter and Mahoney, "Analyzing Organizational Fraud," 35.

13. *See* note 6,. 50.

14. Anthony Green, "Risk Retention and the Legal Department: Volunteering without Raising Your Hand," *Chief Legal Officer* (Spring 2002), 33.

15. *Id.*, 34.

16. Itamar Sittenfeld, "Federal Sentencing Guidelines," *Internal Auditor* (April 1996), 60.

17. David McNamee, "Targeting Business Risk," *Internal Auditor* (October 2000), 47.

18. David B. Crawford, "Levels of Control," *Internal Auditor* (October 2000), 43.

19. *Id.*, 43–44.

20. *See* note 6, 53.

21. *See* note 7, 58.

22. Samantha Linsley, "Implementing a Financial Compliance Response," presentation at the Managing for Fraud Prevention Conference, Royal Institute for International Affairs, Dorchester Hotel, London, March 7, 1995.

Chapter 10

1. Stephen Doherty, "How Can Workplace Violence Be Deterred?" *Security Management* (April 2002), 132–143.

2. *Id.*, 132–143.

3. Howard W. Hallman, *Grass Roots Government*, (Beverly Hills, CA: Sage Publications, 1974), 15–16.

4. *Id.*, 20–21.

5. Milton Kotler *Neighborhood Government: The Local Foundations of Political Life*, (New York: Bobbs-Merrill Company, 1969), 8–11.

6. Barry S. Leithhead (ed.), "Managing 'People' Risks," *Internal Auditor* (December 1998), 66–67.

7. Mark M. Cicz, Book review of *Are Your Employees Stealing You Blind?*, by Edwin C. Bliss with Isamu S. Aoki (San Diego, CA: Pfeiffer & Company, 1997), *Internal Auditor* (April 1997), 22–23.

8. Balkaran, "Curbing Corruption," 45.

9. Balkaran, "Management Fails," 11.

10. Miller, "Wanted: Ethical Environments," 13.

11. Michael Stamler, "Screening For Fraud," *Internal Auditor* (October 1997), 67–68.

12. Miles Z. Epstein, "Employee Background Checks Pay," *Commerce* magazine (Commerce and Industry Association of New Jersey), (February 2002), 28–29.

13. Ann Davis, "Suits Challenge Methods, Data Used to Check Workers' Pasts," *The Wall Street Journal* (April 19, 2002), A-13.

14. Ann Davis, "Northwest to Halt Use of FBI Data in Some Instances," *The Wall Street Journal* (May 1, 2002), D-3.

15. "Who Are Those Guys?" *Law Enforcement News* (February 14, 2002), 1. Reprinted with permission of *Law Enforcement News* (John Jay College of Criminal Justice, New York: 2002).

16. Condon McGlothlen, "Hiring and Legal Risks," *The National Law Journal* (April 29, 2002), A-28.

17. Bratton, *Turnaround*, 156.

18. Glazer, "Does Better Policing Reduce Crime?" in Reichel, 94–95.

19. ACFE, *2002 Report to the Nation*, 22.

20. *Id.*, 25.

21. Carol Hymowitz, "Just How Much Should a Boss Reveal to Others about a Staffer's Firing?," *The Wall Street Journal* (March 19, 2002), B-1.

22. *See* note 17, 149–150.

23. Robert D. Putnam, *Bowling Alone: The Collapse and Revival of American Community* (New York: Simon & Schuster, 2000), 118–124, 287–290. For Putnam's original article, see: "Bowling Alone: America's Declining Social Capital," *Journal of Democracy* 6, no. 1, (January 1995).

24. *Id.*, 21–25.

25. *Id.*, 438–439.

26. *Id.*, 296–330.

27. *Id.*, 283.

28. *Id.*, 148–149. For an example of Wuthnow's work in this area, see: Robert Wuthnow, *Sharing the Journey: Support Groups and America's New Quest for Community* (New York: The Free Press, 1994).

29. *Id.*, 404–414.

Chapter 11

1. Natalie Angier, "The Urge to Punish Cheats: It Isn't Merely Vengeance," *The New York Times* (January 22, 2002), F-1.

2. Paul H. Rubin, "The Death Penalty and Deterrence," *Phi Kappa Phi Forum* 82, no.1 (Winter 2002), 11. Becker's work is found at Gary Becker, "Crime and Punishment: An Economic Approach," *Journal Of Political Economy* 76, no. 2 (1968), 169–217. Reprinted from *Phi Kappa Phi Forum* 82, no. 1 (Winter 2002). Copyright by Paul H. Rubin, reprinted by permission of the publishers.

3. *Id.*, 11.

4. American Society of Criminology Web site (*www.ACH41.com*). Accessed March 4, 2002.

5. "Racial Profiling Is More Than a Black & White Issue," *The Law Enforcement News* 27, no. 567, 568 (December 15–31, 2002), 11. Reprinted with permission of *Law Enforcement News* (John Jay College of Criminal Justice, New York: 2002).

6. Al Baker, "Commissioner Bans Profiling Using Race by the Police," *The New York Times* (March 14, 2002), B-3.

7. *Religion and Ethics Newsweekly*, Public Television Stations (April 21, 2002), 6:30 p.m.

8. Jack Douglas and Mark Olshaher *Mindhunter* (New York: Scribner, 1995).

9. See note 8, 101–124, for a description of this interview process.

10. Quentin Hardy, "Where Everybody Knows Your Name," *Forbes* (May 27, 2002), 79–82.

11. Steven L. Scott, "All You Need Is Bayes' Rule or, How This Probability Theorem Can Help Your Business," *Marshall Magazine*, University of Southern California (Spring, 2002), 56.

12. *Id.*, 56–68.

13. Beth Robliner, "Borrower Beware: Credit Scorers Are Watching," *The New York Times* (April 21, 2002), BU-8.

14. Michael J. Whalen, "Supreme Court Rulings Acknowledge Practical Considerations of Law Enforcement," *The Police Chief* (April 2002), 11. The Supreme Court ruling cited is *United States* v. *Arvizu* 122 S. Ct. 744 (2002).

15. *Id.*

16. Jennifer S. Lee, "Welcome to the Database Lounge," *The New York Times* (March 21, 2002), G-1.

17. *Id.*

18. Edward Ip, "Data Takes Shape," *Marshall Magazine*, University of Southern California (Spring, 2002), 49–53.

19. Wendy Taylor and Marty Jerome, "Expose Yourself: Consumers Will Tell You Anything If You Make It Worth Their While," SMARTBUSINESSMAG.COM (May 2002), 17.

20. *Id.*

21. "A Neglected Law Enforcement Asset," *The New York Times* (editorial) (May 9, 2002), A-38.

22. Albrecht, "Employee Fraud," 33.

23. *Id.*, 35.

24. *Id.*, 35–36.

25. "Security and Civil Liberties," speech by Jacob Perry, former Director of General Security Services, State of "Israel, at Israel's Security Industry: Technologies and Strategies for Homeland Defense and Counter-Terrorism" (conference), New York City, February 19, 2002.

26. David Stout, "9 Hijackers Drew Scrutiny on Sept. 11, Officials Say," *The New York Times* (March 3, 2002), 20.

27. "Workplace Security," The Wall Street Journal Reports, *The Wall Street Journal* (March 11, 2002), R-1-16.

28. Curtis C. Verschoor, "Reflections on the Audit Committee's Role," *Internal Auditor* (April 2002), 30.

29. Wayne C. Manus, Vivian L. Polak, A. John P. Mancini, and John M. Nonna, "Now More Than Ever, Cybersecurity Audits Are Key," *The National Law Journal* (March 11, 2002), C-8.

30. Ernst & Young LLP, *Global Information Security Survey 2002* (March 2002).

31. Carpenter and Mahoney, "Analyzing Organizational Fraud," 37–38.

32. Jeffrey Rosen, "Silicon Valley's Spy Game," *The New York Times Magazine* (April 14, 2002), 46.

33. "Letters," *The New York Times Magazine* (April 28, 2002), 14–16.

34. All references and attributions are found in Sandra Blakeslee, "Hijacking the Brain Circuits with a Nickel Slot Machine," *The New York Times* (February 10, 2002), F-1.

35. *Id.*, F-5.

36. "Persuasion," *The Economist* (May 4, 2002), 77–78.

37. *See* note 34.

38. *Id.*

39. *Id.*

40. Adler, "The Thrill of Theft," 51–52.

41. Emily Eakin, "Penetrating the Mind by Metaphor," *The New York Times* (February 23, 2002), B-9.

42. *Id.*, B-11.

43. *Id.*, B-9.

44. Sylvia Nasar, *A Beautiful Mind* (New York: Simon & Schuster, 1995), 115–122.

45. Hal R. Varian, "Economic Scene," *The New York Times* (April 11, 2002), C-2.

46. Frederick S. Hillier and Gerald J. Lieberman, *Introduction to Operations Research* (New York: McGraw-Hill, 1995), 470.

47. *See* note 44, 14. Nasar's reference to Cournot is based on Harold Kuhn (ed.), *Classics in Game Theory* (Princeton, NJ: Princeton University Press, 1997); John Eatwell, Murray Milgate, and Peter Newman, *The New Palgrave: Game Theory* (New York: Norton, 1987); and Avinash K. Dixit and Barry J. Nalebuff, *Thinking Strategically* (New York: Norton, 1991).

48. Martin Gardner, *The Colossal Book of Mathematics*, (New York: W.W. Norton & Co., 2001), 471.

49. *See* note 45, C-2.

50. *See* note 44, 374.

51. Christopher Oster, "Can the Risk of Terrorism Be Calculated by Insurers? 'Game Theory' Might Do It," *The Wall Street Journal* (April 8, 2002), C-1.

52. *See* note 46, 485-486.

53. Adam M. Brandenburger and Barry J. Nalebuff *Co-opetition*, (New York: Currency/Doubleday, 1996), 4–8.

54. *Id.*, 41.

55. *FraudInfo Newsletter* 4, no. 6 (February 6, 2002), published electronically by the Association of Certified Fraud Examiners.

56. Marci Alboher Nusbaum, "Blowing the Whistle: Not for the Fainthearted," *The New York Times* (Februof 10, 2002), B-10.

57. Argyris and Schon, *Organizational Learning*, iii.

58. *Id.*, 2–3.

59. *Id.*, 11.

60. *Id.*, 3.

61. *Id.*, 9.

62. *Id.*, 39–40.

63. Lory Hough, "A Meeting of the Minds," *John F. Kennedy School of Government Bulletin*, Kennedy School of Government, Harvard University (Spring, 2002), 34–35.

64. "What's News," *The Wall Street Journal* (April 11, 2002), A-1.

65. Bratton, *Turnaround*, 138.

66. Cassell Bryan-Low, "A Sullied Profession Discovers It's Hip to be Calculating," *The Wall Street Journal* (March 26, 2002), A-1.

67. Gretchen Morgenson, "The Enforcers of Wall St.? Then Again, Maybe Not," *The New York Times* (June 20, 2002), C-1.

Chapter 12

1. Campbell's remarks can be accessed at this time from the Web site of the National Food Service Security Council, (*www.nfssc.org*).

2. *Id.*

3. *Id.*

4. *Id.*

5. *Id.*

6. Cited in Dayton Fandray, "Pay Attention!" *Continental Airlines* magazine (May 2002), 26.

7. *See* note 1.

8. *Id.*

9. Dennis Drent, "The Quest for Increased Relevance," *Internal Auditor* (February 2002), 51–55.

10. *Id.*

11. "IFAC Initiates Anticorruption Dialogue," *Internal Auditor* (August 1999), 13–14.

12. Carpenter and Mahoney, "Analyzing Organizational Fraud," 36.

13. Larry E. Rittenberg, "Lessons for Internal Auditors," *Internal Auditor* (April 2002), 32.

14. Campbell, "Focus on Cyberfraud," 31–32.

15. Brandenburger and Nalebuff, *Co-opetition*, 12–13. Their reference to the Lincoln Highway is from *The Lincoln Highway: Main Street Across America* (Iowa City: University of Iowa Press, 1988).

16. *Id.*

17. *Id.*, 32–33.

18. *Id.*, 71.

Chapter 13

1. Brandenburger and Nalebuff, *Co-opetition*, 71.

2. Joe Sharkey, "Spy vs. Spy Is Now Spy vs. Traffic," *The New York Times* (April 24, 2002), C-6.

3. *Id.*

4. Henry, *The COMPSTAT Paradigm*, 245–256.

5. Uniform Crime Reports,*www.fbi.gov*. Accessed February 13, 2002.

6. Clark, *Crime in America*, 30.

7. National Incident-Based Reporting System, *Volume 1: Data Collection Guidelines*, U.S. Department of Justice, Federal Bureau of Investigation, Criminal Justice Information Services, Uniform Crime Reporting Program, August 2000. Available on Uniform Crime Reports, *www.fbi.gov*. Accessed February 13, 2002, 8.

8. *Id.*, 9–10.

9. Roland Chilton (University of Massachusetts at Amherst), Victoria Major, and Sharon Propheter (FBI), *Victims and Offenders: A New UCR Supplement to Present Incident-Based Data from Participating Agencies*, paper presented at the 1998 annual meeting of the American Society of Criminologists, Washington, D.C. Available at Uniform Crime Reports, *www.fbi.gov*. Accessed February 13, 2002, 2.

10. *Id.*, 3.

11. Lorne C. Kramer and Mora L. Fiedler, "Beyond the Numbers: How Law Enforcement Agencies Can Create Learning Environments and Measurement Systems," *The Police Chief* (April 2002), 164. *The Police Chief* is published by the International Association of Chiefs of Police.

12. "As Albuquerque Switches to NIBRS, Memphis Offers Tips from Experience," *The Law Enforcement News* (February 28, 2002), 1.

13. See note 4, 287–298.

14. National Fraud Center, "The Growing Global Threat," 14.

15. *Id.*, 7.

16. "Ethics Resources," *Internal Auditor* (December 1999).

17. "Victims Often Fail to Report Hacker Attack, Survey Finds," *The New York Times* (April 8, 2002), C-3.

18. ACFE, *2002 Report to the Nation*, 22, 25.

19. Shover and Wright, *Crimes of Privilege*, 49.

20. Elizabeth Moore and Michael Mills, "The Neglected Victims and Unexamined Costs of White Collar Crime," in Shover and Wright, 51.

21. *Id.*, 52.

22. Doherty, "How Can Workplace Violence Be Detered?" 134.

23. Richard M. Titus, "Personal Fraud and Its Victims," in Shover and Wright, 57.

24. Anne Jenkins and John Braithwaite, "Profits, Pressure, and Corporate Law Breaking," in Shover and Wright, 223.

25. Curtis Lavarello, "Police in Schools: Improve Safety, Prevent School Violence," Quantico, VA.; FBI National Academy Associates, Inc., *National Academy Associate* 4, no. 2 (March/April 2002), 13.

26. David G. Banks, "Get M.A.D. with the Numbers!," Austin, Texas: The Association of Certified Fraud Examiners, *The White Paper* 14, no. 5 (September/October 2000), 19.

Chapter 14

1. Fara Warner, "Think Lean," *Fast Company*, (February 2002), 40.

2. All references to Bedbury and his theories appear in Scott Bedbury, "Nine Ways to Fix a Broken Brand," *Fast Company*, (February 2002), 72–77.

3. Lardner and Repetto, *NYPD: A City and Its Police*, xiv.

4. Markey, "A Breath of Fresh Growth," 35–36.

5. Dana Beth Ardi, "Knowledge Workers Unite!," *Forbes ASAP* (March 25, 2002), 29.

6. Henry, *The COMPSTAT Paradigm*, 281.

7. Ann Quigley, "Fast Companies," *Continental Airlines* magazine (Winter 2002), 56.

8. Mayor Tony Williams was the guest speaker at the monthly meeting of the New York City Crime Commission, January 23, 2002, New York City. The author was in attendance.

9. Ridley, "Worth Repeating," 41.

10. Norman Marks, "The New Age of Internal Auditing," *Internal Auditor* (December 2001), 45.

11. *Id.*

12. Clare Ansberry, "In the New Workplace, Jobs Morph to Suit Rapid Pace of Change," *The Wall Street Journal* (March 22, 2002), A-1.

13. Steve Lohr, "In New Era, Corporate Security Looks Beyond Guns and Badges," *The New York Times* (May 27, 2002), C-1.

14. J.N., "Now Wire Me a $1 Million Refund," *Forbes* (May 27, 2002), 52.

15. *See* note 13.

16. Monte Burke, "Corporate Confidential," Forbes (May 27, 2002), 48.

Chapter 15

1. Ridley, "Worth Repeating," 39.

2. Michael Barrier, "Relating to the Audit Committee," *Internal Auditor* (April 2002), 29–30.

3. Christy Chapman, "Raising the Bar," *Internal Auditor* (April 2001), 55.

4. *Id.*

5. Eakin, "Penetrating the Mind by Metaphor," B-11.

6. Mike Tannenbaum, "Risk Management in the Limelight," *Risk Management* (March 2002), 6.

7. Carol Hymowitz, "Business's New Agenda," Workplace Security, The Wall Street Journal Reports, *The Wall Street Journal* (March 11, 2002), R-6.

8. *Id.*

9. Barsky, "From Triple-X to Just Extraordinary," A-20.

10. Blakeslee, "Hijacking the Brain Circuits," F-5.

11. Marks, "The New Age of Internal Auditing," 44.

12. Terry L. Cooper, *The Responsible Administrator* (San Francisco: Jossey-Bass Publishers, 1990), xiv.

13. George Greanias and Duane Windsor, "Corporate Governance: the Legal Framework for Institutionalizing Ethical Responsibility," W. Michael Hoffman, Jennifer Wills Moore, and David A. Fedo (eds.) in *Corporate Governance And Institutionalizing Ethics* (Lexington, MA: D.C. Heath & Co., 1984), 96.

14. R. Kenneth Andrews, "Difficulties in Overseeing Ethical Policy," in Hoffman, Moore, and Fedo, 27.

15. Amar Bhide and Howard H. Stevenson, "The Cost of a Clean Conscience," *Harvard Business Revue* (Spring, 1991), 42.

16. John A. Rohr, *Ethics for Bureaucrats: An Essay on Law and Values* (New York: Marcel Decker, 1989), v.

17. Frank J. Navran, "Making Ethics Part of a Company's 'Mythology'," *Ethikos*, no. 4 (January/February 1991), 12–13.

18. Lloyd G. Nigro and William D. Richardson, "Between Citizen and Administrator: Administrative Ethics and PAR," *Public Administration Review* (November/December 1990), 627.

19. Terry L. Cooper, "Ethics, Values, and Systems," *Journal of Systems Management* (September 1979), 10.

20. D.M. Randall and A.M. Gibson, "Methodology in Business Ethics Research: A Review and Critical Assessment," *Journal of Business Ethics*, no. 9 (June 1990), 457–471.

21. Henry Mintzberg, "The Manager's Job: Folklore and Fact," *Harvard Business Review* (March/April 1990), 163–176.

22. Ethics Resource Center, (1990), I-1–I-2. Obtained from Ethics Officers Association Web site (*www.eoa.org*).

23. Thomas L. Peters and Nancy H. Austin, *A Passion for Excellence: The Leadership Difference* (New York: Random House, 1985), 6.

24. Kirk Hanson, "Institutionalizing Ethics in the Corporation," in Hoffman, Moore, and Fedo, 188–189.

25. John E. Fleming, "Managing the Corporate Ethical Climate," in Hoffman, Moore, and Fedo, 225–226.

26. Mark S. Frankel, "Professional Codes: Why, How and with What Impact?" *Journal of Business Ethics*, no.8 (February/March 1989), 111–112.

27. Brooks, "Corporate Ethical Performance," 35.

28. "Assessment of Ethical Performance of Organization Members: A Conceptual Framework," *Academy of Management Review* 16 (1991), 667–690.

Chapter 16

1. "CEOs Are Mixed on Terrorism Concerns," *Security Management* (April 2002), 16.

2. Carpenter and Mahoney, "Analyzing Organizational Fraud," 37.

3. Richard A. Oppel, Jr., "Official Says S.E.C. Is Strained, with Duties Exceeding Budget," *The New York Times* (March 6, 2002), C-13.

4. Michael Schroeder, "Senate Panel Seeks Sweeping Change for Auditors," *The New York Times* (March 7, 2002), C-1.

5. Rebecca Buckman, "Cyber-Sleuths: Dogged On-Line Investors Are SEC's Top Source in Internet Probes," *The Wall Street Journal* (August 4, 1998), C-1.

6. Glenn R. Simpson and Jathon Sapsford, "New Money-Laundering Rules to Cut Broad Swath in Finance," *The Wall Street Journal* (April 24, 2002), A-1.

7. Elizabeth Bartels, "Who (Or What) Drives the Crime-Policy Bus?" book review of *Crime and Politics: Big Government's Erratic Campaign for Law and Order*, by Ted Gest (New York: Oxford University Press, 2001), in *Law Enforcement News* 28, no. 573, 574 (March 15–31, 2002), 15.

8. Michael Scott and Rana Sampson, "Building a Body of Knowledge: The Problem-Oriented Guides for Police," *Subject To Debate*, newsletter of The Police Executive Research Forum 16, no. 4 (April 2002), 1.

9. Chet Epperson, "The Riddle Of The 1990's Crime Decline," book review of *The Crime Drop in America* (Cambridge Studies Iin Criminology), by Alfred Blumstein and Joel Wallman (eds.) (Cambridge, U.K.: Cambridge University Press, 2000), in *Law Enforcement News* 28, no. 573, 574 (March 15–31, 2002), 15. Reprinted with permission of Law Enforcement News (New York: John Jay College of Criminal Justice, 2002).

10. Jennifer S. Lee, "Once Bamboozled, Now a Bloodhound: On the Trail, Online," *The New York Times* (March 7, 2002), G-7.

11. Pinkerton, "Top Security Threats," 13.

12. "Business to OSHA: 'Ouch!'," *CFO Magazine* (January 2001), 16.

13. *Id.*

14. W. Michael Kramer, "Corruption and Fraud Stunt Third-World Growth," *The White Paper* 16, no.3 (May/June 2002), 22–24.

15. Schon, *Beyond the Stable State*, 123.

16. Jonathan Alter, "Six Months on, the Fog of War," *Newsweek* (March 18, 2002), 20.

17. Joseph S. Nye, Jr., "The Paradox of American Power," Undermining Terrorism conference, Harvard University: Cambridge, MA (May 2–3, 2002).

18. James S. Bowman, *Ethics in Government: A National Survey of Public Administrators*, *Public Administration Review*, no. 50 (May/June 1990), 345–353.

19. *Government Executive* magazine (September 1990), 7.

20. Geoffrey Y. Cornog, "Developments in Public Administration," *Public Administration Review*, no. 22 (Spring 1962), 99–101.

21. *Annals of the American Academy of Political and Social Science*, no. 297 (January 1955).

22. Del Jones, "Many CEO's Bend the Rules (of Golf)," *USA Today* (June 26, 2002), 1-A.

23. Dave Richards, "Envisioning Our Future," *Internal Auditor* (August 2001), 61.

24. National Fraud Center, "The Growing Global Threat," 12–13.

25. *See* note 2, 35.

26. Robert F. Meier, "Geis, Sutherland, and the Development of White Collar Crime," Austin, Texas: The Association of Certified Fraud Examiners, *The White Paper* 15, no. 6 (November/December 2001), 37.

27. *Id.*, 42.

28. *Id.*, 43.

29. Robert Putnam, "Bowling Alone: America's Declining Social Capital," *Journal of Democracy* 6, no. 1 (January 1995), 75.

30. *Id.*

31. The university closed the Washington Public Affairs Center in 2001, after almost three decades of operation. For those who participated in the WPAC experience, such as I, it was an invaluable learning opportunity.

32. *FraudInfo Newsletter* 2, no.42 (October 27, 2002), published electronically by the Association of Certified Fraud Examiners.

33. Hymowitz, "Managers Must Respond," B-1.

34. *See* note 2, 38.

35. Carol Hymowitz, "How CEO's Can Keep Informed Even as Work Stretches across Globe," *The Wall Street Journal* (March 12, 2002), B-1.

36. Lisa Guernsey, "Where Tips Meet Truth (Sometimes)," *The New York Times* (February 21, 2002), G-1.

37. Judith Burns, "SEC Fields Tips Linked to Fraud at Record Pace," *The Wall Street Journal* (February 20, 2002), B5N.

38. "Enron Returns: Fund Trustees Will Take a Harder Look,Union Leaders Say," Work Week Column, *The Wall Street Journal* (February 26, 2002), A-1.

39. Jacob M. Schlesinger, "O'Neill Weighs Stricter Corporate Penalties," *The Wall Street Journal* (February 25, 2002), A-3.

40. John Harwood, "Public's Esteem for Business Falls in Wake of Enron," *The Wall Street Journal* (April 11, 2002), A-6.

41. Joann S. Lublin, "Boards Seek Advice to Avoid Their Own Enron-Style Mess," *The Wall Street Journal* (April 24, 2002), B-1.

42. U.S. Sentencing Commission, Organizational Datafile, FY2000, cited in *FraudInfo Newsletter* 4, no. 15, (April 10, 2002), published electronically by the Association of Certified Fraud Examiners.

43. *See* note 3, C-13.

44. "The Reputation of CEO's Is Important," report of survey conducted by Burston-Marsteller, USA Today Snapshots, *USA Today* (February 27, 2002), 1-B.

45. *CALEA Update*, Fairfax, VA: The Commission on Accreditation of Law Enforcement Agencies (February 2002), 24.

46. "10 Minutes With," *Continental Airlines* magazine (March 2002), 47.

47. Brandenburger and Nalebuff, *Co-opetition*, 10.

INDEX